God's Country

By

J.T. Ringo

Copyright © **2024 JT Ringo**

All rights reserved. No part of this publication may be reproduced, distributed, or transmitted in any form or by any means without the prior written permission of the author.

ISBN:

978-1-962210-29-4 Paperback

978-1-962210-30-0 Hardback

Dedication

This book is dedicated to all who struggled to find peace in new lands,

and to all of those who still struggle to live peaceably on their own.

Acknowledgments

Special thanks to;

- My brother, Donny, who dedicated hours and hours of research to prevent me looking ignorant.

- The County Seat, Carrie, and all the gallons of coffee.

- Prescott, AZ for always reminding me of the history, struggles, and stories of the peoples who call it home.

- Most importantly, my wife and daughter, who continually remind me what "home" means and what love looks like.

Contents

Dedication i
Acknowledgments ii
Chapter 1 1
Chapter 2 25
Chapter 3 53
Chapter 4 72
Chapter 5 91
Chapter 6 122
Chapter 7 144
Chapter 8 164
Chapter 9 176
Chapter 10 184
Chapter 11 197
Chapter 12 229
Chapter 13 238
Chapter 14 253
Chapter 15 270
Chapter 16 282
Chapter 17 308
Chapter 18 322
Chapter 19 334
Chapter 20 353
Chapter 21 363
Chapter 22 379
Chapter 23 397
Chapter 24 428

Chapter 1

Andras remembered it being cold. He had clung to the scarf his grandmother had made him, twisting his fingers into the loose knitting. Ma used to pinch his thigh when he stretched and tugged at the knitting, but the closer they got to leaving, she cared less about the scarf, and she clung tighter to Andras's hand each time they left the house. Andras remembered hearing gunfire from the city, not constant barrages of cannons and mortars, but pistols and rifles ringing over the white and gray hills of twisted gnarled trees. Pa said the Russians wouldn't quit until they controlled everything, and the only chance at a new life was across the Atlantic.

Every month brought new, more unbelievable, fantastical imagery of a new world with gold spilling out of well springs and food falling off of trees. Miles and miles of farmland just waiting to be tilled. While Pa had heard scalp-tingling stories of the savage practices of the aboriginal Americans, he could not be dissuaded from his dream of owning land in the Colorado territory. Ma didn't display the same enthusiasm. As the days drew nearer, she watched the slushy road turn to mud, looking out the window at anything that sounded like an approaching rider or cart. At night, her prayers lasted longer, as true divine desperation accented her words with faith.

That winter's chill reached through wool and linens, and Andras pulled Ma's coat tight around himself. Pa had handed Ma the tiny sack of coins and the note, but Andras's reading wasn't too good yet, so he only recognized a few of the words; *Walenty, Poland, family, and dock.* He'd been practicing his reading with Baba's old bible, but so many of the names discouraged him from wanting to learn more. If reading was so difficult, why did Ma enjoy it so much? There's not even much to look at except the first page of each new section. The intricate calligraphic lettering and gilded images of ancient heroes holding random nonsense or being killed in ways that made Andras feel unsafe. The dock master was a thick, burly man with a mustache that reminded Andras of a walrus. As well as his face. And his chest. The man took the tiny sack of coins and the note and nodded, telling Ma when they would be departing. Andras didn't hear because he had gotten bored after the first few words and was watching a terrier chase a wily rat trying to board the gangway of the ship.

The ship was the biggest thing Andras had ever seen, a huge wooden ship with a smoke stack that belched smoke even as it sat in port. While the huge water wheel protruding from the center of the ship was fully functional, Massive off-white sails sat furled against the mast, waiting to be needed. The crew members, all bundled in thick woolen jackets and caps, loaded with loud guffaws and quiet hummed songs with the sweet smell of tobacco smoke pushing through the musty scent of the water. The ship captain gave a tight-lipped smile to Andras who politely returned the same nicety and looked at the ground.

Ma was a strong, silent woman whose gentle hands taught better than her words. Not that she was ever harsh or violent, but a hand on a shoulder or a pinch on the leg was enough to discern the error of your ways. Ma loved Jesus and the church, and she was always cooking for sick people in the church and the unfortunate on the street. "Nie są bezdomni. Zagubiły się i szukają domu. Jezus przygotował dla nich obiad. *They are not homeless. They are lost and looking for a home. Jesus prepared dinner for them,"* she had told him once after she had pinched his thigh for swiping a biscuit. Andras remembered looking at the people living under bridges and on the street corners differently after that. He would want strangers to help him get home if he was lost.

Ma was always smarter than she'd let people assume. She knew almost three full languages, including a little Spanish from her time as a launder girl in Spain when was young. Ma and Andras spent much time alone together when Andras was younger. Pa was a shepherd in a group of shepherds who would watch over a herd that was sometimes far away. Sometimes Pa would be gone for weeks at a time, but when he came home, he would spend every moment with them, holding them close and kissing them both. Often Ma would shove him away with a shy grin, telling him to go bathe, "Pachniesz jak prawdziwy pasterz!"

Pa spent evenings telling Andras stories his uncle used to tell him. Sometimes he would tell silly tales with predictable endings with morals that always had to do with listening to your parents or going to bed on-time. Sometimes he would tell of ancient stories of Andras's great-great-grandfather stealing land from the English and building a home. On nights when Pa was quieter or seemed more tired, Pa would tell stories about the Uprising.

When he was younger, before he had met Ma, a corrupt Polish official forced Pa and his mates to conscript to the military for twenty years. Instead, they rebelled. Pa had spent a year helping Poland fight back against Russia before he met Ma, they had Andras, and Pa spent the last of his Guineas on a new future in America. Pa had purchased thirty-two acres at eighteen cents an acre, and he couldn't stop bragging about what a great deal he got for it.

Andras's favorite story of his father's was one he had told once about a particular shootout he was in during his time under General Rochebrune as a Zouave of Death with the French.

"Vaclav and I had volunteered to stay behind because we knew we were being followed, and with Tomas's foot the way it was, they would overtake us by nightfall. They left us behind on a rocky outcropping with one hundred rounds of ammunition for our rifles each. Vaclav and I laid down behind those rocks and covered ourselves with our blankets and piled snow on top of ourselves so only the barrels of our rifles were out, and we waited. The silence in that canyon was deafening. Every tiny shift sounded like thunder, every rock falling sounded like a gunshot. After a few hours, the first scouts came through the pass on their horses. Vaclav took a shot and punched a hole straight through his big shiny brass button. As the second scout wheeled his horse to turn, I took my shot, hitting him in the shoulder so that it pierced his heart." Pa's eyes were wide as he told his story,

and then he tickled Andras's neck. Andras squirmed away and then got comfortable on his dad's leg again.

"You can shoot a man's heart through his shoulder?" Andras asked, cocking his head. Pa winked at him.

"Not just anyone. But your Pa can." Andras repressed a proud smile as his father winked at him.

"And then what happened?" Andras wiggled, gazing longingly into his father's animated face. Pa closed his left eye and squeezed an invisible rifle against his shoulder.

"They sent another group of scouts to try and sniff out where we were hiding, but we were too well hidden and too smart for them. Eventually, they stopped sending scouts after us when there were twenty four men dead on the ground!" Pa fired his invisible rifle, making dramatic *Pshew!* noises as imaginary recoil jarred his body.

"What were they planning, Papa?" Andras asked enthusiastically, knowing exactly what they were planning. He wanted to hear it the way his father told it.

"They sent a demon after us." Pa said, his eyes hauntingly wide, his fingers twisted into claws that leapt forward and tickled Andras's ribs. Andras yelped and squirmed, screaming a loud laugh.

"What did he look like, Papa?"

"I never got to see him up close. He was a demon from the Serbian wasteland sent to enslave Poland. He was as quiet as a shadow, and

his skin was invisible. Before we even knew how much danger we were in,--"

"*Vaclav's rifle exploded!*" Andras interrupted loudly, throwing his hands in the air, mimicking a dramatic explosion.

"*Vaclav's rifle exploded! In a loud crunch of black smoke and fire, Vaclav's rifle was ruined. The Serbian demon had shot a bullet into the left side Vaclav's gun, igniting the charge, sending black powder spraying all in Vaclav's eyes.*" Andras gasped and reached for his eyes. "*We were so surprised, we didn't even know what to do. The Serbian had gotten above us to the left and was firing down on us from our left side! Vaclav's gun was useless, and he could barely open one eye. His face had black stains and angry, red burns from the shot, and he knew he couldn't stay, but I had to cover his retreat. In a mad dash, we broke from cover, and sprinted back nearly one hundred yards, darting between trees and boulders, slipping and sliding like baby deer on a frozen pond.*" The imagery of a baby deer was humorous, but the intensity of his father's tale had him riveted. "*I could hear the whizz of the Serbian's bullets through the trees, and I prayed to the Christ that none of the bullets would find me, and he heard my prayers, and I escaped with my life.*"

"*Did you find bullet holes in your coat and pants, Papa?*" Andras asked, wide-eyed. His father nodded gravely.

"I found bullet holes in my coat and in the fabric of my pants. The whole time I was running, I was narrowly avoiding death!" Andras gasped and pulled his bear skin comforter up to his chin.

"Did he kill you?" Andras asked nervously, prompting the next chapter of the story that Berle had told so many times.

"No. Lord knows, he tried. Instead, I killed him."

"How, Papa? He was invisible and had the devil's own eyes to aim with!"

"I waited. I was patient. I didn't move for two whole days!" Pa froze as he spoke, remembering as well as dramatizing. "Once I thought I knew where he was hiding, I pointed my rifle that way and I waited."

"And then what happened, Papa?" Andras almost whispered it. Andras had had nightmares about this part of the story before. Dreams when he felt the skin tear from his bones and felt his throat stab with pain from screaming.

"After three days. I was near fainting from starvation, but then I heard a loud yelp, a shriek, and the low swelling howl of a wolf who had found its next prey. As more wolves approached, the Serbian demon cried and screamed for help, and that night, the Christ had put some softness into your Pa's heart, and I shot that demon before the wolves could tear him apart." Andras's imagination was dripping in red and sticky, matted gray fur and long stained teeth. Andras's father was so brave, and a strong soldier who fought for what he knew was right.

And now Pa guarded the town goats and sheep with the other brave men.

The day finally came for them to leave for Ameryka, and Pa was insistent they not leave anything behind. *"Anything not in Ameryka when we arrive is behind us now. In nine days, we will be Amerykanz. A new life."* Pa's eyes sparkled with wild fantasies of the future. Andras couldn't help but feel inspired by his father's optimism despite his mother's insistent warnings to be careful.

The ride to the dockyard was exhilarating. Just like royalty, a carriage awaited them, a darkly-painted wooden carriage with cushioned seats, pulled by four horses! Andras had never gone so fast in his entire life! His mother clung to him, an arm around his chest, holding him closely with every jarring bump and bouncy pothole. Andras could smell the sea before he saw it.

The musty, salty smell of the harbor with the squawking yelps of the seabirds. His heart caught in his chest, and he had to be free of his mother's grasp. He twisted free of her arm and lunged forward towards the open window on the door. Throwing back the silken shutter, he beheld the massive ship they would be riding to a new life. The sails were furled, and the smoke stack gushed dark black billows. Like before, the dockyard was milling with workers and travelers, all with their own important business to attend to.

He spied a trio of fancy men, each with thick, curly mustaches and black bowler hats. They spoke elegantly to each other in a lilting language that caused two of them to guard their mustaches with a chuckle. An even stranger traveler carried two luggage bags with a long robe made of colorful thread. Her hat was unlike anything Andras had seen before, tassels and bangles that chimed as she walked. When they boarded the ship, Pa shook the captain's hand and lingered behind to speak with him as Ma and a few crew members lugged their bags below deck.

Andras was surprised to only see a few passengers below deck. There was a family of dark brown, almost black-skinned people with curly black hair and dark brown eyes like his. They were speaking a language that Andras recognized as French, but he didn't know it. Another family sat in a corner of the long room. They had clothes like Andras and Ma, and they smiled at Ma as she approached. They were friendly to Ma, and the father spoke very fancily to Ma in Polish like he had heard the English and other rich people speak.

Ma pulled Andras aside and kneeled in front of him so they were eye-to-eye. She spoke low and gently, somehow more calmly. Andras noticed Ma had been more relaxed since they boarded the ship, and he was grateful for it. She wasn't clinging to him and glancing over her shoulder anytime a noise sounded behind them.

"This is our home for the next few days, and these people are our neighbors." Andras's eyes swept over every inch of the cabin, over every board, exposed nail, and detail of the tools and supplies against the wall. Ma touched the middle of his chest with one soft finger, and his eyes locked-on to hers. *"Do you understand?"* And Andras

nodded earnestly and honestly. A carriage and a ship in the same day? This was the best day ever.

Another small group of people followed in behind them, a very proper and well-dressed mustachioed man who was unmistakably English based on the wafting tannins of Earl Grey and flavored tobacco in the air. He removed his hat as he entered the cabin and sniffed appraisingly at the slowly crowding room. Behind him were two valets, also dark-skinned people, two men who looked as old as the teenagers in Andras's village. They lugged a trunk and several small bags into the room behind him. They also were well-dressed, although not as fancily as the Englishman. He smoothed the bottom of his mustache with the back of his forefinger and waved at a wall.

"Tenneson, Howard: let's set up camp along that starboard wall. That way, the sun will not disturb our mornings," and the two black-skinned boys set up a cot and a small folding table large enough for tea and a novel. The Englishman did his share of the work, double checking the supplies for the sixteen-day journey across the Atlantic. He was not harsh to his two valets as he had seen some other people before, but he spoke to them as a supervisor overseeing two apprentices. He praised excellence and chided laziness. He spoke in platitudes and cliches about leadership and doing it "the English way". When they had completed their tasks, he encouraged them to sit and gave each of them a cut of cheese, and he ate a piece as well. They chatted quietly amongst themselves.

After a few quiet moments the same walrusy man as before entered the cabin and removed his cap. He cleared his throat and spoke in gruff, accented Polish.

"Greetings, passengers. I'm captain of this vessel, Einjar Klep. Please call me Captain Ein or Captain Klep while aboard. During our journey, this cabin will be your living area. Meals will be served in the galley three times a day at..." and Andras became bored. The captain didn't have black and golden teeth or fingernails for armor, he didn't even have powder fuses smoldering in his beard. Andras found his first real ship captain to be quite boring. He would have been satisfied with a bent and notched sabre on his hip.

In his young, innocent ignorance, Andras allowed his eyes to wander the cabin as Captain Klep listed rules and expectations. He noticed the Englishman's valets whispering with the teenagers from the French family. They smiled as they whispered, and Andras was surprised by how happy their smiles made him. Big, bright teeth surrounded by beautiful chocolate skin forming into genuinely joyful smiles. Andras stretched his mouth into a wide smile like theirs, and it felt alien and strange on his face. Andras smiled and laughed plenty, but he could recall no one in Poland who expressed joy like them. Perhaps he could be happy like that if he could work for them and learn their secrets.

When the captain had finished his speech, he approached and shook the Englishman's hand, and they exchanged a few words in English, a strange, mixed language like Ma's Spanish and the language the

German family down the street spoke. Andras saw the kids at school sometimes, and they spoke their own language when the teacher wasn't nearby. Andras liked to listen to it, and he wished he knew another language. Andras considered the logistics of befriending and learning French from the Englishman's valets. The captain shook the professor's hand again and tipped his hat to Ma and him. Andras copied the action, lifting an invisible hat, and nodding slightly. When Pa arrived again, he was out of breath like he had been walking up and down many stairs, and he clapped the captain on the shoulder with a smile.

"What a beautiful ship! Have you explored at all, Andras?" Pa asked enthusiastically. Andras shook his head, his messy hair tumbling all over. Pa looked more excited than he was to be on a ship, but he was pretty sure Pa had been on a ship before. Andras looked to his Ma who smiled and gently shoved him playfully towards his Pa. The Hungarian professor winked at Andras and said in fancy Polish,

"Worry not, young one. We shall watch carefully over your mother while you explore." The professor's wife nodded and scooted closer to Ma, who turned to talk with her. Andras sprinted to his Pa who scooped him up, and they zoomed up the stairs to the top deck where a dozen men carried bags and barrels and secured ropes and nets. The whole ship creaked as the mooring line was loosed, and the enormous vessel drifted away from the dock. Andras wanted to feel the surge of the engine sweep them over the waves, but for several agonizing minutes, the creaky, busy ship merely drifted slowly away from the

land. Andras could only feign excitement for several minutes before he asked his Pa one of the thoughts that had been on his mind.

"Pa, when will I know Amerykanzi? I want to be able to talk to the other kids and the Indians when we arrive." His father chuckled.

"What do you know about the Amerykan Indians?" Pa asked with curiosity. He put Andras on the deck, and Andras rested his chin on the wooden railing and watched Poland slowly rise and sink behind waves. The engine below deck finally rumbled to life, and the smoke stack coughed plumes skyward. The ship began to press through the shove of waves northwestward.

"Ma borrowed a book for me, and I looked at the pictures inside. They wear feathers in their hair, and they live in big triangle houses, and their skin is brown, and they paint it sometimes to disappear in the trees. I think I'd like to be one." Andras recalled the detailed etchings from the book, tall, proud men with piercing eyes and angular faces. Their hair was like black silk, and it was adorned with beautiful handmade beads like the ones he'd seen the church priests pray with. They carried weapons like the warriors of olde; axes, bows, and shields. If America's Indians were anything like Poland's ancient warriors, nobody would be able to stop them. Pa laughed and patted Andras on the back.

"An Indian is not something you become, Andras. They were born Indians. They were Indians long before any Europeans came there.

Ameryka is their home." Andras gazed out over the gray waves and squinted to see the twisted chimney smoke from his childhood home.

"The Indians are Amerykanz?" Andras looked up at his father who looked equally confused.

"Huh. Yeah, I suppose they are." Pa scratched his chin, his prickly cheeks rasping under his calloused fingers.

"Is Amerykan hard to learn?" Andras asked.

"English."

"English? Why English?"

"That's what they speak in Ameryka. English."

"The Amerykan Indians speak English?"

"Well, no. They speak their own languages."

"All the Amerykan Indians speak their own languages?"

"Each tribe, yes."

"And we have to learn all the languages?"

"No, Andras, only English." Andras was very confused, and he wasn't following Pa's logic, but he stopped asking questions. At least he wouldn't have to learn dozens of new languages, but how would he speak to the Indians when he met them?

"When can I know English?"

"Want to start now?" Andras nodded enthusiastically, and Pa began to think of all the English words he knew.

For days, Pa had done nothing but speak about "Kholo-raedo, Khenses" no matter how many times the Hungarian professor corrected him with that fancy accent of his, "Kolorado na terytorium Kansas, mój kolega," emphasizing the proper vowel sounds. Pa would wave his hand at Istran and then shake Istran's knee affably with a chuckle. "Polak, Węgier – dwa bratanki, i do szabli, i do szklanki! *Pole and Hungarian—two brothers when it comes to the sword and the glass!*" Istran would laugh and berate him on the importance of keeping one's traditions close in America, warning him, "Ty także utoniesz w amerykańskim tyglu. *You, too, will drown in the American melting pot.*" Pa looked him in the eyes with a genuine gleam of hope, "W Kolorado na terytorium Kansas możemy to mówić, jak chcemy. To jest Ameryka! *In Colorado, Kansas Territory, we can say it however we want. This is America!*" and he would laugh that ridiculous guffaw.

Traveling and living on the ship was exhausting for Ma. By the second day, Ma was pale and clammy, seasick as he had ever heard someone becoming. Her face was always sweaty, and she either slept or went above deck for fresh air and sunshine.

They'd been at sea for three days, and Andras had decided that he would not mind living on a ship for the rest of his life. He had already grown bored of staring out at the waves, but he had found games to play with each of the other passengers and some of the crew members. The ship's cook, a thick man the other crew members called "Śledź," suddenly believed he was going mad after his knives and utensils began disappearing and reappearing in strange places. Andras and Lele, the youngest of the French family, got caught once by a crew member who asked what they were up to in a stern voice that smelled like medicine and tobacco. When they told them, he laughed loudly and told them to be sneakier in the future.

At night, he began to understand the rules of a card game called *poker* that many Americans played on the frontier. Pa was immediately interested when he heard that. Pa assured him it wasn't gambling, only research. Ma spent most of the time in bed, feverish and clammy, and she could barely keep any food down. The French family offered Ma some laudanum, and she felt better for an evening.

That evening, Pa told stories about the uprising that made the professor cover his mouth and the Englishman's valets lean forward suspensefully. Ma was not stirred by the intensity of the tale of his three day shootout with fifty Russian marksmen. She rested sleepily on his shoulder, an arm wrapped around his, her peaceful smile that lingered when she stopped fighting the weight of her heavy eyelids. Andras thought she looked very pale and fragile, like a small china teacup.

Usually, Ma's skin was warm and light like cream, her eyes were the brightest blue, like a snowstorm's sky or an icy lake in the sun. Now, her skin resembled the pages of Grandmother's bible, and her eyes were the color of road snow three days after a storm. But she was smiling. Looking at her, he wasn't sure if she was awake or not, but she was smiling and not cringing in discomfort. Droplets of sticky sweat clung to her forehead, but she seemed peaceful. As Father's story continued, he thought he spied Ma's hand tighten around Pa's arm more.

After six days of arrhythmic slapping and unstable footing, Ma's constitution had had enough. She spent as much time above deck as the crew members and their work permitted. She would lean on the railing and gaze westward.

In the days leading up to the end of their voyage, Ma was getting worse. Andras couldn't understand or properly know what he should feel. Ma had never been sick before, as far as he could remember, and Pa spent more and more time at her side. Each night, he encouraged Andras to hug his Ma tightly and tell her he loved her. Andras always did because he did love her, and he knew in his stomach that it was important she knew. Pa got sad as the days went on, and the ship's most knowledgeable crew member tended to her as much as he could. Andras found it increasingly difficult to sleep after hugging his Ma goodnight. Each night, her hugs were a little weaker until he caught Pa helping Ma put her arms around him during a good-night hug.

One night, Ma fell asleep particularly early, and Pa had him go in and kiss her good night. She didn't strain and struggle to sit up as she usually did, but she did turn her hand over and look into Andras's eye. She hadn't said anything yet. Andras scooped up her hand in his and traced the lines on her palm with his other. Looking into her eyes made him so sad and scared lately. They were so close to their new home, and he knew that, if she could just rest until they got to Ameryka, Ma would be fine.

Andras wasn't sure if it was the heavy hand of his father, or the rush of cool air that woke him up, but when he sat up, he felt his dad's strong hands under his arms lifting him onto his shoulder with a near-inaudible grunt. Andras closed his eyes again and rested his head on Pa's shoulder. He could feel urgency in his father's gait. When Pa put him down, Andras had barely opened his eyes when he was hugging his mother. Pa was holding her hand, and Ma was resting on the bed. Disappointed by the change of position, Andras snuggled closely to his mother's shoulder, his father's hand heavy on his back. After a few moments, he felt Pa lift him again and carry him to bed.

The next morning, the ship's crew member who had been caring for Ma played a song on his pipe while the rest of the passengers watched a rolled bundle of canvas lifted overboard. Pa's eyes streamed with hot tears that didn't stop and soaked Andras's shirt. Andras didn't know what else to do but hold Pa even tighter. Ma was gone. Her bed was empty, her things were packed in her suitcase, and Pa couldn't muster a smile.

The next morning, Captain Klep told all the passengers that they would be arriving at New York port by morning. Andras didn't know much about New York, but the way Lele spoke about it, it was a kingdom of science, business, and castles. Pa was quiet and thoughtful like he was when he returned from long trips. Andras wasn't sure how to help, so he learned to fall in love with curry and naan. He was inspired by goat milk and spiced vegetables, and did everything except think about where Ma was right now. Pa was quiet for a few days before he finally began laughing with Andras again. He wasn't ever as silly as he was before. Pa was changed.

Andras noticed the change in the smell of the air first, then the color of the sky, then in the frequency of other vessels. They were approaching a heavily-populated area, and he thought Pa would be more excited. Andras made sure all his things were packed and ready to depart before his father even found the strength to rise from bed. Lele pointed out buildings that Andras couldn't track, and she excitedly told him about an exciting deal America and France made for a statue. Andras did his best to pay attention, but he was relieved when he was alone with Pa again.

Ma was gone. His brain had put it together a day or two before; the bundle of canvas was his mother. Ma was dead, and they buried her at sea instead of a muddy hole. Andras thought for a moment before he decided that a burial at sea was better than a shallow grave in untenable farmland, faded into the native landscape.

The guests packed their meager items slowly, dragging the process out so they wouldn't be sitting around waiting to make landfall without somewhere to sit or a book to read. Pa packed quickly and efficiently, like a soldier who had just received marching orders. The Hungarian family lingered nearby as Pa packed quickly, watching him closely as the stoney expression on his face melted into a molten visage of tears and a broken heart. Istran placed a firm, supportive hand on Pa's back, and Pa let him leave it there while he collected himself. He grabbed the violin case from their small pile of belongings and held it out for the professor to take, offering it to him as if to give it to him. Then Pa said something to him in Hungarian that sounded serious. Andras had never heard his dad speak Hungarian, nor had he ever seen his father look so powerless and pathetic. Istran appraised Andras sadly. Istran took the violin case and felt the weight of it. The professor opened his mouth to speak, but nothing came to mind. He looked to his family who looked equally perplexed.

"*Pa?*" Andras asked, taking two side steps toward his dad, looking between the silent parties. Pa finally looked away from Istran to look at his only son.

"*Andras, tomorrow, you will be Amerykan. You are creating a brand-new life with all the bad things and sadness behind you. You can be anything you want! What do you want to be? Think. Anything...*" Pa looked at him with those wet, shiny, tired eyes and forced a smile. Andras could tell it was one of those "be strong for Andras" smiles. He knew they were fake, but he appreciated the strength and love behind them nonetheless. Andras thought hard. He'd thought about this hundreds of times before, maybe even hundreds of times while he was on this ship.

The Hungarian professor and his family were staring at him, the professor holding Pa's violin case in his left hand. Istran kneeled to meet Andras's eyes, but said nothing. The professor looked unsure and confused. His fear put Andras on edge. Andras took a small step closer to his father who pressed him again.

"Anything you want, my love. A baker, a hunter, a miner, a mayor! You can build your own town." Pa's enthusiastic words were kind, but not comforting. Andras was missing an important part of the situation, but he didn't know what to ask. He stepped toward Pa again.

"*I…*" Andras began. "*I want to…*" his voice caught in his tiny throat. He was too young to feel the weight of a decision, to feel the burden of each syllable uttered.

"*Go ahead, baby bear. What do you want?*" Pa pressed him again, rubbing his back. A lone tear escaped his father's tired eyes, and skated down his cheek. Andras felt a surging of emotion, a great welling up of burning hot tears, scared and sad.

"*I want my daddy,*" Andras said as his eyes went blurry with confused, heartbroken, scared tears. Andras couldn't imagine a future without his Pa. His Pa's strong, rough arms scooped him up and pulled him close. Pa smelled like seawater, tobacco, and home, and Andras wrapped his arms around his father's neck and sobbed loudly. Istran put down the violin case, whispered something in Hungarian, and patted Pa on the back before stepping away silently. Andras never asked his Pa about that moment, but the Hungarian family watched him closely after that.

Later that day, all their luggage and belongings were brought to the main deck in preparation to be unloaded onto the New York dock.

The ship was abuzz with excited commotion, not only for the successful conclusion of their nine day voyage, but the prospect of a new life, a new beginning. Even the crew members seemed excited at the chance for some shore leave. A dark haze of warm smoke and civilization hung over the bustling streets and avenues filled with people, carts, horses, wagons, and crates. Everywhere he looked, there were people dressed in all different colors and textiles. Some men wore beards and hats while some went shirtless and carried boxes. Some people had colorful tattoos on their skin while some had strange and exotic animals in boxes or even carried on their shoulders. He saw one tall man with a long black coat and a tall black hat like a stove pipe with a monkey on his shoulder chewing on a piece of orange fruit. Andras could not look away from each new exciting thing that revealed itself as they neared the shore.

America was such a stark contrast to the gray, war-torn, colorless avenues of Poland. The streets of America looked more fantastical than anything he could have imagined. Flags hung from buildings with red and white stripes and stars in the shapes of numbers. Even the people were colorful and diverse. He saw skin colors across the whole spectrum, even an American Indian far off with tall mohawk and painted face. Andras craned his neck to peer through the crowds, but he was gone.

He felt his dad's warm hand on his shoulder and looked up at him. Pa's face was the brightest he had seen since before Ma's funeral. His eyes glinted with the hope of new futures. Pa had their bags slung on his back and staged on the deck in front of them. He held the single English book he owned in one hand and the battered violin case in the other. Andras dug into his smaller bag, pulled out his identical hat, and pulled it tightly onto his head, just like his father's.

When they finally came to a stop, and the crew members had moored the vessel to the crowded dock, the commotion and psychosis of international travel overtook them, and Andras was lost in the human current with only the strong hand of Pa as his compass. Pa lifted him off of the ground and held him on his hip so that he could see further. They had joined a long queue of travelers who each held papers and luggage.

"What are we doing, Pa?" Andras asked, wondering why they weren't riding horses across the open golden plains yet.

"We have to sign some papers to become Amerykanz, Andras. We can be patient, can't we?" Andras nodded. They took four small steps closer every few minutes until they finally reached the threshold to a long room of doctors and aproned nurses carrying trays of bottles and tools. The doctors inspected each of the travelers and asked them questions. They looked under their arms, at their backs, and inspected their eyes and tongues. Finally, they signed a paper and handed it back. Being Polish at the New York port earned a scornful look from the man with a ledger. Either that, or he was angry that Pa didn't speak much English beyond a *"Hullo"* and *"Please, I'm Berle, and this my son."* Ma knew a little English. The lines at the New York Port were endless it seemed. Sitting in a tiny room with eighty other people with

only grease paper over the windows to keep out flies made Andras sweaty and Pa grumpy.

On Pa's lap, gripping a bit of soft fabric, was Andras, a handsome young boy, five or six years old with hair that looked as if it hadn't decided if it would be blonde or brown yet. His eyes were not stunning or breathtaking in a way that would make one look twice. They were two brown pits, holes in the earth. His skin was pale and had a sickly pallor that made the wet-handed doctor spend extra time checking under his arms and his scalp for parasites, boils, or some indication of something communicable. The doctor had looked him over, scribbled a note, and passed the wrinkled piece of paper back to his father. It was impossible for Andras to keep track of everything that was happening, and at some point, he had fallen asleep on Pa's shoulder, his arms around his neck so he wouldn't be gone when he woke up.

Chapter 2

Andras woke up to a hard bump, a jarring *thunk*, and a creaking bounce that made his eyes flutter open and him sit up. Pa's hand was there, immediately on his shoulder, a heavy comfort. Andras was sitting in the back of a cart being pulled by a tall brown horse with floppy blinders and jingly bridle that the horse chewed absently.

"Hey, my boy, you slept for a long time! We're still in New York getting a ride to one of Pa's friends' houses to stay for the night, how does that sound? Are you hungry?" Pa looked at him with a tired, calmer face, turned around on a bouncy bench beside a man whose back was still turned. He had a bald head shiny with oil or sweat, Andras couldn't tell, but it was cold, so he had a guess. His clothes were many different colors like so many of the other Americans in New York. He held the reins lazily and piloted the horse through the streets. They spoke and laughed together like old friends in Polish, joking, laughing about old times and memories. Andras had never seen this man before in his life, but he spoke to Pa like they had known each other for years. Andras divided his attention between the bustling city street and Pa's conversation with his friend.

The street they bounced down was less crowded than earlier, the buildings were not as tall, and the air smelled better. The street was still wet and muddy, but snow was not piled on the sides of the road in gray ziggurats of snow and ice. Andras was surrounded by Pa's, Ma's, and his own bags as well as a crunched basket, a thick pane of green glass, and a very lazy dog that Andras didn't notice until last because it hadn't moved. The dog looked as if it was melting with droopy ears, loose skin, and large, sad eyes that gazed up at him. As Andras made eye contact with the floppy canine, its tail swept the floor of the cart in a pathetic wag. Andras waved tentatively at the dog. He had never owned a dog, and most of the dogs in Poland ran in the streets and barked at you as you passed. This dog was not like the sharp-eared fast dogs of the Russians, but the complete opposite. Instead of dark fur to blend in with darkness and foliage, this saggy sack of sadness was a splotchy mix of brown and white spots. Andras wasn't sure if the dog was sick or if something was wrong with it. Pa's friend spoke up to Andras over his shoulder, and Andras noticed some faint scarring etched into his cheek and around his eye.

"Say hello to Lincoln, Andras! Lincoln is my dog. He is a very good hunting dog." Andras looked at the dog and tried to imagine it chasing down a stag in the black forest. He could only imagine it trundling along, struggling over fallen trees and stepping on its own ears, traveling at a leisurely pace on its stubby legs.

"Hello," Andras said quietly, doing as he was told.

"I'm your father's friend from Poland from a long, long time ago, before you were born." Pa's friend turned back around to face the muddy avenue. Pa turned and pushed Andras's hat back down onto his head and smoothed down one of his sandy blonde eyebrows that had stuck up while he was sleeping.

"*This is your Uncle Vaclav, Andras. Remember from the stories?*" Andras's eyes widened at the realization, and he looked at the back of the shiny head of the cart driver. Vaclav was a recurring character in Pa's war stories. Andras's favorite story featuring Vaclav was the one about the Serbian demon. In that account, Uncle Vaclav had received the very same scars he had just glimpsed. Andras stared at Vaclav's back while he recalled all the stories he had heard about this heroic man. Andras nodded in response to Pa's question, and he looked at Lincoln the dog with a new air of respect. Now he imagined that saggy sad sack of slobber and skin on Uncle Vaclav's heel in battle, attacking Russians and hunting Serbian demons by his side. He slowly reached toward the dog who had only moved his eyes and tail since Andras noticed him. He patted the dog on the head three times gently and spoke sweetly to the dog.

"*Hello, Lincoln. Good dog.*" Andras spoke softly. The dog's tail swept the cart again and its nose sniffed the air. Uncle Vaclav and Pa chatted the whole way to Vaclav's home, a second-floor tenement apartment with a view of the hazy city and the ocean beyond.

Lincoln hopped off the cart and summited the stairs before Pa had even lifted Andras off the back. They lugged all their bags and belongings up the stairs and into Vaclav's home. It was dim and sparsely furnished. The walls smelled like tobacco and he had shelves of books. On one wall, three long-guns leaned in a rack, barrels to the ceiling. He had a painting of a very old, tall building that reminded Andras of the big, old churches back hom–back in Poland.

Andras put down his bags in the doorway and looked around. Vaclav opened a window and began restarting the fire. Lincoln found a spot by the fireplace and plopped onto the ground, his loose skin and ears flowing away from him like soft wax. Pa picked up Andras and placed him in a creaky rocking chair. Andras resigned to rock in the chair for a little while instead of tiptoeing through a stranger's home. Pa began to make up the canapé like a bed for Andras for the evening while Vaclav began to thinly slice potatoes and drop them in a pot. Now that Andras was fully awake, he was listening to Uncle Vaclav and Pa's conversation.

"All the supplies and wagon are waiting with the farrier. Josef's family is moving as far west as California, so Josef will swap out the mules with you in October." Uncle Vaclav was discussing the plan with Pa, and Pa nodded slowly as he listened.

"Josef knows we will be in Kholoraedo?" Pa confirmed.

"Colorado, yes, I will write them again to be sure. I see Josef's daughter once a week for bread, so they will know." Pa nodded again. Vaclav glanced at the violin case that leaned against the wall. When he spoke again, it was not in Polish. "Ya tak dumayu?" Pa glanced over at the violin case and nodded with a smirk. Pa picked up Andras and laid him down on the makeshift bed and pulled a thin blanket over him. The fire was warm, and the cushions were softer than the cot he had been sleeping on in the ship. When he laid his heavy head down on the faded red pillow, he watched Pa and Uncle Vaclav smile and chat.

They found such comfort and peace in each other. Andras didn't know what they were saying, but he wasn't sure if it was because they were speaking a different language or because he was falling asleep faster than Lincoln, who was already snoring with one eye open. Pa opened up his violin case, pulled out a long metal tube and the stock of a rifle, and assembled them, showing his hunting rifle to Uncle Vaclav who hefted it with admiration. He fell asleep listening to Pa and Uncle Vaclav whispering at the table.

In the morning, he awoke to the sound of his father in the kitchen failing to make breakfast quietly. He bonked wooden spoons off of dark iron pots and spilled hissing liquid on the stove top that bubbled and made a sharp burnt smell that made Andras open his eyes and sit up. Pa smiled at him and rasped a whisper.

"Hey, Andras! It's your first morning waking up an Amerykan. How do you feel?" Andras yawned widely and rubbed his eye with a limp-fingered hand. Blinking away the sleep, he stared at his Pa blankly and nodded weakly. Pa chuckled and pointed to a steamy plate of *placki ziemniaczane,* potato pancakes. Andras nodded a heavy head and swung his legs over the edge of his makeshift bed. As he took in Uncle Vaclav's house, there was much more to it than he saw in the dark last night. The windows of his second story home peered over the schoolhouse next door that also doubled as the town hall for this small corner of metropolis. To the east, taller buildings blocked out pieces of the watery horizon. The streets below were less crowded than the dock area where they landed yesterday.

Andras remembered yesterday and was astounded by all the events that had transpired the day before. He took stock of how he felt. His body felt slow and heavy, his clothes felt like they were stuck to his skin, and his hair felt…chunky. He always hated bath days, but now, he wouldn't mind a dunk in that old metal tub, Ma scrubbing his skin raw. He thought about his mother for several moments before he pushed the sad feelings away, images of Ma ebbing away like a tide.

Andras crossed the dusty floor and sat in the wobbly chair that shifted each time he did. He picked up the placki and chewed it slowly, staring at the wood grain patterns on the table. Andras would often look for faces or animals in the shapes of the wood grain and knots. Pa put a warm, heavy hand on Andras's head and kissed his forehead. Pa sat across from him and munched a bigger pancake silently. Together, the two American men ate in silence thinking of Ma and what today would hold for them. Uncle Vaclav emerged from the bedroom wearing a warm coat, a frayed scarf and a flat cap cocked to the right, ready to head out. He patted Andras on the head with a tight-lipped smile, gave him a friendly wink, and stole a potato pancake off the table. Over the stove, Vaclav dumped a small box of black powder into a black metal pot that steamed and rattled on the stove as it prepared whatever was inside.

"When do you want to pick up the supplies and wagon?" Pa asked between chews. Vaclav tugged the small silvery chain emerging from his pocket, swung his watch into his hand, and popped it open in one fluid movement. He shrugged and considered the watch face.

"*I'd be ready to leave as soon as the* coffee *is done.*" Andras looked at the rattling pot on the stove. Coffee. So very American. He imagined the hot drink being sweet like molasses and making him feel warm all over like the California sun, or so he'd heard. Pa nodded and hurried his breakfast. "*Want some coffee?*" Vaclav offered a small tin cup identical to the one he held in his other hand. Pa shook his head, making a face at the pot of coffee.

"*Bleh,*" Pa said, sticking his tongue out in disgust, "*I'll just have some tea or some brandy if you have it.*" Vaclav laughed and sipped the coffee in his cup. He waved a hand vaguely at the cabinet with the brandy bottle.

"*Uncle Vaclav, I want some coffee,*" Andras spoke up, his first words of the day raspy and faint. Both Vaclav and Berle looked at him with an amused smirk. Berle studied his son for a moment before glancing at Vaclav who was awaiting silent permission from Andras's father. Pa's smirk prompted Vaclav to half-fill the other tin cup and place it in front of Andras.

It smelled of wet earth and smoke and something…sweet, like an orange being opened in July. The steam curled up from the motionless black surface and disappeared in front of his eyes. He could feel the warmth of the drink as he wrapped his hands around the gray metal cup, and the pain that flashed on his fingertips made him pull away slightly and look up at Pa who maintained his smirk and rotated the cup so the curled handle faced Andras. Andras grabbed the handle with both hands and moved the cup to his mouth. As it traveled slowly toward his face, he felt distinctly different. This is what it feels like to be an Amerykan. Sitting in an apartment in New York City with his family, no gunfire or cannons far off, a cup of coffee in hand; this is what Pa had been talking about. He wished Ma was here.

When the warm metal cup touched his lip, he sipped a tiny bit of the dark, American liquid, and his face and throat immediately recoiled from the heat and flavor simultaneously. The flavor reminded him of the air when the vulcanized tire factory caught fire and burned for two weeks. The heat made the tip of his tongue feel rough and raw, like a knee that had just scraped brick as one was climbing over a wall. His jaw clenched from the bitterness, and he opened his mouth and let the coffee dribble down his chin and onto the lap of his trousers.

Both Pa and Uncle Vaclav were laughing hysterically. Andras immediately giggled churlishly, felt embarrassed, and then was completely distracted by his father and uncle. They were not sad immigrants struggling to survive in a country that was being snatched up like biscuits at a bake sale. They were a family, laughing together in a moment, unworried about invading armies and oppressing empires. Nobody was keeping watch by the windows or listening for patrols and dogs. Andras pushed the cup away and savored his first experience with coffee.

They bounced down the street in Vaclav's cart, the tall brown horse clip-clopping down the uneven roads as it had dozens of times before. Andras did not dare sleep this time. He was sitting up in the cart, drinking in every color, texture, figure, person, and sight. To Andras, he was in a magical, fantastical land that his Pa had teased him about in stories for years. Each person they passed had inherited a great prize of existing in such a ripe garden of hope. They passed a cobbled intersection, and Andras smelled the most delicious baked delight he had ever encountered. He sniffed the air and looked for the source. Across the way was a warmly lit bakery with ovens and a busy pastry chef within, not yet open for the day. Andras tapped his uncle on the shoulder and pointed to the delicious-smelling building.

"Co to znaczy? *What does it mean?*" he asked, referring to the sign.

"To piekarnia! *It's a bakery!*"

"Nie, co to znaczy? *No, what does it mean?*" Andras leaned forward and pointed to the sign specifically.

"Oh. To znaczy, Palwicz Pastries." Vaclav pointed at the sign. Andras saw his Pa leaning to listen to Vaclav's brief lesson as well. Andras continued to point out signs, and Uncle Vaclav would point to it, and read the English words back to Andras. Andras reckoned he would be an English-speaker long before they reached Kholoraedo.

The farrier was not some broad-shouldered sooty beast as Andras had expected, but a woman whose straw colored hair clung to her forehead. In the heat of a forge, she hammered a horseshoe in a dress and checked it for straightness before patting the big palomino horse twice on the flank. The horse lifted its foot, business as usual, and she pressed the hot horseshoe into the hoof. After the smoke had subsided a bit, she dipped it quickly in a small tub of oil and nailed it to the hoof while it still steamed and smoked. The horse lowered its foot and tested the fit a few times before continuing to chew. The woman wiped sweat from her forehead with the sleeve of her dress and tugged a bonnet off of the other, smaller anvil and tied it under her chin.

"Folks, can I help you gentlemen find something?" Her voice was strong and deep and reminded him of the commanding voice of the priest from Ma's church back in Poland. Uncle Vaclav removed his hat and smiled.

"Pardon, ma'am. We're here to pick up an order. A wagon, a team, and some supplies including one special package for my friend. Should we conclude business with the man of the house?" Uncle Vaclav's English was very good. His American accent barely contained any remnant of Polish except when he accidentally bit into those double-u sounds. She nodded and stepped inside for a moment and returned with a bill of sale, signed and folded. She opened it, scanned it, and handed it to Vaclav. He nodded and handed it back. She pocketed the note in a pocket on her dress and thumbed over her shoulder.

"The man of the house is still sleeping. I have the wagon and team all ready to ride with spare wheels and supplies ready. The other supplies you ordered arrived yesterday, and they're waiting to be loaded in the barn as well."

"*Is something wrong?*" Pa asked Vaclav who waved him off casually. They followed Eunice to the other barn where the large covered wagon sat with two mules already pawing anxiously at the straw-strewn floor. Andras's mouth split into an excited grin as he looked up at the two mules.

"*Do they have names?*" Andras asked without looking away from the mules. Vaclav translated for Eunice. She nodded and walked to the front of the wagon where the two shifted impatiently from one hoof to the other. She crouched in front of Andras and pointed to the first one.

"Buck." and then pointed to the next, "Peter." She smiled at him, and Andras smiled back, pointing at each mule.

"Buck and Piotyr," he repeated softly with a smile. She nodded, smiled back, and stood again. Addressing Vaclav and Berle, her voice changed back to the strong, professional woman.

"Freshly watered and fed this morning. I left a small satchel of apples and brown sugar lumps in case Buck gets bitey. He's a spoiled baby boy who gets grumpy when he feels neglected, so give him lots of pats and he'll pull you all the way to Judgement Day." Almost as if he could understand English, Buck swung his thick head and showed his long yellowy teeth. Andras giggled at the animated beast and nearly vibrated with excitement at the prospect of traveling to their new home with Buck and Piotyr.

Uncle Vaclav and Berle began packing the wagon while Andras meandered around the barn, playing with a pair of barn kittens that had come to investigate the visitors. For a while, Andras sat in the back of the wagon and asked, "what is that?" in English for any item he wanted to learn the English word for. He would then repeat it back as best he could and try to internalize it. Some words stuck better than others; sugar, horse, wheel, hat, pot, trousers, and rifle.

When nearly all the crates and boxes had been loaded, a sleepy-eyed man with a thick mustache and scruffy chin wandered into the barn and waved a hand at the men lifting supplies. When he spoke, Andras and Berle could only stare in confusion at the most unrecognizable version of English they'd ever heard.

"Marn' luds! Yarr aff thi' morra?" The man asked as he approached. Uncle Vaclav smiled and shook the man's hand, responding as if he had understood the slurred garble of phlegmy consonants and pitches.

"As soon as we've loaded, and I've had the chance to see your poxy mug. How ya' been, Hann?" Vaclav released the hand and handed him a sack of flour to load.

"Aff te fine yon Hameldaeme. Aye, naye nobla'. Yon aye hail at the hert, Pol'. Ah ken tell bot thems: thon laddies had muckle powstie. Am no sad bot loosin' thissen neigh, he's a bauld-daur. He'z tea's oot, and Ah've ben bet bah hem fur tha' last time." The man patted Buck's flank as he rounded the mule, and Buck rolled an eye at him and chewed the bit, perhaps remembering the last time he bit him.

Andras didn't realize he was staring aghast, open-mouthed at the man's strange English that Uncle Vaclav could not only understand, but was holding a conversation with. It sounded as if they were speaking two separate languages, but they laughed at the same moments and answered each other's questions.

Andras resumed assembling his space within the wagon. A small pile of boxes was his chair that he could lay down on and rest his head on a flour sack, if he got tired. He had a crate for a table and an empty tin cup on the table that had fallen out of a pack earlier. Andras decided that this would be his cup for the duration of the journey. A can of sugar was nearby his makeshift mobile campsite in case he wanted to swipe a finger or two.

The man that Uncle Vaclav had been talking to appeared at the back of the wagon, locked eyes with him, and began to communicate to him in that loud dialect he spoke. Andras stared and tried to glean a syllable of recognizable language, but to no avail. At one point, he thought that the man had said a word in Polish, but he was pretty sure that was just the man's accent. Besides, why would he be talking about crickets? Andras looked down shyly, and the man laughed and patted the wagon. Pa passed the violin case up into the wagon, and Andras set it down gently.

"Rifle," Andras said in accented English. Berle's eyes squinted in a proud smile, and Pa grabbed his shoulder and shook it with a squeeze.

"Yes. Rifle." Pa responded back in the same accent. Andras blinked and tried to think through the next correct English words.

"Rifle...why...why vee-oleen?" Andras's words were fragmented, and inconsistent, but Pa understood. He responded in Polish so Andras would understand.

"The violin case keeps the rifle safe. And a safe gun keeps people safe. Do you understand that?" Pa touched the middle of his chest with one soft finger, and his eyes locked on to his. Andras nodded.

"A safe gun keeps people safe. I understand." Pa had taught Andras to respect and fear guns since he was big enough to pick one up. Andras had not learned to shoot yet, but he knew how to measure out powder and that felt wadding was better than paper, but paper was more readily available. Andras knew how to put percussion caps on the nipples of the older rifles and that conical bullets worked better than balls, but it was easier to make balls in the field.

When the wagon was loaded, Hann, Uncle Vaclav, and Pa worked together to raise the white canvas covering that reminded Andras of the sailing ships they had come on only days ago. Now this canvassed vessel would carry them over amber waves of grain to their new home. The mules knickered and swayed impatiently, ready to not be stationary any longer than necessary.

The wagon was stacked with supplies and tools, food and clothes, and everything remaining of their life in Europe. And Ma's things. Pa had thought, for a brief moment, about leaving her things here, but he decided against it, saying, "*I want as much of her to stay with us as* long as possible. We'll bring her things to our new home first. Yes. Yes, then we'll figure out what to do next." Andras nodded and agreed.

Uncle Vaclav pulled out two more packages, both wrapped in paper and secured with lots of itchy brown twine. One was long and thin while the other was a thick triangle shape.

"What's this?" Berle asked with a wry smile upon noticing the last two parcels.

"They are gifts for you," Vaclav replied in English, "to celebrate new beginnings."

"New beginnings." Berle echoed back slower and thoughtfully. Vaclav nodded. He handed him the smaller parcel first. Pa broke the string and handed the twisted bundle to Andras who began picking at one of the knots while still glancing at Pa's gift. He peeled back the layers of noisy paper revealing bright silver and blued steel. Andras stopped fiddling with the string and watched Pa unwrap the most impressive pistol he'd ever seen in his six years of life.

"Rifle," Andras said and looked up at his Pa. Pa smiled at him for a moment and then looked quizzically at Vaclav.

"Your eighteen-sixty? Why would you give it to me?"

"Because there's no more Russians to kill in New York." He laughed and closed Berle's hands around it. "Take it, friend," he said in English now, "Where you're going, you will need it more than me."

"Because Indians?" Berle asked.

"Yes. And worse." A shiver ran through Pa's right arm as he cradled the pistol in his hand. Inside the paper was also a pouch with rounds of pistol load; powder, wadding, and round. Another tiny pouch of percussion caps jingled as Pa put them all in his satchel. He palmed the handle and wrapped his fingers around the smooth wooden grip. His finger rested along the side of the trigger guard as he half-cocked the hammer, rotated the cylinder with his fingertips, and then pulled the hammer all the way back and listened as it click-click-*snap*ped five more times. He tested the ramrod for several rotations.

"You kept it…cleanly." Berle complimented him, searching for the right words. *"I'll make you a deal: I'll hold onto it for you until you come to get it."* Vaclav nodded in agreement and put a hand over his heart in silent promise.

"Open the next one, Zimo. This is the one I am most excited for." The second, longer, larger parcel unwrapped much more slowly. Pa's hands seemed to recognize the weight and feel of it, so he cradled it as skillfully as a mother would hold their own child. When the paper fell away, Pa was holding a gleaming brass and blued steel rifle with a dark wooden stock and grip. Pa's fingers glided over the bright yellow metal and deep twisting wood grain. He held it up to his shoulder, and his hand found the loading lever, and he pulled it down. What followed was one of the most aurally-satisfying experiences Pa had ever had as the rifle's bolt slid open, revealing where the cartridge would be ejected after firing.

"Repeating?" Pa asked, focusing on the most important words of his phrases. Vaclav nodded and showed him how the tube under the barrel opened to receive the forty-four-caliber cartridges. Pa cycled the lever a few times, making a satisfied smile each time to Vaclav who nodded in agreement.

"This one has never been fired. It was a survivor from the Americans' civil war, and I thought it might be a good, you know, start-over, new beginning, yes?" Uncle Vaclav pulled a box of cartridges out of his coat pocket and set them down on the back of the wagon. "And maybe Andras can learn to shoot with it too. It doesn't kick quite as hard as our old muzzleloaders." Pa glanced over at his violin case and nodded Andras to go retrieve it.

Stoically, almost religiously, Pa opened the case where the three pieces of the rifle lay. He felt the weight of the trigger and the hammer. He double checked the screws' tightness and lifted the rifle to his cheek. It was shorter than his Whitworth forty-five, but also lighter and more easily-maneuverable, perfect for firing from horseback or from the seat of a wagon. Andras thought excitedly about when he would get the chance to learn to shoot with the new golden rifle.

"*Vaclav, I don't know what to say–*" Pa began, not masking his desire for the rifle. He held the rifle close, knowing it would be needed.

"Just say thank you, and that you promise to keep yourself and Andras safe out West. It's a different kind of danger altogether. In Poland, we fought Empires and armies. In America, you fight America."

With the wagon fully loaded and ready to depart, Uncle Vaclav shook Hann's and Eunice's hands again, offering more money for their kindness and troubles. Of course Hann and Eunice declined, but Vaclav insisted, and he ended up giving them five extra dollars after much indiscernible protestation. The three of them mounted up in the wagon and Pa took hold of the reins, calling out to Buck and Peter, letting the long, thin reins guide their powerful heads onto the worn, dusty road. Eunice had already resumed her place at the anvil, her bonnet lying untied beside her. Hann had donned a heavy leather apron and waved in wide, smiling arcs to them as they pulled away down the road. The three Polish men sat on the splintery bench of the wagon together, each pothole or stone a squeaky bounce.

Uncle Vaclav had agreed to ride with them for a day, stay the night outside of town, and then Berle and Andras would set off alone in the morning. Andras thought about continuing the journey without Uncle Vaclav, and he found that he was sad to think about Vaclav leaving.

"Uncle Vaclav?" Andras began.

"Yes, Mr. Walenty?" Vaclav responded with a smile.

"You have to stay here? Do you want to come with us?" Andras didn't look at him because he already knew the answer. Vaclav sighed sadly.

"I wish I could. But my work is here, and I have built a good life for myself in the best city in the world! And you and Zimowa will build the best life for yourselves together in Colorado. I have no doubt. But now that I have a friend out west, it gives me an excuse to go visit. And I suppose I could visit your Pa too while I'm there." With a wink and a smirk, Vaclav and Andras laughed together. Pa elbowed Andras playfully.

Andras was surprised by how suddenly the New York metropolis disappeared, making way for familiar-looking villages and towns. Andras felt at home again, surrounded by muted colors and hard-working simple folk who don't fear blisters and sweat. Before sunset, they arrived at their final stop before setting out into the great unknown. The farmstead they pulled up to was picturesquely idyllic with beautifully manicured hedges surrounding a freshly painted porch and three gorgeously crafted rocking chairs.

As the wagon came to a stop, a man emerged from the screened door, shading his eyes from the glare of the sun. For a moment, Andras recognized an image of the American countrysiude stretching on to the horizon with the grizzled frontiersmen posed on the porch. Andras felt as if he was in a story, a fantastical fictionalization of his dreams. Even the tragedy and loss of their crossing fit into the poetry of the American immigrant tale.

Pa lowered him onto the ground from the back of the wagon and straightened his clothes. Vaclav jumped down from the driver's seat and called out in terrific English.

"Vernon!" He smiled and waved. "I sure hope Helen let you know that we was calling upon y'all tonight, meanin' no imposition, sir." Vaclav removed his hat and held it in front of him. Vernon, the man on the porch, wriggled his nose in a derisive sniff, his mustache sweeping to and fro like a shop broom. He inclined his head slightly toward the interior of the house and called in.

"Ma, we expectin' o'ernight company?"

"Yes, Vern'," a call from inside the house replied.

"Callers for Mary?"

"Yes! Who else? Me? I'm too leathery for gentlemen callers anymore. Anyone calling on me anymore is the lenders. Bring them in, for Saint Peter's sake!" Ma's voice became more irritated and louder.

"It's that German-or-some'ot feller and two more looking like him, one's a lil'un." Vernon extrapolated further.

"Vernon, if I have to leave this kitchen to smile at our guests before you do, you're going to be cooking dinner for us and our guests collectively." Vernon sighed in concession and welcomed them warmly into their home with a barely noticeable nod of his head and a lazy arm waving them in to follow. The home was comfortable and sensibly assembled, all the chairs and furniture put exactly where Andras would have thought to put them in his own frontier home on the prairie. The kitchen smelled of bread and cooking fruit, a sweet fruit that Andras had definitely smelled before. Opposite the kitchen, a small, petite woman wearing a lovely green dress with a lovingly embroidered pattern and tiny white beads like pearls. Her hair was the color of Ma's eyes in the sun and it was pinned up in a neat bun. She was smiling as she emerged, beaming excitedly at Vaclav who returned the smile and nodded politely to her.

"Good day, Vaclav. You are wishing well today and your clothes," she spoke with the clumsy caution of a child learning to read. Mary was learning Polish, presumably with the help of Vaclav who was gazing at her like someone who was hearing music for the first time or had just witnessed something rare and beautiful to be cherished forever, to have and to hold. The air between them seemed to hold its breath as they both recovered from seeing each other.

Vernon shuffled through the electric air and waved a fly away that had followed him from outside, dispelling the charm of the moment. Vernon lowered himself into a wooden chair that had been worn smooth and stained dark from Vernon's consistent reliance on it. Vernon swirled a tin cup, tipped back the contents and swept his mustache back and forth once more as he studied the guests in his house.

Mary had been boarding with Vernon and Helen for most of the past year when, much to Vernon's displeasure, she met a charming Polish veteran working at a stable in town. That next week, Mary suddenly became interested in learning to ride and insisted on lessons. Much to Vernon's displeasure, a charming Polish veteran had agreed to tutor Mary for the price of riding out to join him for a picnic once her lessons were completed. While he was not overly enthusiastic at the prospect of Mary sharing a private picnic with this Polack, he also disliked the idea of prolonging her lessons longer, so after five riding lessons, Vaclav took Mary on a lovely picnic of fruits he had bought from the docks. They rode out to a small pond encircled by willows and ash trees where he told her of his heroic exploits against the Russians. Berle even appeared in a few of those stories, his antics being underplayed so as not to overshadow Vaclav's heroism.

Mary was delighted to meet Pa and Andras, being already excited to meet friends of Vaclav. Since the romantic picnic following the riding lessons, Vaclav had come calling on Mary at least once a week. Whenever Vaclav had come to visit, Vernon was always in the final stages of preparing a chore or project that he would need Vaclav's help doing. Of course Vaclav never minded, enjoying the chance to be around and build rapport with Helen and Vernon as well. Vernon's distracting chores did not keep Vaclav away from Mary but instead made him a regular fixture and reliable source of help when he came around.

In fact, Vernon was the only one not beaming when Vaclav arrived. This visit just happened to coincide with the day Vernon was planning on tarring the roof of the bunkhouse. He informed them that they were welcome to stay in the bunkhouse if they got the roof done by dusk. When Helen began to protest and offer up the sofa for Andras to sleep, Pa spoke up in his best English.

"Thank you so very much, all of you. The bunkhouse is good. We are happy to…" His voice trailed off, and he looked to Vaclav with a stumped face. "*Odwdzięczyć się?*" he asked.

"Repay." Vaclav prompted. Pa snapped his fingers with a smile.

"We are happy to repay your kindness," Berle finished with a smile. "Yes?" He confirmed with Vaclav who nodded to him. "Yes."

The rest of the evening, Berle and Vaclav spread hot tar across the roof of the mostly finished bunkhouse. They broke for a supper of tomatoes and bread with coffee that Helen brought on a tray. Andras spent the evening inside with Mary and Helen, carrying loads of linens to launder, fine dishes to carefully put away, and books to read to Helen while she rocked in her chair with her eyes closed. Mary brought her language learning books for Andras to read as they were the only books in the house containing Polish. Andras struggled with the words, finding the familiar phrases and verbs as he stumbled through the sounds and consonants.

When Helen began to snore and the rocking ceased, Andras perused the English words and lessons, sounding out the strange words the best he knew how, but he was sure it was all nonsense. After lunch was all cleaned up, Mary came gently into the room with a kind smile and curious eyes. When she spoke, it was clunky and slow-tongued, but Andras was so happy to be able to speak to someone besides Pa and Uncle Vaclav.

Mary was kind and very interested to talk to Andras. She knelt on the floor and spoke slowly, choosing her words carefully, and not getting upset or offended when Andras would correct her or help her pronounce the trickier words. She asked him about Poland and about the ship they traveled on. He told her about the black people he saw on the boat as well as the fancy Englishman and the Hungarian family.

"Polish is very hard for me. I did not learn to read English until I was eleven, and now I think I will not learn to read Polish until I am very old." She laughed and Andras shook his head enthusiastically.

"I think your Polish is very good for an Amerykanzi." He patted her knee encouragingly like Pa did when he got frustrated. *"Uncle Vaclav is helping me to learn English until we leave tomorrow. Then Pa and I will learn together while we ride to Coloraedo. I was hoping to learn to talk to the Indians we meet on the path."* Mary made a dramatic face with a comically scared expression.

"Talk to the Indians? Why would you want to talk with them?" Andras could not think of a reason why he wouldn't want to talk to them. They could teach him all about his new home, the trees, the animals, which mushrooms were safe to eat, and which berries to bake in a tart. He wanted to learn about what America was like before he came and whatever else he could! They knew more about living in America than any of the other people from Europe.

"I want to learn how to live in the prairie like them! I want to see mountains and the golden plains!" His voice rose with excitement,

and Helen snorted loudly from her chair and then resumed sleeping loudly. Mary and Andras both muffled a snicker.

"The Indians are dangerous. Be careful, Andras." She said, with a dire look on her face, emphasizing the foreboding seriousness of her statement. Andras wondered if she meant what she said.

"Why are they dangerous?" Andras asked.

"They don't like people coming onto their land. They like to scare people away" she explained. Andras pondered that.

"Where is their land?" Andras asked, intending to avoid their land and respect their wishes.

"It's the whole country. They don't want anyone living anywhere near them. The Pawnwee and Mohawk Indians have put up a fight, but the army has settled them down with their cannons and soldiers." Andras thought about the Russians, how they invaded and started telling people what to do, forcing Pa to fight. Pa told him once that a man should defend his home with his blood and final breath. *"A man without a home is always lost"* he had said.

"If we live in Coloraedo, will the…Pawneen-mohock be angry?" Andras's mouth moved strangely around the foreign words. Mary giggled and covered her mouth, apologizing in English.

"I'm sorry–er, I mean– *I'm sorry. Pawnee and Mohawk are two different… two other states?"* Her confidence waned as she searched for the correct word. Eventually, she quit trying to remember it and instead taught Andras a new English word. "Tribe," she said in

English, *"like a town or village."* Andras thought for a moment. It was a strange word, *tribe,* but if it was like a town or village, but not quite,

"Family?" Andras suggested. Mary considered for a moment, and then nodded.

"Yes. The Pawnee and Mohawk are two different families of Indian. They speak different languages and wear different clothes." As Mary explained this concept of family groups being distinct from the other, Andras thought about the other families in Poland and how they all dressed similarly to him. He was excited to see all the different Indian families, and he began to imagine wildly the different things they would wear and do.

The images he had seen of the Indians were always stern-faced, dark skinned people in simple clothing, beaded and adorned with skillfully-made and hand-carved effects made from nature's finest resources. One man in particular had a smoking pipe made from the pronged antler of a deer, and the stem of the pipe was wrapped in a dark brown pelt like a rabbit or squirrel. When Andras got a pipe, he wanted it to be just like that.

When Pa and Uncle Vaclav returned from roofing their lodging for the night. They all shared an evening dinner of roasted potatoes, baked chicken and carrots, and Vernon brought out a set of jars that he filled with a drink that almost looked like water. Pa struggled to get the proper English words out.

"What is this?" Pa had asked.

"It's my own special mash," Vernon explained as he sat down in his smoothed wooden chair and swirled the glass like it was a fancy wine. He sipped it, coughed, made a face, and then seemed to settle into the chair, melting a little like a piece of cheese too close to the fire.

"Yes, thank you," Pa replied. "What…what is…this?" Berle asked, not knowing how to ask Vernon what it was made of, what it resembled, or if it was safe for human consumption. Vernon took another gulp and a heavy exhale like he had put a piece of too-hot potato in his mouth. Convinced, Pa took a sip and considered the drink for a moment, swallowed it, suppressing a cough, and then took a second gulp. He shrugged and nodded with a strange face of analysis and then swallowed the cheek of mystery spirits. He nodded and shrugged. Vernon seemed offended by Pa's lack of reaction, and Pa's indifferent face broke into a smirk, and then a high, mocking giggle directed at Vernon who was swirling his own glass and considering the ramifications of downing the rest of the glass as Berle had done.

Andras watched this ridiculous interaction between two adult men with a scientist's analytical eye. As Vernon tried to keep up with Pa's constitution, the room relaxed into friendly laughs and relaxed conversation. Pa's words slipped back and forth between English and Polish, and Uncle Vaclav couldn't stop giggling and muffling bursts of laughter that climaxed when Vaclav covered a laugh, and a booger leaped from his nose. The whole room erupted in laughter, Andras laughed along, and his eyes felt warm and heavy. Andras remembers

Pa bringing the blankets up under his chin, and Andras fell asleep to the sound of his Pa, uncle, and new friends all laughing together.

Chapter 3

The next morning was a blur of getting dressed, loading the wagon with more supplies, and then he was sitting next to Pa on a wide bench that creaked and bounced as it navigated the well-worn wagon trail. Pa hummed a familiar Polish tune as he smiled passively under the brim of the wide hat that Vernon had loaned him, as long as he "took care of it." Pa had agreed and pressed the hat down onto his head with a satisfied smile.

The trail could be seen reaching out for miles, bisecting hills and cutting a swathe through the grassy fields and trees. This morning, the sun warmed their backs and a slight cool breeze blew behind them, keeping the sun's rays from getting too hot. Other wagons were on the trail ahead of them, winding in swaying lines that reminded Andras of ships on the sea, their billowing white canvases filling and flapping as they skated across the landscape. Behind them, three wagons matched pace with them as their passengers sang songs in unison with sweeping verses and choruses that reminded Andras of the Spring birds that lived in the Winter trees and sang the snow away.

"Alright, son." Pa spoke up in his thick accent, "Now that we are on the trail, we speak English." Andras's face flushed as he frantically reviewed all the English words he knew in his head.

"Yes, Father." Andras replied with a stern tone. Berle smiled and ruffled Andras's hair lovingly, and Andras rested his head on his dad's arm. Andras loved the first few days spent on the trail. During the day, Pa would drive and sing and tell stories, stopping to pee, marvel at America's beauty, and assist other travelers. Pa had started pointing out different kinds of flowers while they were on the trail, and sometimes Andras would leap from the wagon's roost and sprint out to pluck a new flower or plant, and then sprint back to Pa where he would help Andras find a new page in his grandmother's bible to slip in the flower. Andras would then smoosh the book closed and tighten the belt around it to preserve the specimens. In the coming evenings, Andras found comfort in one of his mother's shawls that kept him warm in chilly evenings and smelled vaguely of her as he fell asleep holding it.

At night, they would light the lanterns that hung on the front and back of their wagon, and Pa would pull off the trail, usually near fellow travelers. The other travelers on the trail were typically hospitable and kind, offering to share their fire and food in exchange for stories or songs from their home. Andras always insisted that they camp near new people each night. He loved meeting other children with their own games and jokes and songs.

For several nights they traveled close to a family from Ireland. Harrison was a thick man, not from laziness or overindulgence of fine foods, but from decades of hard labor, savage combat, and distilled liquor to forget the latter. His wife, Hanora, was a kind woman who had a laugh that bounced off the hills and sounded what Andras wished lightning sounded like. She always cooked meat for her husband and two sons, John and James. John and James were much older than Andras, and they didn't express any interest in playing with Andras or even chasing him around the wagons when he tossed grass blades at them from atop the canvas covering.

When Pa and he had first joined Harrison by his fire aside his sons and wife, Andras's eyes were drawn to the knotted, empty pant leg. Harrison noticed Andras's gaze and patted his stump of a leg.

"War's a nasty, evil thing. Everyone on that battlefield leaves part of themselves behind. I got lucky and only lost my leg. At the end of the day, there were just a lot of dead Americans on American soil. I took a bullet in the knee as we were charging across a field out of a treeline straight at a line of cannons. I was the luckiest bastard God ever loved that day. There I was, lying on the grass with my blood pouring out of my leg, all my brothers and fellow soldiers dying around me like there was nothing else to do. The Union boys found me and saved my life, but old lefty was the price of my life. I may be alive, but that surgeon made sure I don't ever charge up any more hills, bayonet affixed, reckon?" Andras was not scared of the man's missing leg, but instead was more curious as to where they were heading. If he fought to defend his home, why not stay?

"Berle, why don't you tell us a story of Poland? Andras mentioned you fought in a war as well." Harrison had asked between puffs on his corncob pipe. The moon was perched behind a low hill, slowly sliding skyward. Above, the stars were a glimmering sheet of diamonds that nearly provided ample light on their own for Andras to see the knotted pant leg of the old soldier elevated.

Berle scooted more securely onto his tiny camp stool, a folding seat that fit nicely in the wagon. He tipped back his hat and squinted his eyes as he stared at the fire. Andras looked up at his father who searched the dusty tomes of violence and protecting his beloved for years. As he began, Andras could already feel himself growing sleepy from the familiar timbre and phrasing of his Father.

"I…remember one early morning, we had been marching all night, and we were very tired. A small group of us had been assigned to cause problems for the Russians on their supply routes and bridges, and the Russians had been chasing us. The morning was as foggy and white as cream, and we heard a church bell ringing from the west like God was calling out to us himself. When we finally stumbled into the church, it was empty except for the parson who had rung the bell. By the time the Russians…" Pa's voice slowed and then trailed off as if distracted. Andras's lethargy melted away at his father's sudden silence, and he glanced up at him. Pa was focusing on the moon as it rose above the hills and rising mountains. Harrison turned to look as well, and Andras heard Harrison's breathing change. What was wrong with the moon? Andras squinted at the celestial body as it glowed warmly in the dark sky, trees and riders silhouetted–riders. Andras saw them. Three horses with riders astride sitting atop the hill with the moon to their backs. They looked like knife blades made from shadow against the eerie glow.

"How many are there?" Berle asked Harrison without turning to look at him. Andras counted three riders on the hill, so still they could be statues. One of the horses nodded its head silently.

"I'd wager around ten or twelve." Harrison answered gravely. He reached for his range rifle, essentially a revolving pistol with a long barrel and stock.

"Ten? Really? That's not the scouts?"

"Yes, really. The scouts probably spotted us at sunset. If you're seeing them now, consider it a courtesy, a warning. They're letting us see them, so we know whose land we're crossing through."

"Are we in any danger?"

"Oh yes, grave danger, but the *in-jun* don't let you see them a'fore they open up your throat and make a toupee out of you." Berle leaned to grab his shiny new rifle from Vaclav. Andras found that he was gripping Pa's coat when he leaned, afraid to be too far from him. The brass plate on the rifle caught the flickering light as tongues of fire pawed at the sky.

"Will they attack?" Berle asked. Harrison's eldest son, John, rejoined the fire with a pistol in hand.

"No telling. They might not even know themselves yet. Reckon they're out there in the dark, skulking and spying, seeing if we have anything of value asides our women."

"But Andras and I brought no women." Berle countered.

"And they don't want what Hanora has. They might think they do, but they don't." Berle barely choked out a laugh, a human moment in a tense situation. Harrison chuckled in response, checking the caps on his rifle. John, whose accent was near perfectly American, helped his father up onto his last leg and handed him his crutch, trading the rifle for the pistol.

"Should we start tacking the ox, Pa?" John asked Harrison warily. Harrison nodded and patted his son's shoulder reassuringly.

"Might as well. Either way, they don't want us here, and I don't rightly feel like sleeping here anymore." The two families packed their wagons quickly and silently, hitching their teams and loading their belongings within the hour. Andras silently protested with frightened eyes when his father told him to stay in the wagon, out of sight, and to try to get some rest. Andras could not sleep. He lay on the floor of the wagon on his side, watching his Pa, his head resting on the violin case. Ma's scarf was pulled tight around his head. Every bump or mule nicker made Andras start, jerking to alertness. Behind them, the sound of Harrison's rhythmic ox-song and whistling comforted him. Just knowing they were behind him gave him peace.

After what felt like hours, Andras noticed that he felt calm. Pa swayed lightly with the bump of the road, and a cool breeze blew through the wagon. The only sound he could hear was the rattle and squeak of wood and metal, and the crunch of the road below them. He glanced out the back, and his throat caught.

Harrison was not sitting on his wagon, singing to his oxen. Where before, the hobbled veteran sat, dark maroon stains glinted in the swinging light of the wagon. Blood visibly dripped from the seat like the bench itself was bleeding. Across the rump of one ox, a twisting line of blood-splatter sparkled.

Visible beneath the wagon, John's arm dangled, his finger caught in the trigger guard of the pistol that dragged along the road. When the wheels straddled a stone that caught the pistol, John's arm toppled into the road, a twisted, bloody ragged stump where the rest of John used to be.

Andras reeled back in horrified revulsion and he cried out in his most infantile scream, crying for his Papa. As he scrambled towards the front of the wagon, the seat was empty. Pa was gone, and only his rifle lay on the bench, half-cocked. Again, Andras cried out, huge, hot tears rolling down his dust streaked cheeks, saliva flying from his parched, cracked lips.

He turned to retreat into the wagon and was paralyzed by the glint of two inhuman eyes sunken deep into the skull of a human face curtained by long black hair adorned with bones and beads. His face was painted red with the blood of Harrison and John and his father, and before Andras could turn to run, the man was on him. Andras shrieked in pain as he felt his hair tugged backwards and he was thrown to the floor. The man pounced on him, twisted blade in hand, and pressed the blade to Andras's forehead and whispered horribly in Russian to him as he began to cut.

Andras woke up in the wagon, the morning sun warming the white canvas that fluttered gently in the slow breeze. Pa's hand was on his shoulder, and Andras clung to it like a lifeboat.

"*Hey, hey, Andi, I'm right here. You were having a nightmare, my love.*" His father's voice in his mother-tongue calmed him immediately and he nodded, wiping the sweat from his brow. Behind them, Hanora drove the oxen with her younger son, James, beside her. The dream was already fading from his memory, but the pitch black silhouette of the hair shrouded man with glowing eyes lingered in his mind.

"*Pa–* Pa," he corrected himself, switching to English, "Did you see any Indians?" He saw only a small corner of his dad's face from where he sat, but he could tell he smiled.

"Yes, I did, Andras. Mr. Harrison and I drove straight out of their territory, and we saw them on hills, watching us, guiding us towards the safe roads."

"They did not try to kill you or threaten you?"

"They are people just like us, Andras. They fight to defend their home like we have. They protect what they have and love their families just like us. The least we can do is leave when they ask us to leave. If they try to hurt us or steal from us, we'll set them right, but until then, they're just our nervous neighbors. Do you understand?"

The fantastical image Andras had of the indigenous Americans was in flux. While in Poland, he had seen many pictures of them and Ma had read parts of books to him concerning the red men, but he had never seen them as an actual threat before until last night. They appeared in the darkness like they were part of the wilderness, and, without word or action, chased off two wagons-full of settlers. They may be people just like us, but they were not exactly like us.

"Are we afraid of them?"

"Yes. We would be foolish to not be afraid of them."

"Why?"

"Because this is their home. They would be afraid of us in our home." Pa said with confident finality that made Andras believe and agree with it. The natives would fear and respect him on his own home territory. He would know every rock and tree and every secret path. Nobody would be able to invade his home and steal his land once they arrived. Andras imagined scenarios of himself sprinting through the woods, rifle in hand, surprising the invaders, causing them to panic and flee without a shot fired. Andras took note: he needed to learn how to scare off invaders by standing ominously on a hill. Strangely, Andras had yet more respect for the Indians than he did before.

By midday, Pa pointed at a wide, roiling river, and said, "See that, Andras? That's our ride to…" and he took his time on this next part, "Co-Lo-Rah-Do." The Ohio River was not a frothing canyon of raging currents, but a silvery avenue of smoothly churning water that was more inviting than daunting. Andras thought that he might enjoy a swim before he considered how cold the water would be. Further below, Andras saw a boat casually navigating the water, one of the passengers dropping a line in the water.

"What about Buck and Piotyr?"

"They're coming too. They will ride on the boat with us. It's a big boat." Andras thought of the last boat he was on. He thought of that final evening with Ma, when Pa roused him from sleep and allowed him to hug her and say goodbye. If Andras had known that would be the last time he would have seen his mother, he would have held on longer and kissed her one more time on the cheek the way that always made her smile, and her eyes would squint shut, and she would bump her forehead against his. Andras's eyes felt hot for a moment, and he rubbed his nose with his sleeve.

The wagon squeaked and swayed down the winding hill to the wide, flat river ferry like they had in Poland. Poland had many ponds and rivers, and a ferryman could always be found nearby when a bridge couldn't. One warm summer, Andras had dreamed of becoming a ferryman, spending his days fishing in the cool summer streams and swimming.

The ferryman was a black man, older with a round curly white beard that almost seemed to gleam in the streaks of sunlight between the branches of the swaying willows. He removed his drooping wide-brimmed hat and raised a vague hand in greeting. Pa waved back and halted Buck and Piotyr.

"Y'all heading west down the river?" he asked. His voice was smooth and deep like molasses. He looked them both over and assessed the wagon and team.

"Yes, sir. We're trying to reach Colorado, and we've heard that the Santa Fe trail may be the best way to get there." Pa responded in near-perfect English. Andras had heard Pa practicing his English in the evenings when he was supposed to be sleeping, and Pa seemed to be more proficient daily. English was not an easy language to learn.

"You heard right, friend. You Ukrainian?"

"Ukra– no, no, no. Poland. We're from Poland."

"Poland! That's good too!" He smiled widely as he reached in his pocket and opened a small notebook and penciled-in what he could only assume was *Poland*. "Never had Poland before. Welcome aboard!"

The ferryman helped them load the wagon and animals and shoved off down the river. He sang as they drifted, songs about pain, hope, work, masters, and far-away homes. Andras never learned any of the words of the songs, but he loved listening to the old man with black skin and white hair. Mr. Andrew, the ferryman, was born in North Carolina before the American war, and had been enslaved until he was grown.

"I'll tell you what though, missuh, Summer o' sixty-five, *that* was my best birthday. I remember the first beer I had, dressed in all blue in some Goddamned–oh, sorry, son, beg your pardon–some damned cornfield in Tennessee. I still got a piece of that bottle too." Sure enough, Mr. Andrew produced a worn shard of brown glass, worn smooth from years of handling. "Once the war was over, it was time for me to get my own piece, be my own person, work for my own table, Lord knows." Pa nodded deeply in agreement as he listened. The two of them brushed the mules as they chatted.

Mr. Andrew and a few of the other ferrymen on the Ohio River had a running competition, seeing who could meet the most people from the most places. It was a charming exercise that encouraged them to show kindness to everyone who rolled down their path. There was nothing more neighborly than being immediately interested in someone you just met.

The river trip was long and boring. At one point, Buck became restless, bucking and complaining in his tack until he vomited all over the deck of the ferry. Pa sat Andras on Buck's back and told him to sing and stroke his back to make him feel better. Mr. Andrew and Pa cleaned up the mess together, merely tossing it overboard. Pa patted Buck kindly and scratched him behind the ear. Andras mimicked his father and scratched Buck behind the ear in the same way. The mule nodded and sighed heavily, flapping his thick, hairy lips and settling back down.

One morning, Andras awoke with a start. He had heard a loud noise, and he paused and listened. He could hear the echoing timbre ringing in the air. A gunshot? Pa and Mr. Andrew could be heard moving and shuffling outside the wagon. Andras heard the smooth cycling of Pa's new rifle followed by a very quiet sigh and exhale, and suddenly thunder! Before the smoke cleared, Pa had stepped behind cover. And another round was cycled. A crack of thunder, and the wagon's canvas shivered as a hole punched through it. Andras rolled backwards over himself, falling out the back of the wagon and landing hard on his side. Someone grabbed him hard by his shirt and yanked, lifting him back into the wagon. He was relieved to see Mr. Andrew, a handful of Andras's shirt in one hand, a pistol in the other. He recognized it as Uncle Vac– as Pa's pistol.

"What's going on?" Andras asked Mr. Andrew who was hesitant to rise above the edge of his cover.

"Cut-throat bandits trying to rob us before we can reach St. Louis. Stay hidden, Andras!" Another sharp crack of gunfire, and a shower of splinters tumbled onto Andras's head. Mr. Andrew brushed splinters away from his face and laid a heavy hand on his head.

"You stay down now, you hear? Nod your head, son, say something that you understand me, boy." Andras nodded quickly and turned with an agile slither of his small body, and hugged the floor of the wagon. He scooted and shimmied to his place among the crates and pulled Pa's violin case close to him.

Andras did not squeeze his eyes shut and whimper while hot tears streamed down his face. Andras listened and forced himself to not flinch when a bullet *whizz-popp*ed over his head. Pa needed a brave warrior right now, not a child that needed tending to. Each crack of gunfire was another chance of death for any of them. He could hear Pa and Mr. Andrew talking back and forth, calling out what they saw.

"Watch left, Andrew," Pa said clearly, "Those marksmen are hanging back to get an angle as we move further down-river." Pa's voice was stern and calm. He didn't convey panic or fear, but a familiar confidence.

"Shit, Berle, I'm getting pinched over here with them shooting from both sides!" Andrew shouted to Berle, not calm at all. " And I'm getting down to... eight shot left."

"Head down, Andrew, I'm going to fire over you." Pa spoke slowly, and he heard the same quiet breath and slow exhale. Pa's brass-beauty kicked hard into the crook of his shoulder, and he watched the man in the blue shirt stumble and double-over, tumbling onto his shoulder, and flat onto his back. From the center of his chest, a dark red stain blossomed across the blue of his shirt. As Berle exhaled, he breathed out the old words like a curse over the man's final quivering. *Kistka do kistky, krov do krovi, mudak.* His father taught it to him, and his father from him, and so on all the way back to swords and longships. He cycled the rifle, and the gleaming metal casing tumbled to the deck of the ferry.

The next man–no, a boy! A boy no older than fourteen reeled in the loose sand of the river bank, reconsidered, grabbed the pistol off the dead man's hip, and fired a blind shot towards the ferry. Berle didn't even hear the hiss of the bullet. He turned his attention back to the other three assailants who were emerging from cover and lining up shots again. One of them even fired a shot wide and high before looking over the rotting log they crouched behind.

Americans fight so differently than Russians or Polish or Hungarians. They leap, hoot, and holler, without any military discipline or formation. Their comfortability with repeating weapons makes their attacks dangerous, chaotic, confusing, and altogether frustrating for an ill-prepared defender. Fortunately for Berle, Andrew, Andras, Buck, and Piotyr, their lack of military discipline was also reflected in their accuracy. If Andrew and Berle put any sort of pressure on these wild bandits, they would dive between covers and neglect aiming, fighting to keep pace with the ferry that was slowly drifting away to St. Louis and then Westport beyond that. Home seemed so close now, and these yelpling assholes weren't going to stop them.

He ducked behind the wagon's wheel again, two of the wild shots coming closer than he felt comfortable with. A splash of water and a low *thunk* of a bullet hitting heavy wood. Berle raised his rifle and fired at a sprinting man, his pistol dangling from a piece of rope around his neck as he ran. The bullet puffed a sandy explosion as it missed its target. "*Kurwa.*" He cycled another round and exhaled slowly again. With a sharp kick and a puff of smoke, the brigand tumbled to a twisting halt, sprawled in the sand. *Kistka do kistky, krov do krovi, mudak.* Berle sniffed, cycled a round, and searched for his next target. He could sense retreat in their attacks, and he wanted to send them running.

Inside the wagon, Andras opened the violin case and subconsciously withdrew his hands reverently. The wooden stock was darker, where Pa's hand and cheek rested. Andras had seen a tired-eyed Pa come home after a long day, disassemble his rifle, clean it, count the bullets and powder spent, and then Andras would crawl into his lap and poke him in the face to keep him awake. It was a fun memory.

Andras wrapped his small hands around the cold metal of the barrel and wooden stock, surprised at the weight of it. Pa always wielded it with such ease. He fitted the three pieces together and made sure the screws and pins were tight. Like Pa, he pulled back the hammer and held it nearer his head. He closed his eyes and listened as he squeezed the trigger, like Pa always did. The hammer's *snap* was barely audible over the gunfire, shouts, and lapping of water. Piotyr knickered and reared with a small hop. Andras took three bullets and caps, and he slid the first over the nub with his thumb. He packed the load tight and turned back onto his belly to crawl to the back of the wagon. Mr. Andrew sat on the deck of the ship, tipping black powder into the cylinder of the pistol. His clothes were disheveled, and his hands were shaking.

Pa, on the other hand, looked every part the epic frontiersman hero. His wide brimmed-hat was tilted to the left to allow him to squeeze the rifle close to his shoulder and cheek. His loose linen shirt, hardly touched with sweat, fluttered open in the breeze. When he gazed down the rail of his rifle, he kept both eyes open. There was no hatred or malice in his eyes. His face was the same as that of a farrier making horseshoes or a baker sifting flour. When he squeezed the trigger, the crack felt more like lightning than real lightning. Goosebumps ran up Andras's arms, and he held his father's rifle closely. Andras saw two of the lawless bandits high-tailing over the hill as quickly as they could through sturdy bushes and rooty shrubs. Mr. Andrew aimed the pistol at them and braced his arm over a box that once held cloth bolts. When Berle didn't fire at them, he glanced over, his left eye squeezed shut.

"We're letting them go?" Andrew asked, relief almost audible in his sigh. Berle paused and looked at them shrinking away over the hill.

"Should we not? Do they have something we need?" His confusion was genuine as he began reloading his repeater faster.

"No, but…ain't we afraid of them coming back for us?" Mr. Andrew was thinking more about his many future trips on this river, and the likelihood of encountering the same band again, now with mistakes learned from, and tactics honed.

"Maybe stay in St. Louis for few days. Wait for them to feel the sting of their wounds and weigh their gold. Perhaps they will choose to stay home instead of facing off with Andrew Ferryman again." Pa winked at Mr. Andrew and held out an empty hand, offering to reload the pistol. He chuckled and handed him the pistol.

"'Feel the sting of their wounds.' I like that. Maybe I will do just that. 'Got some friends in St. Louis I've been meaning to visit since I said

I would seven years ago. Ain't that just the way life is, huh?" This time Pa chuckled and nodded.

A low *whizz-snap* hissed past them followed by the most awful keening shriek Andras had ever heard. This desperate, begging, pleading, awful, crying wail that Buck squalled made Andras feel sick and his skin crawl. He heard Buck's screams in many of his nightmares for years to follow. Gushes of hot, dark blood splashed on the deck as Buck twisted and fought his tacking to see what had ripped him open. A deep hole in his side was the inspiration for this awful blood-splashed nightmare from which Andras could not look away. Buck was dying, and Piotyr fidgeted and kicked beside his old friend, helpless to do anything but watch him scream and writhe, weaker and weaker by the moment. The metallic smell of Buck's blood was all that Piotyr could focus on.

"Berle! One more is still shooting at us! They shot the neigh!" Mr. Andrew dropped to the deck again, covering his head. Pa's eyes spread wide and glistened as he looked at Buck and then to the source of the shot. It was the boy he overlooked earlier. He had picked up a rifle from one of the bodies of his dead friends and abandoned their original directive for a new one: raging, boiling, scalding, terrifying, awful revenge. The kind of revenge that feels like justice at first, but then feels like murder and shame every night for the rest of your life as you're trying to sleep.

Berle snapped the receiver tube shut and locked eyes with his son who was hugging his old rifle like a child would cling to a blanket or toy.

Berle moved towards him in one fluid movement and inspected his rifle. He smiled a roguish half-smile and cupped his son's chin in a hand, squeezing his cheeks playfully. Berle shook his head in disbelief as he knelt and raised his old friend to his cheek.

"*Biegnij do domu, chłopcze,*" Andras heard his dad whisper over the sobbing wails of Buck's dying. Another bullet hissed past them through the air. Andras could see the boy pausing to reload, and then run a dozen yards before firing again.

"Tato…dlaczego on ciągle przychodzi? *Dad…why is he still coming?*" Keeping the rifle pressed to his cheek, Pa stood and moved to shield Andras.

"Obserwuj dalej, synu. Patrzeć. *Keep watching son. Behold.*" Andras saw the final gunman, a boy, running to keep pace with a ferry gaining speed, firing his last bullets without thought of tomorrow. "Amerykański wojownik nigdy się nie poddaje. *The American warrior never gives up.*" Pa said those final words in their heart-tongue like someone seeing the ocean for the first time. Pa's old rifle rang less like a clap of thunder, and more like the boom of a slamming church door. When the swirls of black smoke subsided, the pursuing form of the vengeful boy was replaced by the shrinking shape of a dead child, enwreathed by crimson rites and dead friends. *Kistka do kistky, krov do krovi, mudak.*

"*Mudak,*" he echoed his father's last syllables to the rapidly shrinking bandit. Next stop, St. Louis, and then home.

Chapter 4

Seventy one. Seventy two. Seventy three. Seventy four. The rhythmic rocking and predictable noises of the American steam train nearly lulled him to sleep. A mean feat to be sure, but made impossible by Satan himself in the form of a sniffly, ancient woman sitting across from him, snottily knitting what she muttered to him would be a quilt for sick cats? He did not care. Since he landed in Boston two weeks ago, he found he could not sleep on trains.

Feet up, hat placed over his eyes, statuesquely still. *Sleep, dammit.* **Sniff.** *Seventy five. Isus Hrist.* He lifted his dark hat from his face. Lifeless black eyes, doll's eyes, set in sharply angled bony features. His hair was cut short, shaved after an initial delousing. He had a thick, black mustache that covered the white, root-like scars that lanced across his already pale face. The old woman, *the sniffer*, paused and locked eyes with him. She didn't sniff. He sat up and leaned close to her. She did not move. His voice was a harsh, raspy whisper, like the sound of shifting snow on a mountain or the wind outside your window.

"I heard your sniffing while I was trying to be sleeping, and I wanted to ask," he paused and cleared his throat, "what plighted cacophony born of incest and poor hygiene created the rotted sphincter that summoned you here to torment me?" The withered woman gasped, aghast at the slew of rude words and insults from this strange, dead-eyed man. All she could muster was a weak, "Well, I never…How…I would…" She stammered as she gathered her knitting close to herself, leaning away from him. He sniffed loudly, animalistically, and sighed.

"You're almost there, sister. Keep the faith. You will see the Lord soon enough." Her face went pale, and she began to shakily rise from her seat. "Good, girl. Let me sleep," he hissed at her. He settled into her old spot and put his black boots up onto his old spot, pushing his hat back over his eyes. The rocking and repetitive movement of the train began to slow his breathing, and his head felt heavy once more.

He wasn't sure how long he had been drifting or sleeping, but when he heard the high squeal of locomotive brakes and the rhythm of the train change, he began to stir again.

Ogden was an ugly name for a place, but he was here on business. Yes, the business was personal in nature, but business all the same.

A few years back, he had been left for dead on a snowy mountainside, ripped open, bleeding out, already exhausted from fighting and traveling for so long. Vukašin had come from Niš to hunt a monster the Russians had come to call "Zimnyaya Gadyuka, *Winter Viper*," because of the way he would strike lethally and then disappear into the snowy countryside. The Viper had been harassing and hunting Russians for months before the Russian general had sent for him. Vukašin had killed rebels and monsters in Austria, Hungary, Serbia, Russia, and Poland before, but the Russian leadership seemed scared and frustrated.

He followed a supply convoy of Russian troops for two days before the Winter Viper finally struck. Vukašin only watched. A hillside once gleaming with white, flawless snow now lay enshrouded in smoke and ruin, upsought by the Winter Viper and his companions. As the Russians below him died, he watched the hillside with didactic fascination. The way he moved and fired, how he took aim, the way he hugged trees as he advanced; all of it would help him kill the Winter Viper. For months, Ilić watched Russian convoys. Most of them left unaccosted, but the ones that were ambushed on the road, Ilić watched from afar.

Eventually, the time came for Vukašin to test his mettle against the Viper's. For three days, Vukašin tailed a detachment sent to hunt the Viper. It was a savagely bitter cold autumn, and winter was threatening to be even more unforgiving. Months of watching the Viper strike gave him the clairvoyance to pick a steep valley passage to strike.

Vukašin scouted ahead and set up his blind high-up on the northern ridge. On the second day, Vukašin saw two Polish resistance fighters settle onto a ledge, awaiting the Russian convoy. He would wait. He cared less about the Russians troops than he did the Winter Viper. He wasn't hired for security detail. He was hired to kill a monster. He wasn't on overwatch; he was hunting, and his quarry was wily. He had gathered a lifetime's worth of information on the Winter Viper in the past months.

He knew he was local and that he probably lived in one of the nearby towns. Nobody moves through a forest like that unless they grew up in it. He knew that he made his own bullets, typically out of melted lead bits, sometimes still clinging to the paint of what it once was. Ilić knew he was a hunter before he was a soldier. His patience, carefulness, and skill weren't something that could be beaten into you. No, skills like that can only be honed on an empty stomach with your boots full of snow and your father breathing heavily next to you, whispering, "Pažljivo…pažljivo…naći srce… srce. *Carefully… carefully… find the heart… the heart."*

Memories of that autumn flooded his thoughts as he readied himself and straightened his clothes to depart. Outside the window, there was no train station or bustling township to greet them. On the other side of the glass, beautiful Utah countryside with picturesque jutting mountains. The trees grew tall and thick, and the rivers were all churning with frigid white water. Perhaps Ogden could be a fine place to live after all.

"What the hell, this ain't Ogden," one of the other passengers said.

"What's going on, why did we stop?" another said.

"Is the track out? Did the engine detach?" More passengers began to stand and raise their questions and theories as to their premature stop. *Dammit. He hadn't slept at all.*

Ilić hefted his gun belt and fastened it around his hips, patting the pistol that rested against his leg with a friendly hand. A man eyed him with a glint of suspicion, and Ilić smelled fear. Ilić winked at him and sat back down. Who knew when they would get moving again? This might be the perfect opportunity to get a few minutes of sleep. The passengers murmured and droned for several minutes before one brave man volunteered to make the walk to the engine to figure out exactly what the hell was going on. The man tugged his waistcoat flat and he tidied the bottom of his mustache with the back of a finger.

As the hero approached the wooden door with the small window, the door jutted open with a splintering crack, bashing into the mustachioed hero's face. He tumbled to the ground, his forehead and chin bleeding already. Through the door, a filthy man walked in, the bottom half of his face covered by a strip of burlap. He had a short-barreled shotgun and was aiming it at the man bleeding on the floor.

"Get the hell up, idiot!" The bandit kicked the man in the leg and motioned to a seat with his shotgun. A woman gasped and another screamed. Two more similarly filthy outlaws followed in, a skinny woman with few teeth and a thick man with a pistol. The woman held out a flour bag as the thick man waved a pistol in their faces, kindly asking for valuables, and pistol whipping those who had nothing to offer. Three people were already on the floor in differing degrees of bleeding and unconsciousness.

Ilić sighed to himself. Looks like sleep would have to wait a little longer. He felt a heavy thud against the bottom of his boot, and heard a thick voice.

"Wakey, sleepy duck. Time to hand over your valuables or get whipped." With one hand, Ilić raised his hat very slowly and lazily opened one eye to look at him.

"Hm? Are we there?" Ilić rused.

"Yo–" Ilić's other hand flashed to his pistol, drew, cocked, and fired it before the thick outlaw could utter his first word. The center of his face was a leaking hole. His nose was gone, replaced by a fleshy tunnel that led to a larger opening on the back of his head. The bandit's eyes fluttered, and he collapsed backwards. The compartment became a cacophony of yells and blasts. Ilić scooped up the man's pistol from his limp hand and fired it into the chest of the skinny woman. She yelped and fell backwards, clutching at her chest wound. He fanned three more shots into her from his hip, and she lay still. The shotgun-wielding outlaw wheeled about and trained his barrel on Ilić. He faked left and dove right into an empty row of seats. The shotgun shook the windows and filled the compartment with a noxious black smoke. Two bystanders fell over, wounded or dead, as the wide blast shredded through rows. Ilić pulled his own pistol and emerged from the bench, his pistol aimed on the shotgunner's head. He pulled the trigger, and the cabin fell silent except for the wet dripping of the man's brains sliding down the wall.

There had to be more than three. These three didn't have the air of criminal mastermind to them, but he didn't feel like playing vigilante gunman today. Nonchalantly, at the pace of a man perusing the shelves of a store, he emptied the empty shells from his pistol, licking his fingers each time. He reloaded the gun, holstered it with a spin, and tipped his hat to the shell-shocked occupants still waving shotgun smoke from their faces.

"If anyone knows the Winter Viper," he began, his voice like a knife on stone, "tell him that Vukašin Ilić is back from the dead. Tell him that *Hush* has an old score to settle." Ilić snatched his long winter coat off the seat back and draped it over his shoulder, the collar and interior a beautiful gray and brown fur, and on the shoulder, like an epaulet, the head of a wolf.

He stepped out of the train car and breathed in the beautiful Utah air. Several cars down, he heard more shouts and the muffled shot of a pistol. From the opposite direction, a horse swayed and whinnied.

"Ah, the American stallion. How majestic," he rasped. He approached the horse slowly, his hand extended to smell. The horse eyed him unfamiliarly and extended its neck to smell. In a single motion, Ilić snatched the reins and pulled the horse closer, still allowing it to smell his hand afterward. He swung a leg over and kicked hard with the skill of an experienced rider. The practiced horse jumped forward and raced along the stopped train, not pausing for the bewildered outlaws further down the line.

There was a town somewhere at the end of these tracks where he could buy a bath, some real food, launder his clothes, and finally fucking sleep. Thinking about sleep made him yawn. He'd been running on coffee and snuff since he had left Boston. He'd snatched a roll of bread from a passing cart before he'd boarded the train, but it had been several hours, and now he was riding a strange horse in a strange land to a city he'd never been to kill a man he'd never met. Perhaps lunch was in order.

Ogden was a warm, busy town of loud, strong people. Churches gleamed white in the Utah sun, and a wide main street lined with craft shops and stores. At the end of the row was a wide, rust-colored barn with an anvil and coal forge along the side. Inside, a short thin man with thin stringy hair atop his head nodded in greeting.

"Howdy, friend. Corral and clean your rig?" He looked over the horse and rubbed its neck kindly.

"Yes, and I'm looking for somewhere to stay while I search for someone," Vukašin explained. The stableman nodded and pointed down the street to a building with a balcony draped with flowers and ivy.

"Reckon the cafe down yonder has a room for rent, and the kitchen makes up a fine dinner. They also pour a fine nip behind the bar." Vukašin nodded and handed the reins over. He rifled through the saddlebags until he found a bill fold filled with busy-looking currency.

"How much, par'ner? For the tack and shine?" Vukašin growled. He saw each value had a different pompous looking American on it. The stableman rubbed the top of his head.

"Well, the brush up and rig is normally just two bits. We got a pasture out back, and I can put her up in a stall at night with some hay. Some of the boys come and turn out the stalls twice a day, so it stays real clean. How's… three and a half sound?" He rested his hands on his hips and looked up at Vukašin. Vukašin pulled out a five note and handed it to the small man.

"How's about we settle on five, and you treat my old girl here real nice?" He rasped with a smile that tugged the spidery scarring up his neck. The man smiled back widely and snatched the note from him and pocketed it with a cheerful nod.

"You got yourself a deal, friend. You're gonna be able to see your face in that saddle, you're not gonna' wanna' sit on it. What's the old girl's name?" The stableman held the reins and a stirrup for Vukašin as he unmounted. Vukašin smiled again, his grin showing more teeth than normal for a smile.

"Clara. Call her Clara," his whisper like a cautious step on ice.

"Lovely name. We'll treat her like our own, sir. Let me know if there's anything else I do for you," said the stableman. Vukašin reached past him and removed his wolf-skin coat and long gun in a cinched-shut canvas sack. He slotted the sacked-rifle into the sheath on his back, draped his coat over one shoulder, and tugged his hat down snugly.

"There is one more thing you can do for me, Mr…" Vukašin paused expectantly. Understanding, he started,

"...Oh! Brigham. I'm Brigham Holson."

"Brigham," he hissed, "Do you know of anyone who goes by the moniker Winter Viper?" The name hung in the air like a foul scent.

"Winter Viper...Hmmm. It's not ringing a bell. Has he been running with anyone in the territory?" Brigham rubbed the top of his head again, thinking.

"Perhaps. You may also know him by the name 'Berle Walenty'." Ilić held his breath, watching for even the slightest indication of recognition. His face twisted in agonizing cognition, the rusted gears and stonework grinding in unfamiliar patterns.

"Berlioz Valentino, maybe? He's that Mexican feller from *Gwarahluharra*."

"Describe him."

"He's got real dark tan skin and black hair–"

"No."

"No?"

"No. He's a murderer from across the sea. He is light-skinned and has lighter hair. He may be traveling with a younger boy."

"What's the boy's name?"

"I don't know."

"You some kind of...bounty hunter?" Brigham asked, a little sourness in the way he said *bounty hunter*. Vukašin studied his face for a moment. Brigham shivered and looked away to shoo a fly that Vukašin did not see.

"Nothing quite so…formal." Vukašin took a step backwards towards the barn door. "He thinks I'm dead. He shot me once. I wanted to tell him the good news and return the favor." As Vukašin pulled his collar away from his neck to reveal more of the scar, Brigham winced. The pale white lines like cracked glass all coalesced to a malformed mass of scar tissue and flesh pulled tight. The main part of the scar looked like meat that passed through the grinder only once. The white pale shock of it was disturbing and intriguing to look at. Vukašin covered the scar again. "You'll let me know if you hear anything?" Brigham nodded gravely.

"I will." Vukašin extended a hand that Brigham took warmly.

"You're a good friend, Brigham," Vukašin hissed to him. He turned and left the barn.

The ground felt soft and uneven under his boots. Down the avenue, the cafe was a loud establishment filled mostly with the local color. A few road-weary travelers rested at the bar, exchanging news of the territory. A high flight of stairs with brass railing led to a second floor of more patrons playing cards, drinking, and resting. The second floor had all the available rooms for rent while the first floor had the kitchen and bath.

He entered the bar fairly unnoticed. A server looked him up and down and smiled as he walked in, and the barkeep waved and nodded as he entered. Vukašin leaned against the bar and scanned the menagerie of men on display. Most wore clean clothes and light coats. There were no rifles or munitions on tables, and the piano did not swell with songs of victory. In fact, only a few of the patrons wore weapons openly. He assumed there were more weapons hidden away, in pockets or behind the bar, but the people of this town enjoyed relative peace.

The barkeep polished a glass and placed it on a shelf before draping his rag over his shoulder and leaning against the bar. Barkeeping was a universal language shared by all human cultures. Every town had a pub just like this with a bartender indistinguishable from this one.

"What'll it be today, sir? We've got some hot cornbread just out of the oven, some roasted potatoes in stew, hot bath, and full-sized beds upstairs." This man was probably one of the partners or long-time employees.

"A little bit of all of it I suppose. I've been on the road a few days, and I haven't had a proper meal or slept since I landed in Boston." His voice was heavy and harsh like a rasp on fine china. The barkeep leaned in to hear his whisper, and caught a glimpse of the scar etching from under his collar. "I'd like to rent a room while I look for someone. I've got my horse corralled down at the livery, and I think I need a bath." Vukašin draped his coat on the bar and placed his hat on top. He sighed as the cool air of the saloon washed over his head.

The barkeep filled a tin cup with cool water and brought a plate and bowl of steaming food. The moment the plate was in front of Vukašin, he remembered how long it had been since he had real food, and he was overcome. He ravenously attacked the food, spooning gravy with bread, drinking broth, and tipping his plate into his mouth. He brushed his mustache with his hand to clear it of any scraps and surveyed the carnage of his meal. The barkeep stood nearby, impressed.

"There was a moment there I thought I was going to have to stop you from eating that fork, friend. We've got a hot bath gettin' drawn up for you down the hall o'er there, and here's the key for the green room." He handed him a thick iron key that had been painted green many times. He took the key and pocketed it and glanced down the hall.

"Do you have anything else back there besides this fine meal?" Vukašin asked, arching an eyebrow.

"Like what? Anything in particular?" the barkeep asked, clearing away the already mostly-clean dishes.

"Maybe something our temperance sisters out east might have missed," Vukašin whispered with a devilish smile. The barkeep smiled and nodded.

"No need to be afraid, sir. Nobody's going to come axe your whiskey in here." They shared a warm chuckle.

"In that case, do you have any mash-spirits back there?"

"Sure do! A man here in town distills it himself. He's an old Russian feller come this way 'bout a decade back." The barkeep presented a small glass and a fancy decanter of pink-tinted liquid. "Makes it from beets. Grows them himself! I was unsure of it at first, but after my first sip, I tell him, I say, 'Vic, I need a crate of this immediately. And then make a second crate for the bar.'" He laughed at his own cleverness as he poured. Vukašin picked up and eyed the small glass. Beets? Hm. On the other hand, alcohol. How different from vodka could it be? He smelled the pink liquid: it smelled like vodka. There was the tiniest hint of spice, but that could just be from the food. He sipped it, and let it pass over his tongue. Spicy. Bright. Then smooth and sweet. He swallowed and looked at the glass in impressed disbelief.

"Nosi se! *Get the hell out of here!* That's good!" The barkeep topped him off and nodded, walking away to help other patrons. Finally, he found something in this filthy country that he liked.

He sighed. He had a room upstairs, a warm bath waiting, a full belly, and a new favorite drink. He looked down the bar again at the other guests, looking for the next hint of a trail. He stroked the wolf head on his coat absentmindedly, finding the bullet hole that killed the wolf and saved his life.

He remembered the moment he realized he was beaten out in the snow. Days. Days without moving, without sleeping. He had been pushing snow into his mouth and letting it melt for water, and he had salted pork in a small pouch on the stock of his rifle. It was salted pork that attracted the wolves, he thought. A small group of them, three or four came sniffing around the first night, but they kept their distance. When they realized he wouldn't flee or fight, they decided to make their move.

At dusk, the wolves moved in silently, the first bite closed on the back of his left thigh, a shaking, pulling bite meant to cripple him. He cried out and drew his knife, but another wolf had his arm while another ripped at his shoulder and chest, fighting for a grip on his throat. Ilíc thrashed and lashed out, punching and kicking desperately.

His knife was lost, he was covered in blood, and he had a thumb buried in the eye socket of a wolf that was shaking him, shredding the flesh and tendons in his neck and shoulder. Hot blood sprayed in his eyes and he tasted fur and drool and blood as he screamed in animalistic agony.

And then an impact like a kick from a horse hit him in the chest, and the snarling and yelping of wolves faded back into the trees. A weight lay on top of him, hot and hairy. The cold stole his heat away, and he could only hear the echoing ring of a rifle shot. He had not but the strength to lift his head. *Where was he? Where was he?* Snow stirred under a shady pine right where he had been looking. Just high and to the right of where he'd been focused.

From across the rocky ravine, the hunched, fatigued shape of a soldier rose from under the tree and began to load a second round. Vukašin grunted weakly to push the dead wolf off of him, but he'd lost so much blood. He didn't realize how much blood he'd lost until he looked at the snow around him. He was lying in a large ring of blood and shredded clothing. A single dead wolf lay on top of him. Maybe some of the blood was the wolf's.

He pulled his thumb out of the wolf's eye socket and found that he couldn't lift his arm. His shoulder was fucked and chewed. It was nearly nightfall again. The wolves would be back, and they would tear him to so many pieces.

He wasn't sure how long he had been laying there, how long he had been conscious or unconscious, but he did notice when he stopped shivering. He noticed when his breathing became shallow, and his eyes felt hot and heavy. He could no longer feel the snow beneath him or the throbbing sharp ache of his neck and face. He finally allowed his heavy eyes to fall shut, and he inhaled as much breath as he could, and blew it out, hoping that his body would be too weak for another. It was better than being ripped apart by wolves or having his lips and eyes picked out by carrion birds. He could see the stars finally, so the moon would soon follow.

The sound Vukašin heard was not the howling of feral doom nor the harp of Saint Piotyr. It was the harsh cyrillic words of Russian soldiers, their casual conversation and relaxed tones mockingly calm for him to hear. The rest of the Russian convoy had finally arrived, and these two must be scouts. At least he was successful in routing the Winter Viper from ambushing the convoy, so it wasn't a total waste of a day. He probably wasn't getting paid though. Vukašin opened his mouth and took another breath. Perhaps they would find him.

As the two soldiers crested the ridge along the tree line, they spotted the bright red battlefield, and the limp shape of Vukašin Ilíc in the middle. Thus began his long, painful recovery, not only of his ripped and broken body, but of his reputation as a shootist. The Winter Viper had bested him, but he was chosen for another chance. He would find him and make him suffer for his sloppiness.

By all accounts, Vukašin should be dead. A mysteriously wet pile of wolf shit. But here he was, being pulled on a cart back to the fort. He had been slipping in and out of consciousness for a while now, catching glimpses of a cart, a barn, a hospital tent, and now another cart. His arm was bandaged to him, holding his shoulder stationary. Half his neck and face was covered in thick wads of gauze that were no longer bleeding through. Having the strength to lift his head, he opened his uncovered eye and took in the small Polish town he was being pulled through. Russians soldiers marched the streets, and he heard the out-of-tune yowling of inebriated soldiers in a nearby bar.

Beside him, a wrapped bundle of brown and gray fur and hide jostled under the bouncing of the cart. With his free hand, he slowly, sorely, painfully tugged the twine that tied the bundle, and the wolf's head flopped down beside him so he could see the clean bullet hole right through the top of the head. *Jesus Christ, what a shot.* He was more than four-hundred yards away with a muzzleloader. He was definitely shooting bullets, not balls, through a rifled barrel. He might be able to track him down again by finding his partner, the one with the freshly-fucked-up face.

None of it mattered for the moment. He was in no state to travel. There they lay, two defeated hunters, both dead and bound in the back of a cart, both put down by the Winter Viper. There, fingering the round hole in the top of the wolf hide-head, he swore an oath. Blood for blood. Bone for bone. He would not kill the Winter Viper for some false sense of justice or loyalty to any government. Plain, old fashioned, vengeance. There didn't have to be a righteous cause or injustice to correct. Ilíc wanted to kill the Winter Viper because, for a moment, he was bested. A Polish freedom fighter– a *farmer*, bested the unkillable Vukašin Ilíc. At least that was still consistent. He was still unkillable.

And then for ten more years, he continued to be unkillable. He learned the Viper's name, assisted in the invasion and razing of his town, and even learned where he escaped to. Ten years dedicated to revenge wasn't as poisonous as he thought it would be. His reputation kept him employed. As soon as he was able to hold a gun again, he was back to the world's oldest hobby. His guns took him all over Europe, Asia, and even to Japan once to help eliminate a particularly bothersome samurai daimyo. But killing the Winter Viper wasn't just another payday. Obviously the original contract for the Winter Viper expired when Ilíc failed, so there was an open bounty out for him. The Russian generals didn't know or care that Berle had fled to America. This was purely personal with the perk of a bounty at the end.

He finished the tiny glass of beet vodka and put a note on the bar. The barkeep left the bottle and went about wiping down the bar. Vukašin took the bottle down the hall to the bath. He soaked in the tub until the water went cold, and then he walked up the stairs in a towel, his boots and clothes in one hand. The heavy green key squeaked in the lock of the green door, and he stepped into a small, warm, pleasant room, dark green walls, sage-colored bed linens, and a vanity with drawers. He blocked the door with the sturdy wooden chair from the vanity and laid his coat and pistol on the pillow next to his. He collapsed onto the bed in the towel and fell asleep almost immediately.

Chapter 5

Berle and Andras arrived at their homestead late in the evening on a chilly spring day. "The warmth hasn't made it over the mountains yet," a local had said. The plot of land was everything Pa had described it to be. Wide open prairie for miles, sparse patches of trees and bushes dotted the countryside, and the famous Rocky Mountains set a gorgeous western horizon. A stream cut through the land, about ten feet wide, five feet at the deepest. There was a nice flat spot near the creek that could make for a great place to build a house. Andras and Berle lay in the back of the wagon together, dreaming about their new home.

"Are we going to grow potatoes?" Andras asked his Pa, sitting up to plan the perfect spot in the fading light.

"Do you want to grow potatoes?" Pa asked him. Andras nodded. "Then we'll grow potatoes. This is your home, too, Andras. We get to build it together."

"Are we going to build our house tomorrow?" He hoped Pa would say yes.

"In a way, yes. We'll start tomorrow. Tomorrow, we'll mark our property lines, and then we'll head into town. There, we can see what's there and hire some hands to help build our house. Maybe we'll buy some seed and Piotyr can help us get some ground ready for planting." They both lay in silence, a cricket and a coyote breaking the sound of the canvas cover rustling in the chilly night air.

"Pa?"

"Yeah, Son?"

"I'm really excited to do all this hard work with you."

"Me too, love."

"Pa?"

"Yes, son?"

"I wish Ma was here."

"... Me too..."

"Pa?"

"Go ahead, son."

"I like talking English with you."

"Go to sleep, Andi-bear. I love you."

"I love you too, Pa."

Berle could not fall asleep. He had dreamed of this moment for so long now, finally sleeping on his own land in America, a place to call his own home, but he didn't feel that soul-healing catharsis that was supposed to accompany this momentous accomplishment.

He had gotten his son here safely. That's what mattered. If he did not feel peace in this moment, he would ensure his son did. Andras would never have to grow up looking over his shoulder, he wouldn't be forced to join an army to fight for some bloated dignitary, he would learn to read and count and plant, and maybe he would never have to kill anyone. That's what Clara would have wanted. Andras loved his ma so much, and Berle didn't know how he was going to raise Andras without her. For so long, all Berle knew was fighting. He could take naps during battles and reload his Whitworth forty-five in pitch black; he could tell where an enemy force would camp for the night just by looking at a map of the area. He wanted none of that for Andras. Maybe Andras could be a banker or work a printing press.

He watched Andras sleep peacefully for a while before finally feeling relaxed enough to attempt sleep himself. He imagined a future where his son was well-fed, well-read, and still flinched at the sound of gunfire.

Berle woke early in the morning and marked off the land boundaries before Andras had even rubbed the gunk from his eyes. The bows of the wagon were leaned against a tree, and the canvas cover was now a lean-to shade near the creek.

Pa was a bright, sunny, mote of happiness, exuding the excitement of a child with a chocolate. He teased and prodded Andras to dress faster so that they could get to town faster. Even Piotyr seemed as enthusiastic and prepared for the trip as Andras. Though Pa had unloaded the wagon, Piotyr still did not love pulling alone. Hopefully, this would be one of the last times Piotyr would have to make the trip alone or even at all. Once the house was finished, Piotyr was free to lounge around the corral and fields as much as he wanted until October when Josef would be by to collect him. Berle cringed and made a mental note to buy another mule or reimburse Josef for the death of Buck.

The road to Foothill was rocky and overgrown, and rabbits and birds scampered away from the approaching wagon. Gradually, the road became more flat and heavily trafficked.

Foothill was a small city that had grown from a large town that was built from a tiny fort made to defend a boomtown. When approaching the city, it was clear this was so: in the center of town was the original mining-camp-turned-main street, saloons, cafes, hotels, stores, craftsmen, and artisans. At the north end of the avenue was the original frontier fort parapet and turret complete with artillery piece atop. Beyond that, small groups of houses formed neighborhoods and a large white church could be seen. The homes thinned out to make way for small fields, barbers, doctors, and what looked to be traveling performers camped on the edge of town.

Two riders on horseback trotted past them, both tipping their hats and extending a casual "Mornin'" and "How'dy." Pa lifted his hat in greeting and smiled at them. Andras smiled and replied with a loud "Howdy too!" in response. Pa laughed and asked,

"What is 'howdy'?" Andras looked at him, puzzled, fully expecting him to have known. To his chagrin, Andras didn't know what it meant either. He'd heard it several dozen times, maybe more, since they had landed in St. Louis. Andras shrugged.

"I thought it was an American 'hello.'" He and Pa both laughed.

On the outskirts of town was a sawmill where Pa had placed an order for the lumber to be delivered for the house and a fence. The lumberyard foreman was the biggest man that Andras had ever seen. He had a thick brown beard like a Cossack, wild and unkempt. He wore no shirt or hat and wore only boots, heavy ranch pants, and suspenders over massive freckled shoulders. Andras didn't know they made suspenders that big. He was covered in muscles like museum statues and carried an ax that was taller than Andras when he rested it on the ground. He shook Pa's hand warmly with a wide smile, a few teeth missing. He led them over to a team of wagons, all with horses and drivers, piled high with lumber.

"Really? I didn't pay for the extra wagons. I don't have much extra. In fact, I was going to ask if I could use the extra I have to hire some of your carpenters to help get us started." Berle looked unsure and stressed, worrying over money and his use of the English language simultaneously. The huge man waved his hands, trying to clear the confusion from the air.

"Mr. Walenty, please, let me clarify. The money you paid covered the team of wagons to transport the lumber. No extra. The team transporting the lumber is going to build your house based on the plans you sent us months ago. My boys will sleep on your property while they build, but they take care of their own." Berle stared at him, mouth agape.

"Mr. Spearman, please, let *me* clarify. Those wagons are going to my property with the wood for my house, and the men driving the wagons are going to build my house for me, all with the money I have already given you." Berle squinted at him, making sure he heard correctly. Mr. Spearman chuckled that gapped grin and nodded.

"Correct, Mr. Walenty. That is what we do. We build good homes with good wood for good people." Berle stared at him, stunned. Andras poked his dad hard in the belly to rouse him, and his dad doubled over and leaned on the foreman. Pa began to laugh, then hugged the huge man. Andras saw Pa wipe his cheek when he let go.

"Let's get on the road then!" Pa said with a cracking voice. The foreman waved as the train of wagons headed off down the path toward their land. Pa and Andras headed off in the opposite direction towards Foothill.

Pa's mood had gotten even better if it was possible. As they rode down the road to the mountain-shaded town, Pa sang songs from the old home, his Polish like a warm memory in Andras's mind.

More folks nodded and tipped their hats at them as they neared town. Even Piotyr seemed relieved at the thought of not having to haul lumber. Main Street was a lively bustling hive of colorful life and thriving people. The clothing in the shop windows was beautiful and looked expensive, like the kind of clothes a queen or an emperor would wear. Andras could smell another sweet shop. He saw the white-painted storefront with pink lettering, and he imagined he could read the words "candy" on the wall. Pa pointed at a butcher displaying cuts of meat. Berle and Andras had been to dozens of towns like this already, and they always found themselves getting excited at their favorite things in each one. Seeing the other's adventurous fire always made each new town or village a new discovery. Foothill was extra special because it was their town.

Technically, they didn't live within city limits, but this is where they would go to buy general goods, pick up their mail, and sell their potatoes. Maybe Andras would learn to read and pray at the schoolhouse by the church. Maybe he would meet a pretty girl who enjoys painting, and they would sit under that tree…Berle found his mind wandering, imagining the future Andras and he would create here. That's the saloon Berle would take Vaclav to when he came to visit. That's the hotel Josef could stay at when they come in October. A kindly looking elderly man, maybe sixty, unlocked a door and tipped his hat in a hello. That's the doctor who would hire Andras to clean up around the shop, but also teach him a few tricks of the trade.

A sharp crack of gunfire stole both of their attention. Two more shots in rapid succession. *Whoever shot first didn't hit his target, and now he's having to dodge,* Berle thought to himself. Andras sat tensely next to his father, ready to reach for the rifle under the seat or run for cover at the slightest hint from his father. Another two shots, and then one. And then one last shot. *Somebody's dead.* Piotyr shook his head and glanced back at Berle.

"What are you worried about? I doubt he's shooting at mules. Go on, hup!" Berle snapped at the mule. Piotyr audibly sighed and trudged forward. Andras was still tense, coiled like a spring. Berle noticed when the cart bounced into a particularly savage pothole, and, instead of bouncing on the bench, Andras absorbed the bounce in his knees and stayed on the balls of his feet, ready to sprint. Berle patted his son's knee and then reached around and squeezed his shoulder.

"Be frightened, but do not worry. This is how cities are, even in America. Yes, there is opportunity, and money, and learning, and new things, but there doesn't need to be a war for men to want to kill each other." Andras nodded. "Do you remember Mr. Gremchen?"

Andras remembered Ma coming to his side as he sat up, his heart pounding and eyes wide. He had awoken to the sound of a woman in desperate helplessness. Her pleas had awoken everyone in the house, and Pa was already walking out of the door, boots, pants, and rifle on his back, buttoning his shirt as he went. His face was stern, almost angry.

Andras had seen that look on Pa's face before, when Russians knocked on the door, when men reached for Ma, and when his shepherd mates would come calling. Pa never looked at him that way. Never once. Andras remembered hearing the raised voices and shouts of neighbors and friends' fathers. Later, Pa came back inside, and he sat next to Ma. He nodded, and Ma began to cry. Then there was a gunshot outside that made Andras jump, and he couldn't stop himself from crying too.

Andras nodded.

"Mr. Gremchen wasn't a soldier. He wasn't a Russian. But he chose to take Russian money in exchange for his own family and people. Do you remember what sin that is?" Pa spoke kindly and softly, trying to gently explain the vigilante execution of their old neighbor in Poland. Andras thought back to his grandma's old lessons of bearded men splitting the sea in half, talking donkeys, and Eliasz running away to a cave because he was hungry and needed a nap.

"Greed. Stealing. Murder." Andras cycled through a few that made sense. He was choosing money over people. That was greed. He was stealing from the local shops to sell to the Russians. That was clearly stealing. He was responsible for the deaths of the people he ratted out to the Russians. Berle considered each answer and nodded slowly.

"Yes, those are against his neighbors and friends, not his enemies. Do you understand?" Andras did not understand. Andras nodded. They passed the avenue where the shooting had happened moments ago. Two people lay in the street, a man with gun-in-hand and a woman in a fine dress. The last man standing was a short, round lawman. He had a faded red shirt and a vest with a tin star pinned to it. He was reloading his pistol and watching the crowd fret over the apparent crime of passion. The wagon rolled past.

"Pa, that was a lady." Andras's voice was flat. Berle rested a heavy hand on his son's shoulder.

"It's sad, isn't it?" Pa asked him, a note of helplessness in his tone. Andras nodded and stored away this memory for a time when his thoughts were ready to process it better. The next street over bustled with relaxed people as if a man and woman weren't lying dead in the street thirty yards away. The city was a strange place. So many things were happening at the same time, each event isolated, causes without effects. So many people living separate, disconnected lives right next to each other. The rest of the day was painted a darker tint after the shooting. The general store was more overwhelming and expensive than exciting and fancy. The sweet shop seemed superfluous to the needs of their new home and land. The stables weren't beautiful and exciting but dirty and frustrating. By the end of it, Andras sat on the jockey bench of the wagon, his Pa's oversized hat on his head, his eyes tired and distant. Pa mounted the wagon and placed the wooden crate of cans and seeds in the back. Pa took the long way out of town, avoiding the crime scene. By the time they reached the outskirts of Foothill, Andras was already feeling better. Bored by the same trees to look at twice, Andras climbed into the back of the cart to take inventory of all they had bought.

"Don't open anything, Andi," Pa drolled without even a glance back, smirking. Andras nodded wordlessly and began sorting through the crates, being sure to stay sitting or low to not get bounced out of the wagon. Food, nails, bullets, oil, grease, a new hatchet, percussion caps, a pot for coffee, a coffee grinder, and a shiny new pail. There were smatterings of other supplies; rope, strips of leather, canvas patches, glass bottles, and other boring things. Among some of the grocery goods was a long, light green, curved food that looked like a vegetable.

"Pa?" He asked, holding up the strange food. Pa glanced back and got excited again.

"Hey! I got that to try from the store! It's called a…a *pamana*?" He struggled to remember the exact name.

"We can eat it?" Andras wasn't so sure. The rubbery plant didn't seem palatable, and it didn't smell like something he'd want to eat.

"Yeah! The food is on the inside. You have to open the outside." It was clear that Pa was nearly as clueless about this strange food as Andras. Andras looked at it oddly before Pa finally took it from him and took his knife to it. He cut it in half and handed the shorter curved piece to Andras. Andras smelled and licked the soft inside and then smiled. The two Americans enjoyed their banana on the ride home from town.

When they finally arrived back home, the lumber wagons were circled, and two of the carts were empty. They had begun measuring out the floorplan of the house with string and stones while others nailed boards together. The remainder of the carpenters and craftsmen set up their temporary camp within the circle of wagons. The horses swayed and chewed grass in a makeshift corral made from rope looped around trees. The men called Pa, "sir" and Andras, "Mr. Walenty". Before the sun disappeared behind the Rocky Mountains, the men made a hearty dinner and sang and drank until the oldest of the carpenters retired to bed. Andras followed to bed shortly after, falling asleep to the sound of Pa laughing with the builders.

The next morning, Andras awoke to the sound of cattle and angry, shouting carpenters. Outside the wagon, more cattle than Andras had ever seen lumbered through their land, lowing and swaying their heads. The dust stirred by this massive immigration made it so he could only see cattle and mountains until a tall rider on a golden horse cut through the dust, swinging the ends of his reins intimidatingly, fearlessly to the cows threatening to wander from the herd. Pa approached the rider, waving widely in large arcs so as not to be missed. The rider kicked his horse, and the charger surged forward toward Pa, and then stopped short in a prancing turn.

Andras felt goosebumps watching the cowboy work the beast. He took off his hat, smacked the dust from it across his knee, and returned it to his head, his light blue eyes catching the morning sun. He was tan and road-worn but youthful and passionate. He couldn't be much older than Pa, but he held himself like a young soldier.

"Y'all are in the way," the rider began without greeting or preamble.

"I beg your pardon, sir, but we didn't know this was in anyone's way. This is our home, I'm Berle Walenty, and–"

"I don't give a damn who you are. We've been grazing this land since my grandpap taught my pa how to ride on these trails."

"We meant no disrespect, sir, I can show you the dee–"

"I don't give a damn what paper no city hall Foothill cooze handed you. Y'all ranchers are trying to snatch up our free-grazing, and we're not gon' stop living our way just so you can live yours." The rider wheeled the horse around, nearly colliding with Pa before riding off to join his other riders. The last of the cattle passed through after several minutes, and the workers and carpenters swore and began repairing the damage the wayward cattle inflicted.

Pa turned and beelined to the head carpenter. Edwin Mathers immigrated from Wales when he was twenty one. He was a stonemason-turned-carpenter, and he had the exacting mind and eye of a master.

"Mr. Mathers, can you explain what just happened?" Andras leaped off the wagon and jogged to keep up with Pa. Ed waved dust away with his floppy old hat and smooshed it down on top of his head again.

"Free-grazers. They're cowboys, pushing cattle from place to place. It's hard, honest work that employs hard, sometimes dishonest people. It's a transient life that a man can disappear into. When something threatens that kind of security, it can't help but feel personal. Once we finish the house and the fence, I'm guessing they'll just go around. It's not like you bought up the mountain range. Thirty-two acres is not a big plot and should be no issue for experienced riders like them. Next time they come through, I reckon they'll see your spread, and think nothing more of it." Ed patted Berle's shoulder and got back to work repairing the fence around the house. Berle watched the dust cloud slowly fade westward.

The house was finished in a week's time. Berle and Andras had come to be very fond of Ed and the others; Mathew's harmonica was the perfect end to a hard day's work. Gershom and Avery cooked some of the best food Andras had ever eaten around a fire. Clive and Froderick could both drive a nail in two hits. Howard kept the men chuckling every night when he would take a few swigs of whiskey and start fabricating the wildest lyrics to songs that never existed.

The day they finished the house and packed up the wagons, Pa cooked placki ziemniaczane for them, and they all spent extra time saying goodbyes and thanking each other. A few of them made plans to meet at the cafe or saloon once they got more settled in. Berle and Andras stood on the porch of their frontier home, watching their new friends ride away back towards town.

As soon as the dust from their wagons had settled, Andras turned and ran inside the house to his room– his very own room. The front door of the house opened into a big room where a small dining table and chairs sat. The kitchen was a simple space, a corner of cabinets and shelves where Berle had wiped and stacked the rest of Ma's porcelain dishes. Their canned foods were in the lower cabinets where Andras could reach and organize them.

The porch had two identical rocking chairs that Ed had built in his spare time over the past week. Berle could not believe that he created these beautiful chairs while he wasn't building this beautiful house. The two bedrooms were right next to each other, and they had an attached outhouse just out the back door.

The spare wood and scraps from the construction sat in the firewood box. Over the stone fireplace that Andras had helped Ed plaster and seal was the golden rifle from Uncle Vaclav. Andras knew that it was loaded. Pa had always said, "What is the point of an unloaded gun? The most dangerous part of a gun is not knowing how to use it."

In his room, Andras had a bed off the floor, a window with a flower in a pot, shelves for books he would get someday, and a desk and chair. Andras closed the door behind him, took out the tiny whittling knife, and carved his name in very straight letters on the bottom of the desk. A thrill of excitement shivered through him: *his room. His bed.* He blew the last of the wood shavings off of his handiwork, and smiled, satisfied.

Every morning, Andras learned a new job, a new skill, a new task, and he and Pa worked all day making sure everything was perfect. Berle couldn't help but be impressed by the young boy's sharp wit and the speed he learned skills. Andras could dig a fence post hole nearly as quickly as him, and easily as well.

Andras cared for and fixed the house like it was his own. By all accounts, it would be his home, but for now, he was just a child, only… six years? Seven now? Berle's heart caught in his throat. When was Andras's birthday? Dammit, Clara was always so much better at such things. He remembered it was cold because, by the time he had brought enough blankets for her and their brand new baby, she looked to be lying in a nest of blankets. It was often cold in Poland, but it only got that cold in the winter. His birthday was in the winter. *Shit.*

Berle squeezed the bridge of his nose and pinched his eyes shut. He forgot his only son's birthday. Berle felt a heavy weight in his chest drop even further, and months of tears pushed behind his eyes, begging to be released. Berle was afraid that if he let himself cry for Clara, he would not stop. He sat down on his bed and did not look in the mirror that sat on his dresser. He held his head in his hands and felt the weight of his fatigue, dragging him to the floor.

Through the wall, he heard Andras humming and talking to himself while he rearranged and pushed his bed and desk to different places in the room. After a moment, he heard the excited footsteps of Andras coming to his room. Andras knocked twice. And then impatiently knocked again. Berle sniffed deeply and wiped his eyes in case anything had escaped.

"Pa, come look at my room! I really think it looks better this way!" Andras called through the door. Pa opened the door and Andras's excited face dropped. "What's wrong, Dad?" Andras's voice was softer now. He heard Clara's tenderness in his words. Tears welled into his eyes again.

Andras approached his Pa silently, and crawled into his lap. He lay his head on Pa's shoulder and didn't say anything. Berle squeezed his son. A tear from each eye streaked a shiny line down each of Berle's cheeks. Andras lifted his head and looked his dad in the eyes. He wiped his Pa's cheeks dry with small, filthy fingers.

"You dripped on me." Andras said. Berle hiccupped a laugh and poked his son in the ribs playfully. Andras squirmed and giggled on his dad's lap. "Are those sad tears?" Andras asked. Ma had asked him this question many times, and Andras could think of no one better to help Pa than Ma. Ma's ideas and words would have to do. Berle bobbed his head side to side considering his son's question.

"Partly sad. Partly happy. Partly tired. But I'm happy we're finally here, and we have this beautiful house. I'm happy we're safe, and I'm happy we met Mr. Ed and his crew."

"Are you sad because of Ma?" Andras felt sad as he said the words, and his lip quivered as he held back. Seeing his Pa so…*soft* was unsettling, but not bad. Seeing his father so raw and exposed amplified his own feelings. A tear rolled down Andras's cheek, and he wiped it away and wiped his nose in a single wet swipe of a loose sleeve.

"Yes, sir. I miss your mother very much." His voice rattled and cracked. Andras listened. "Have I ever told you how I met your Ma?" Andras had heard this story so many times he might be able to tell it in English. Andras shook his head and crawled out of his Pa's lap and lay on his side on Pa's bed, watching his father tell the story. Berle inhaled deeply and transitioned back to Polish as he began. None of those memories were in English.

"Long, long before you were born, my sweet boy, before I met your mother, your Uncle Vaclav and I were just soldiers in the army. The duke had fallen to corruption, choosing to sell his people to Russia instead of defending them. That January, we had been given orders from Russian generals, and the duke was forcing us to join the Russian Imperial army." Andras sat up, crossed his legs, and leaned on his elbows. This was not the story Pa had told him before.

"Vaclav, Tomas, Mav, Gregor, all of us were just so young, and we started talking, and complaining, and planning, and then plotting, and then, before we knew it, we had the entire battalion that had been reassigned backing us up. It was the middle of the night when we emptied the armory of its weapons and munitions, and we fled to the woods. The armory officer came with us actually." Berle was no longer telling a story, but vividly remembering. Andras was enraptured.

"Eventually, the Russians came after us, and we had to stay on the run. We lived like the American outlaw, surviving the wild to fight on another day. When we ran out food and powder, we had to start bartering and trading with other villages and then other cities and countries. The insurrection only lasted a year, but we didn't stop fighting. Your Ma lived in a tiny village on the border of France. I remember when we entered the cafe, and she sent us all back out to wipe our feet. She wasn't afraid of us or our guns. She wasn't going to let a band of ruffians dirty up her beautiful cafe. And it wasn't even her cafe! She just worked there at the time." Pa's face melted into a peaceful smile as he remembered.

"*All the boys tried their hand at asking her to dance or share a drink, but she denied all of them, sending some away red with embarrassment, or embarrassed with a red handprint. I wasn't going to get slapped, so I minded my own business. Later that night, she came and sat by me at the bar, and asked me, she said, 'Why didn't you make a run at me?', and I told her the truth, I said, 'You scare me.' We both laughed and then we started talking... We talked until the owner arrived in the morning to open up the cafe. The guys and I were heading out again, but I wanted to keep in contact with her. We wrote letters back and forth for a long, long time. The next time I saw her, I asked her to marry me. And then a little while later, you came along, and I knew everything would be different.*"

His voice faded off like the end of a hymn. Andras noticed his dad was holding a parcel of letters, all old and yellowed from repeated rereading over the years. He put the bundle down on the small nightstand table by the bed, picked up Andras, and placed him on the floor in front of him. Andras rubbed a sleepy eye.

"Now it's just you and me. We have to care for and love each other like Ma did." Both men understood, but Andras did not respond. He merely nodded. "In the morning, we're going to bury the last of Ma's things and honor her for heaven." Andras glanced at the crate of Ma's old effects. While Clara was buried at sea, all her belongings had ridden in the back of the wagon with Andras. Pa surveyed the land

and nodded. "I just thought of the perfect place. Behind the house at the base of the old oak." Andras imagined the spot. He fumbled into night clothes, let Pa tuck him in, and fell asleep in his bed, in his room, in his house.

The next morning was quiet. The two men ate silently, and Andras went and got more bacon instead of asking for it. Berle looked at him, smiled and then kept eating. Piotyr was munching grass in the short-fenced corral.

The funeral wasn't much of an event. Pa had found an old hat box, gathered the last of Ma's effects and placed them in the hole. Andras had seen plenty of funerals. Now was the time for the oldest and wisest to give a blessing or benediction. Pa held his hat in his hand, and Andras did the same. But Pa did not speak. He stared at the hat box in the hole like he wanted to snatch it out of the hole or take his own place beside it. Andras spoke up after a long moment, his voice watery and forced.

"I miss you, Mama. But we're really safe and happy here. We already made friends, and our house is the best. You would love it."

"Amen," Pa concluded. He started pushing dirt on top of the hatbox, and Andras joined him.

After a hard, quiet morning of working the earth in the garden, Berle appeared holding two guns.

"Andras, today, we learn to shoot," Pa said with that same old enthusiastic pep. Andras left what he was doing and sprinted to his dad. This was what he had been wanting for years now. Pa handed him a pistol as he reached for a rifle, and he accepted it grumpily.

"Alright, a few rules: always, *always,* treat every gun like it's loaded. Not everyone knows what a safe gun looks like or how to make a gun safe. That's why we gotta practice. Next rule, never point the gun at something you don't want to kill, understood?" Andras nodded. "Alright, last rule: one bullet is almost never enough. It's easy to miss." Andras nodded again at his Pa.

Pa explained the different parts of the pistol, disassembling it, and helping Andras to put it back together. Pa held up the gun and half cocked the pistol, rotating the cylinder along the length of his arms as he went. He smiled and put the gun down in front of Andras, showing him how to hold it properly, where to put his fingers, how to pull the hammer back, and the weight of the trigger pull. Andras held it like he was told, accepting the gentle correction from his dad. The gun was heavy, and he could barely hold the barrel straight unless he held it with two hands.

Once he had pulled the hammer back and squeezed the trigger properly three times, Pa explained the loading and timing of each step and emphasized the importance of distance defense. Pa further explained the third rule.

"Sometimes, one bullet doesn't kill someone. Sometimes they get better. At the end of the day, you need to feel safe knowing that person is still alive somewhere, maybe plotting revenge. If you shoot someone, and they're not dead, make sure they are. You should never shoot at someone you don't want to kill anyway."

"Pa, I don't wanna kill anyone," Andras protested.

"I don't want you to kill anyone either." Pa tousled his hair and loaded the pistol in front of him, showing him the steps and the amounts. Andras nodded and concentrated. He wanted to learn all of it.

Once the pistol was loaded, he took it again and noticed how much heavier it was. Pa had set up some cans and bottles on the fence and nodded. This was going to be a disaster. He pulled back the hammer and looked down the sight at the fence and its targets. It was difficult to fix the barrel to one spot, and it got harder the longer he held the pistol. He slowly squeezed the trigger and was startled when the pistol finally exploded, jarring his hands, and leaping upwards. He juggled the pistol in his hands and caught it again, looking at his Pa who had the same alarmed, surprised face. They both laughed nervously.

When the smoke had cleared, it revealed the results of Andras's shot. All the targets were in the dirt, and the fence post had a splintered hole in it.

"Does that count?" Andras asked, unsure. Pa shook his head and replaced all the targets on the fence. They practiced for several hours before Andras could hit a target at ten yards with fifty-five-percent accuracy. Berle picked up his son and squeezed him. Perhaps Andras could grow to be a great hunter.

"Dad, can we learn with the rifle today?" Berle made a dramatically agonized face,

"Aren't you tired, Andi? We've been shooting with the pistol for hours now. We can learn the rifle next time. Is it a deal?" Berle put his son down and extended a hand. Andras instinctively reached, but then relented and smirked.

"Or, a challenge if you're able!" Andras proposed as maniacally as a seven-year-old boy wearing a too-big hat could. "I'll name something, and you have to shoot it. You can get three tries."

"Hold up, partner. I need some parameters. What's my maximum range?"

"I don't know that. I'm only seven."

"Fair enough. But nothing… głupi, *ridiculous*."

"Of course not, Father," Andras patted his father's knee condescendingly. Berle shook his head in amused disbelief at the audacity of this child.

Andras scanned his surroundings, compiling all the different options before every creative, evil, and churlish synapse in his brain all fired at once. Andras leaped up and ran over to the fence, grabbed a green glass bottle and ducked under the higher horizontal beam of the fence. He placed the bottle on top of a big flat rock, squeezing an eye shut and adjusting as he did. Berle watched him with fascination. If he wasn't careful to raise him right, Andras would make a spectacular bank robber. Andras sprinted inside the house. Berle heard shuffling in the house before Andras came running back outside holding a small piece of paper. He affixed it to the backside of the fence so that the card covered the hole from Andras's wild first shot.

"Okay!" Andras yelled as he jogged over to his dad, "Using the repeater, shoot the green bottle through the hole."

"Through the hole?"

"Yeah!"

"The hole you made in my fence with my gun? That hole?"

"Stay on topic, Dad."

"What's with the card?"

"So I'll know if you shot through the hole and didn't just shoot under the board." Berle stared at his son for a moment, aghast.

"Where did you think of this?"

"From a showbill I saw back in St. Louis! There was a shootist who could do all kinds of głupi gun tricks and challenge shots."

"Oh, yeah, I remember that now." Berle nodded and scratched his itchy chin. "He did this?"

"I don't know. We didn't see the show, Dad. There was just a drawer-ing on the showbill of him doing something like it."

"Drawing. What was his name?"

"Draw-ring. I don't know. Blasting Bill. Bill Bang. I don't remember. Are you trying to avoid trying the shot?"

"I'm not avoiding the shot. I'm trying to understand. What's my motivation?" Berle was teasing him, and Andras knew it.

"Either you take the shot, or we spend a few more hours teaching me how to do it." The two stared at each other, waiting to see who would flinch first. Andras couldn't hold a straight face before having to stifle a giggle behind his hands. Berle picked up the Henry rifle and chambered a cartridge with a fluid movement of his hand. The hair on the back of Berle's neck stood on end as he heard the rifle's elegantly machined parts working perfectly.

"You know who you're reminding me of right now?" Berle asked him. He squeezed an eye shut and took a step to the right.

"Who?" Andras asked. Pa still hadn't raised the rifle to his shoulder.

"Your wonderful, creative, tough-as-hide Ma." And Pa fired the rifle from his hip, an explosion of smoke, and the tinkling of glass. Andras's face scrunched as he smiled, amazed and so proud to be that man's son. Berle smirked knowingly. He retrieved the card and handed the ace of spades to Andras, a neat hole through the center.

"Is this from our good cards?" Pa asked. Andras stared at the card in amazement, looking up at his dad through the card like a peephole.

"It's from the cabinet drawer. Do we have other cards?"

"No, we do not."

"It looks more better this way."

"Yeah, maybe it does, but unless we wanna shoot holes in all our cards, we're gonna know which one is the ace of spades no matter what side of the card you're sitting on, you reckon?" Andras turned the card over, his smile shrinking.

"Can't undo it now," Andras concluded before tucking it into his hatband. "Do I look like a cowboy?" he asked his Pa.

"You look like a paddleboat gambler." Berle laughed at his son's creative mind.

"I'll start saving up my bits now. Next time we go to the cafe, I'll play some cards, and I'll buy us our own train, so that we can go to New York and see Uncle Vaclav and Lincoln." Berle almost fell over from laughing so hard. He laid the rifle on the bench where they'd been sitting.

"So, I won. What does that mean?"

"It means I got this neat, new charm on my hat. And we can make supper now." Andras flaunted his new hat accessory.

"Seeing as I won the bet, maybe you should make the supper," Berle teased as they collected the guns and ammunition.

"Dad, I can barely lift the black pan," he countered. Berle rolled his eyes dramatically.

"Fine, but you do the washing-up."

"Deal. But no gravy," Andras countered. Berle paused to consider this last condition.

"No gravy: deal." Berle knew he had called Andras's bluff. Andras liked gravy on everything, perhaps even moreso than Berle. Andras could barely disguise his immediate regret for proposing it, but he stood his ground and shook on it firmly like an experienced oil magnate. Berle admired his shrewd acumen. Maybe he would bring him along on his next business arrangement. Andras's cool, collected professionalism dissolved when he saw the amount of washing up he would be handling alone, so Pa decided to help.

That night, Andras lay on the floor, opening and closing his sore right hand as his Pa sat in a chair and read slowly from an English book. Berle had picked up a copy of "Through the Looking-Glass, and What Alice Found There" after Andras had become transfixed by the images in the book. The book had been an interesting read so far. Andras was particularly interested in the characters of the Tweedledee and Tweedledum. He laughed and asked why they agreed to fight and why they were so scared of a bird. "I've no clue, son. This is all new to me too." Berle was equally as entranced by the character, Hatta, whose sentences were so inundated with superfluous diction and poppycock that the truth was lost. He was excited to see what the book would reveal about him.

"Dad?" Andras interrupted.

"Yeah?"

"The flowers: why are they being mean?" Andras stared at the ceiling at the blotchy knots in the boards above that began to look like faces when he stared at them long enough. Berle looked at the last page and reread a bit.

"It... seems like they're being mean because she doesn't belong there. She sort of wandered in."

"But she's just lost."

"Yeah, Andi, you're right. Earlier, they were talking about her skirt and calling it petals, they called her feet roots: I think Alice is very different from them, and they don't understand her." Berle held his breath between words, careful to take advantage of this amazing parenting opportunity. Andras stopped flexing his achy hand and sat up to face his dad.

"If I saw a flower walking around, asking for help, I wouldn't chase it away and be mean. I would be nice to it."

"Why is that?"

"Because it's new here, and it's probably lost and scared. And I've never seen a flower like that before."

"That's very kind, Andi." There was a quiet moment of warmth between them before Berle continued reading.

The sun had disappeared behind the Rockies, and the sky was still holding on to the last beautiful purple and orange remnants of the day. From outside, they heard a lone call, short and high, but not a coyote or bird. Berle paused and the two looked at each other. The call came again joined, this time, by the sound of beating hooves outside. Berle closed the book and lifted the repeater from the mantle. Andras stayed near the ground and scooted to the window to look outside. Goosebumps crawled down his neck and across his arms.

In a swirl of dust and spinning color was a lone rider dressed in a long white linen shirt with matching linen pants. He had a red cloth around his head that held back his long raven-black hair from obstructing his vision. In his hand, he held a short spear, maybe four feet long, decorated with feathers and small tufts of different colored fur hides. He had a well-worn Winchester cartridge rifle slung across his back.

The horse was a gorgeous, impressive beast. Primarily white, it had brown splotches on its body and face that made it hard to watch when it spun like it was doing now. The rider kicked and whooped as it saw movement in the house, wheeling and spinning his mount in a tight circle. Berle opened up the front door with a sharp jerk. He had that stony expression on his face again.

"Go get the pistol, Andras" was all Pa said before he stepped out the door.

Berle held the rifle in one hand at his side, far from the trigger. The rider made one last rotation before pushing off the back of his saddleless horse. He wore finely-sewn hide boots without spurs that came halfway up his shin. The red cloth around his waist unfurled loosely and draped over one leg. He had a beautiful necklace of many round beads, a pendant made of two long fangs of some mean animal, and a golden coin, rough on the edges, and imprinted with a symbol.

He casually tossed his spear into the ground so that it plunged deep and sat there, waiting for him to retrieve it.

"Hola," he said as he approached, both hands empty. Berle held up one hand, the universal sign for "Hold up, slow it down there, partner." The man was not smiling, and he stopped when Berle held up a hand. "¿Hablas Español?" the strange man asked. Berle shifted his weight uncomfortably. Inside the house, he saw Andras take his place at the window again, this time, armed.

"I'm sorry, I don't understand what you're saying," Berle said clearly and sternly. The man hesitated, thought, and then spoke again.

"My *'indáá-ńne*-talk is not good. I was very small in *Mexíco* and learned their tongue and the tongue of my people."

"I'm still learning English also. It's not an easy language. I thought learning to talk was hard, but reading is worse," Berle responded conversationally. He was feeling out the situation, trying to determine this man's intentions.

"Good for me, I don't read much. The nuns at the Mission tried to make me, but I'm a stone." At that, the man held out a flat hand, unshakable and strong. Berle nodded and raised a hand in greeting.

"I'm Berle Walenty. I recently bought this land and built a home here."

"You, and your child," the man clarified. Berle swallowed. He'd been watching.

"Yes, me and my son. We came here from Poland across the ocean. I don't suppose you speak Polish." The man shook his head apologetically.

"I am Naiche of the Shis-Inday. My people live far from here." He indicated south with his chin. "I heard lots of shooting, and I came to look." Naiche scanned the home, looking for signs of a conflict.

"Yes, I was teaching my son to shoot. He's gotten very good," Berle explained. The man nodded.

"Good. Shooting is important," Naiche stated. Berle nodded in agreement. The air stood stagnant between them.

"Thanks for coming to make sure we were safe. I'm very thankful to you," Berle prompted at last. Naiche nodded and began to walk back to his horse, grabbing his short spear on the way. He grabbed a handful of the beautiful horse's mane and yanked himself onto its back. Berle waved as the man wheeled the horse again and sprinted off into the growing darkness.

"Dad, what was that?"

"An introduction."

Chapter 6

Vukašin Ilíc opened his eyes. He wasn't sure what time it was. He wasn't sure what day it was. He looked at the clock. It said eight thirty-eight. Probably morning. He could see light through the window. The cafe downstairs was already noisy. Apparently, some guests arrived in the night. The green room was not as welcoming and pleasant in the first light of day. He rolled over onto his side and groaned like an old man who had spent his years on the road sleeping on rocks. He pulled on his boots and sat on the bed, staring in the mirror.

"Berle... Walenty..." he said the name like a curse. "Berle... Walenty..." He stared at himself in the mirror hatefully, the words seething in his mouth. He spit on the floor. "Berle Walenty," he growled one more time and swept the alarm clock off the small green bedside table; it smashed into the mirror. Splintered shards of glass tumbled to the ground, and the hateful gaze and heaving shoulders of Vukašin fell away. Like a switch, he was immediately calm and collected. He finished dressing again, secured his pistols around his waist, and walked down the carpeted steps to the cafe downstairs.

A loud group of six men sat around two tables, dusty and darkened by the sun and trail. They drank like men celebrating and had the free spirits of men who lived on the trail. Vukašin sat down at a table with his back to the wall, facing the door. He watched the men carefully for a moment to see if the bender would escalate into something predatory. But the men seemed to know how to handle their liquor well enough. The innkeeper brought his breakfast, and Vukašin nodded towards the loud party of men.

"Who are the breakfast-beer boys?" He asked with a hoarse whisper. The innkeeper looked at them, made a face, and shook his head.

"Nothing but vagrant, drifting free-grazers," was his response. "Don't you worry about them none, sir. They'll be moving on soon enough, probably after they finish their drinks. You need anything else?"

"Another bottle of beet vodka, please, if you would." Ilíc produced a silver coin on the back of his hand like an illusionist, walked it end-over-end across his knuckles, and flipped the coin up with his thumb. The innkeeper caught the coin and chuckled.

"You got it, partner."

Vukašin ate his breakfast slowly, letting the yolk soak his toast. He listened to the cowboys blather on loudly about the vice they got up to the night before. Most of it was just dramatically manufactured retellings of various sad moments from the night before. One stood up from his chair, laid a hand on the table for balance, and indicated he was going out back to take a piss. The others gathered up their things and donned their hats and coats. They loudly shuffled outside followed moments later by their lone relieved companion.

"Where to next, cowboy?" Vukašin rasped to the freegrazer. His bright blue eyes flashed to the stranger, to the gun on his hip, to the scar on his neck, and then to his eyes like open graves.

"Don't rightly know yet. Wherever the work is, I s'pose."

"Where do you call home?" Vukašin sipped his drink casually.

"Dakota Territory–There a reason you're so curious 'bout me?"

"Long way from home. I know how that feels, to feel the…instinctual unsettledness in your bones. Every bed is not 'your bed,' every road, not the one on your street. A man can be driven mad without a place to call his own, you know? We're just like any other animal: we need a territory to defend. A cave to return to. Somewhere to hold up for the long vinters, yes?" A ghost of his Serbian accent whispered out when he said "long winters." The cowboy nodded and glanced at the door awkwardly.

"Yeah, I s'pose I do. Where's abouts you from, stranger? You don't sound like no Coloradan f'round here."

"You've a sharp ear. No, I'm no towny. I come from a very cold place far, far away. Where I come from, there are violent, bloody feuds older than this country. Did you know that? It's a place called Serbia. It's one of the few places in the world you can be sentenced to from another country. The people there are cold and strong. I do not miss it." He sipped his drink again.

"Sounds like a shit place, pard'ner. My condolences to your origins." The cowboy continued walking and left the inn.

The Winter Viper had come West, but no more word or specifics about his location had surfaced. Perhaps he should go back and talk to the Ukrainian in New York instead of just watching him from afar.

Ilíc guessed he would give up at least five fingers to keep his friends safe. The sixth finger was when most "loyal" brethren broke. It was the agonizing transition of finishing one hand and moving on to a whole new set of fingers that shook them. Maybe he would burn the other side of his face to match.

Unfortunately, Vukašin was waiting for that egg to hatch. The Ukrainian was much more valuable as an ignorant compass, mindlessly guiding him directly to The Winter Viper. His woman's landlord, Vernon, didn't even begin the ten count before he spilled his guts about everything he knew. Then Ilíc spilled his guts in that alleyway, and put a bullet in his chest. He turned out the fat man's pockets and stole his watch as Vernon struggled to breathe. They would find him dead…later. Technically it *was* just a robbery gone wrong. Vukašin did rob him. And it all went wrong for Vernon. The ladies Vernon left behind, Mary and Helen, were valuable variables he could add to the equation later if needed.

He finished another glass and tipped himself another. He would need to buy a few bottles of this before he continued searching further West. Obviously, he wasn't finished with this lovely patch of high desert quite yet, but The Winter Viper is slippery, and he's just in his hole right now. Bait him or lull him into a sleepy peace. Then, cut off his head. But what about his son? What about the brood spawn of the Viper? He could leave him an orphan to fend for himself. If the Viper's blood is strong, he'll grow to be just fine. However, loose ends are messy. He'd hate to have to watch his back for the lil' snakelet the rest of his days. That settled it: he would kill the child too. Bullets were cheap in this country and so readily available. He could afford to kill two Walentys.

He stood and left another silver coin on the bar, reached over, and took another bottle of beet vodka for himself. The innkeeper waved in acknowledgment, and Ilíc stepped out into the street of Ogden. He would check with the post office next, he supposed–

"Hey! Hey, you son of a bitch! You killed my brother and his wife! And you stole his horse and saddle! I'm calling you out for murder!" A cracked and wavering voice full of hesitation broke the pleasantness of the morning sun. Ilíc froze, and every muscle in his body tensed as he listened for the brush of steel on leather, the locking of a hammer, the sharp inhale of a marksman, but he only heard alarmed murmurs of townsfolk clearing the way, and the crunch of gravel underfoot.

Vukašin turned slowly to behold his aggressor, or aggressors as luck would have it. The family resemblance was uncanny. Sallow skin, stained fingers and lips, glassy eyes, missing teeth; the picture of American manifest destiny. He recognized them from the train. As he rode away on Clara, formerly known as this-hick's-beatin'-horse, he'd seen these three goons scavenging off the passengers in the train cars further up. Come to think of it, Ilíc had just been thinking about how much he disliked loose ends.

The bold one was angry, stupid with passion, and had a pistol in his pocket. He could see the curved handle from where he stood. The other two seemed to be as equally surprised by the turn of these events as he was. They each had the physique and apparent intellect of gorillas. Thick foreheads, wide jaws, unfocused, inbred eyes; they were the muscle. They didn't appear to be related, by his eye, but they both served the same purpose. They hurt people. They might not be smart enough to make any plans, but they sure-as-hell are dumb enough to carry the plans out. If this moron was dumb enough to clear leather, it would be all-out war for about seven seconds. But he was a coward, and Vukašin was going to make him suffer for that.

He raised his hands, allowing his wolf skin coat to fall open, showing the pistols on his hips and the rifle across his back. The loud idiot moved his hand to his gun, unsure of what to do. Vukašin began taking long strides toward him, his hands still raised.

"There must be some mistake, I just rode into town yesterday on my horse, Clara. I'm staying in the inn; you can check there if you like." Vukašin's ghastly voice hissed out of his shredded throat like a cold hand held on a hot griddle.

"Stop right there, stay back; I'm warning you mister, I'll–" The brim of Vukašin's hat swept the other's hat off as he stood uncomfortably, emasculatingly, terrifyingly close to the man who smelled so strongly of sweat, ass, and alcohol, Vukašin wanted to throw up on top of his pale, thinning head right then. The man moved to shove away, but Ilíc grabbed his throat and yanked him back to uncomfortable closeness.

Ilíc's fingertips dug into the flesh of the man's throat so that Ilíc could feel the man failing to swallow.

He looked at the other two thugs, cheek to cheek with their boss whose face was contorting red into purple, clawing at Ilíc's hand.

"Run. Don't come back," he hissed. "I'm keeping this one." The two cavemen exchanged looks, and the one on the left reached for the pistol on his hip. Vukašin was faster.

He pulled his pistol and fired a shot into the thug's belly. He cried out in a moan and fell onto his side in blinding pain. The last one turned to run as advised. Vukašin stepped behind the purple moron in his grip and flipped him onto the hard-beaten path so that the only sound that came from him was a wet thud and a quiet *uff*. Vukašin fired at the fleeing caveman and saw a puff of pink from his chest. He cocked the pistol, shot the moaning man on the ground in the face so that his head bounced on the ground, and then knelt on the last one's chest.

The pistol in his pocket was gone, flung god-knows-where. His two large backups were dead, and he still couldn't breathe. Black shadows fogged the edges of his vision as suffocation began to set in, then the pressure let off his chest, and he gasped and coughed for the first time in what felt like minutes. In truth, it had only been about seven seconds.

"No, no, keep your eyes open. We're not done," A voice like The Serpent hissed. A sharp slap on the cheek flashed white across his vision. Someone nearby yelled, "Get the deputy!" Vukašin pulled a long double-edged dagger from the back of his waistband, slid it up under his chin, and pierced him to the hilt so that, when he coughed, blood spurted both out his mouth and onto Ilíc's hand.

"I don't even know your name," he whispered like water in hot oil, "that's how little you matter to me. I'm not even sure there's a reward for you. I just like the way your eyes look when you realize that you're going to die in front of all of these people, and they might clap when I wipe my hands on your shirt." And his eyes went wide, wet, and desperate. As the final fraying tendrils of his mortal coil snapped, his eyes dilated, and he heard his own teeth cracking.

Vukašin jerked the knife handle upwards, driving the head back, and obliterating anything on the other end of it. The body went limp with one great jerk. Ilíc sighed deeply. Someone vomited. Vukašin slid his knife free from under the irrelevant man's chin, and wiped it off on the man's shirt. Dammit. Nobody clapped. They would have clapped in Niš.

A man, in what Ilíc could only assume to be an old navy uniform and tin star, approached with the confident stride of military discipline. He held a repeating rifle in his hand, his finger resting alongside the trigger as he marched. He stopped several yards away and pointed the rifle at the ground between them.

"You have one chance to compel me with honesty to keep your life." The deputy was from Georgia. Vukašin was titillated to hear the crowning jewel of the American dialect. He holstered his pistol and stood up. He returned his knife and raised his hands in front of him.

"Deputy," the snake hissed, "I can explain. These… outlaws robbed a train yesterday. During the robbery, I escaped with my life, stealing one of their horses and fleeing here, to your protection. They saw the 'stolen' horse and came for me to finish the job. I didn't fire until they drew on me, officer. You gotta believe me."

The officer scanned the scene and surveyed the faces of the lookers-on. "The train station would be able to confirm any of this." Vukašin lowered his hands. "I'm sure of it. Are these wanted men?" The Deputy gave him an appraising sideways glance and then looked down at the exsanguinated corpse with pink foam dripping out of his mouth.

"Sho' 'nough. Derelict Dan. This'n's Lug-head Larry." He kicked one of the cavemen's boots. "An' I reckon that one's his brother." He nodded to the one who nearly escaped. The Deputy took off his hat and shook his head. "Damn shame…"

"Were you fond of them?" Ilíc rasped. The Deputy spit a gob of brown chaw on Derelict Dan.

"Fuck, no. It's a damn shame waste o' good bullets and an afternoon o' paperwork. But a damn fine sixty dollars spent. That is, assuming you are the same spooky, scarred phantom who killed three robber, and then disappeared with only a warning: *Hush*. That you?" It was Vukašin's turn to spit on the corpses.

"In my defense, my voice doesn't carry well, and there was a very loud couple of moments right before that, but what I said was not a warning."

"I don't rightly care what you said. Let's make this official back at my office." The deputy waved over his shoulder for Vukašin to follow. "Don't worry about the boots, bullets, and belts. You can have 'em, or we can throw in five extra bucks to take the lot off your hands."

"I wouldn't mind trading that sad nag I filched off them for something with a little more…time left," and he chuckled deep in the back of his throat like a thick, phlegmy regurgitation.

"Done. Any of theirs is yours by law, if'n you want them. Anything else?" They walked down four squeaky wooden steps into a recessed sheriff's office above a basement jail. This could be the right angle if he leveraged it correctly

"I have a different idea. What say we settle on sixty-five dollars for the bodies, their horses, minus mine, and their effects? I'm not sure I want anything they had on them. In exchange, I want your help finding someone." The Deputy dropped the money on the table, a small stack of goofy notes again. He smoothed his thin hair and hung his hat on the point of a mounted pronghorn on one wall.

"A bounty?" The Deputy asked, eyeing him once again.

"From Europe."

"Paris, France?"

"Vas- no. What? A rebel assassin coward who fled his home and country. I came here to put him down for good. And he's got a little boy with him."

"He got a name? Or an alias? Or a gang he runs with?"

"I regret to inform you that this is where my trail goes cold. I know he landed in New York, met with some friends, and came out west. He bought a plot while they were still damp with 'in'jun' blood."

"Sounds like a bad guy. Give me a name. He ever been on the sheets?" The Deputy reached under his desk and produced a thick tome of wanted posters held fast with metal rings in a leather cover like a bible. Vukašin produced a yellowing, folded bill, opened it, and handed it to the Deputy. He took it and began to scan it. The depiction of Berle was vague and unhelpful. Cyrillic writing lined the top and bottom of the page.

"I can't read this. Help me out here."

"It says, 'Wanted: Dead or Alive. Wanted for various war crimes in various countries and provinces, in enemy and allied territories. He's killed thirty-seven officers of the Imperial Russian military, and now he's hiding somewhere nearby." The Deputy squinted and studied it before handing it back.

"I cannot recall any such brigand by that name or description. And with a boy, to boot." He rounded the desk and sat on the edge, flattening out his bulging waistcoat. "A lot of people come out here looking for a new start. Maybe your man has turned a new leaf. I guarantee, if he starts any trouble in my town, he'll wish he was back in Russia." Ilíc pocketed the paper.

"What happened to the Sheriff?" he asked, glancing at the empty desk.

"Which one?" he responded absently.

"Um…the last one."

"I suppose it was misleading to ask that. He died. They all died. All of 'em. Cholera, shot, choked, broke neck, malaria, consumption, fell off the roof, conniption, blood poisoning, scalped; all of 'em." He rattled off fatalities on his fingers. "Folk say the office is cursed. Something about a red shaman or something." Vukašin rattled his brain for the word.

"Shaman? Like a sorcerer?" he asked, confused. The deputy nodded and sat back in his creaky chair.

"Sho, nuff. More like a witch doctor. I guess he lives further East, closer to the Rockies. Lots of washed-up Injun like the mountain, say the medicine is good. That's their magic, 'medicine.'" This was getting too off-topic.

"So you'll post these around?" Vukašin proffered the wanted flier again. The Deputy raised his hands,

"Slow down there, partner. Any legal matters like that need to get approved by the marshall or ranger before I can just offer money for your man." Ilíc sighed. How could a nation so underdeveloped and nubile already be so bogged down in bureaucratic bullshit? "Tell you what, friend, I'll write a note telling the train station to check their records for a...?"

"Walenty. Berle Walenty." He gritted his teeth as he said it, holding back hatred. The deputy scribbled a note on a piece of paper and then ripped it off, folded it, and handed it to him.

"The boy in the window is Noah. He should be able to help you."

Noah was a pocky-faced pink child with the appearance and demeanor of a wet cat. His thin hair poked out from under his railway cap, and the collar of his shirt hung loose, although it was buttoned to the top. He gazed with glassy pale eyes at Ilíc, who leaned against the counter at the train station.

"Do you know where they bought their tickets?" Noah asked flatly, like a student reciting lines.

"New York." Vukašin was fed up with the sluggish pace of this hunt. He was not a fucking detective. He was a killer.

"Yeah, but like through an agency, or did they just go to the depot?" When he blinked, his right eye opened first. Every time. Like the hinge on the left one was sticky or something. He wanted to grab his neck and hit him as hard as he could in the face until it opened and closed correctly.

"How am I supposed to know that?" Ilíc growled, a blade through gravel. He spit on the tile floor and stamped it with his boot, squeaking loudly.

"So then, how do you expect me to know it?" Noah countered.

"They don't keep records of their passengers?" Anger sizzled in his voice.

The apathetic lethargy wafting off Noah made Ilíc want to kill him. He imagined stabbing him. He knew he was getting close. He was itching for blood already. He was feeling antsy, irritated, raw, like exposed bone.

"Some of the agencies do, but the depot just hands them out, especially if they rode second class or colored." This was a fucking waste of time. He wasn't trying to find train passengers, he was trying to find residents.

"I don't know. City Hall, I guess?" was what Noah said when Ilíc asked him where the permit office was.

Down into a basement, a lantern and city clerk in tow, he opened the heavy wooden door to the records room. The room was large for a basement, and the ceiling was higher than he was used to. The dry room was filled with floor-to-ceiling bookcases along the walls and several long, low shelves in the middle. Massive lecterns for studying the myriad tomes were spaced around the cool basement.

"Why would a church need these kinds of records?" Vukašin asked, stunned.

"You misunderstand. These don't all belong to the church here. All the wards exchange books and share. These have been in the hands of thousands of faithful all over." The city hall clerk seemed to be intimately acquainted with the Mormons. Perhaps he was one of them.

"Thanks so much," Vukašin rasped at him. He handed him a twenty-dollar note and closed the door behind him. He perused the books and found himself drawn to many of the irrelevant books. Thousands of years of genealogies, financial records, land permits, family recipes, recovered artifacts and treasures, and more that Vukašin could not believe. Why the Mormon faithful would be so concerned about the West was a mystery to him.

No proper faith would strive for Earthly gain. God does not send men to war or to conquer and steal; kings and governments do. If a king does something in a god's name, it is in vain. Nevertheless, Vukašin could not help but think that, were he to gain power someday, he would rule as he wished and convince the people that it was god's will. Anyone who opposed him would be worse than a traitor: they would be a heretical apostate. There would be no room for dissension in god's empire because to dissent from god was to be *evil,* if such a thing existed.

He chuckled to himself. There he went again, philosophizing.

He had been searching for nearly thirty minutes before he found a book titled *Cheyenne Land Acquisition 1861-1876.* It was handwritten in rows with the name of the family or owner, the size of the plot, and a number corresponding with a drawn map of the area. The entries were not organized in any discernible order besides numerical.

As plots were sold, whoever was updating this record assigned them the next number.

Vukašin had no indication of when The Winter Viper would have purchased the parcel, but it would have been after the uprising was quelled in sixty-four and after he discovered his wife had fallen pregnant. The boy wasn't older than ten yet, so that reduces the range to a few years. He flipped to the middle and began scanning.

He'd been reading the swoopy cursive letters of the author for nearly an hour when he paused, his nose tickling with the air's dust and particles. He waited.

He'd been sitting in a dark basement reading line after line of names and land sizes and numbered locations, and all for what? So he could find and kill one man who had no clue he was alive? For vengeance on a moment that should have sent him to hell?

The stairs creaked. Someone was coming down the stairs. A voice, not raised in warning, but low in conversation. Multiple people.

His nose tickled, his eyes squinted, and he could feel the sneeze coming. He drew his pistol and pointed it at the door. The door creaked open. He pulled the hammer back.

The door swung open, and Vukašin was pointing his pistol at the open doorway. He held up a finger in polite excuse and then sneezed violently. Dust shook off his wolfskin coat. He sniffed and looked down the barrel of his gun.

"I beg your pardon," Ilíc dabbed his nose politely with the back of his hand, "I wasn't expecting company."

"God bless you, you spooky fuck," the sun-kissed cowboy from before, his hair like burnt sand and eyes like a mirage, said, his hands raised. Vukašin cocked his head like a predatory bird studying a rabbit.

"Are you following me? You looking to put a bullet in my back? Who were you talking to?" Another of the free-grazers appeared behind him, his hand on his pistol.

"Not quite. We ain't so concerned about no Russian mutes." He smirked a handsome, churlish half-smile. Vukašin returned the smirk and snapped the hammer forward safely, spinning the pistol once on his finger before letting it spin into its perfectly formed holster. He wasn't going to tell this trail-scholar that Serbia was not in Russia. The cowboy lowered his hands.

"What do you want?" Vukašin growled at them, the skin around his collarbone and Adam's apple pulling taut so that the quickening pulse in his neck was visible.

"We came down here to pull some permits, look at some land that recently got bought up. Ain't nothing that concerns you." Vukašin's grasp of the English language was good, great even compared to most other foreigners, but this particular dialect vexed him.

"By all means," he held out a hospitable hand to the other books in the cellar, "help yourself."

The cowboys split up and began perusing the titles. Ilíc watched them peripherally for a moment before returning to his mindless scanning.

"Boss, the German's got the map we need." He heard one cowboy whisper to another. They approached and looked at the map cautiously, careful not to disturb the stranger wearing a wolf. He sighed like a father trying to read in the presence of children. He turned the map with a quick twist of his wrist.

"By all means…" he hissed like piss on a fire. The lead cowboy extended his hand in a confident greeting.

"The name's Rhodes," he announced like a town mayor. Ilíc stared coldly. "Appreciate the gesture," said Rhodes, saluting casually with the rejected hand, and he bent over the map. He traced an unmarked path across the Colorado map and stopped on a tiny blip in the center of an untouched sea of Colorado landscape East of the mountains near a town recorded as "Foothill."

"There." Rhodes indicated to his fellow. The other nodded and craned his neck to see the number scribed inside the tiny square. Rhodes took the book from in front of Vukašin and flipped two pages back. "Says here it was… originally signed by a…Vaclav Sarna, but the owner is a…Berle Walenty."

Before the name was completely out of his mouth, Vukašin struck with the raging ferocity of a caged animal, starved, deprived. He slammed Rhodes's head against the map, kicked the table they both leaned against, and drew his pistol. He waited for them to recover and notice the final fraying fiber of sanity that held the hammer back on his pistol.

"What the flying fuck…" Rhodes grumbled painfully and then froze.

"Hold up, mister," the other began. Vukašin drew a second pistol from the back of his gun belt and pointed it at him.

"What do you know about Walenty?" His question cut through the groaning of their stunned recovery.

"Nothing. We don't know nothing, sir. Please don't kill us," Martin pleaded, his hands raised. Rhodes wiped his nose, spit on the floor and straightened his shirt.

"Don't fucking beg, Martin. He ain't a judge or your daddy," Rhodes sniffed and cursed as he checked the integrity of a tooth. Martin fell silent. "We can take you to him. But we want a cut."

"A cut?" Vukašin cocked an eyebrow. A bold move for a bleeding man staring down six bullets.

"Yeah. A good, fair cut. Whatever you're up to, it's unsavory, and I want to help you get rid of that greedy fucking farmer. My boys are good for it. We split it…thirty-five, sixty-five. We ride with you and help you…do whatever you're doing." The pause was loaded and primed.

Vukašin glanced at the map that now lay on the floor. That tiny speck on the map was the den of the Viper, at last. The mountain range that divided them was a jagged, misshapen scar with no observable paths or passes on the map.

"Seventy-five, twenty-five, and you get paid after Walenty is dead. If any of your men cross me or try to subvert my plans, I'll kill you first." Vukašin's voice was steady and unwavering with no hint of remorse or hesitation in those airy syllables.

"You don't need to worry about my boys. They're along for the ride no matter what. If they do anything stupid, you can rest easy knowing I'll kill them first. I'm assuming the reward for this is…substantial?" Rhodes spit a wad of pink foam on the cool basement floor.

"You negotiate without any thought of the value? You are very foolish–"

"Yeah, well, maybe this ain't about just the money, alright?" Rhodes snapped back, annoyed. "But…it'd be nice to be recompensed for services rendered." Vukašin nodded, lowered both hammers, and stowed his guns. These barbarians would prove useful guides and companions in the unfamiliar countryside, and their personal connection to the land bound them tighter than any extrinsic motivation.

"Seventy, thirty, and when we find him, you do exactly as I say. This last part is most important," Vukašin began, and he made his tone unmistakably dire. "When the time comes, I kill Walenty. No one touches him but me." Martin glanced at Rhodes. Rhodes nodded and stood.

"If he's as dangerous as you're making him out to be, I'd be glad to let you handle him." Vukašin folded and pocketed the map of the Colorado territory with the Viper's den marked.

Rhodes and Martin introduced him to the crew; Rhodes was boss, Hank Rhodes, after his father, Henry. Martin's last name sounded like poetry to his ears, but he could not get his tongue around the intimately-acquainted consonants. "Xochuitl-Tlajuillakan" was not a word he had learned yet. The remaining four he met were Barnabus Rowe, Jack "Stoney" Jackson, Asher Milan, and Ben Sanderson.

Vukašin surveyed them as they were introduced, feeling the calluses on their hands as they shook, the strength in their arms. He took note of Rowe's slight head tilt as Rhodes spoke: hard of hearing. Jack nodded as he listened to Rhodes's plan, fidgeting and looking at the others imperceptibly. He was untried, maybe the youngest. His name was associated with one of the generals of their civil war, the losing side, if he remembered correctly. Benjamin Sanderson was the knowledgeable one. His neckerchief was tied with a lariat loop, and his boots were worn on the sides where the stirrups rubbed for thousands of hours. Asher seemed to be the gunhand of the crew. He was the only one to carry a long gun, a cartridge rifle with a long thin scope on it. He wondered if Asher had ever killed a man before, but he could sense that Asher had felt the rush of blood on his hand as he stabbed something. He was at least a fine hunter.

"We'll leave after dinner," Rhodes told his crew. "We'll make camp and then make dust for the old goat trail. It's a slog, but it'll save our horses, and it's got a few springs to spot at. Is that acceptable to our guest rider?" Rhodes motioned toward Ilíc. He knew the importance of a strong image in front of his direct reports. Ilíc nodded wordlessly. He'll let the chips fall as they may, but he wanted to make sure he was the only one ready to cash in when the cards were down.

Vukašin went back to the stables for his new horse. The outlaws' horses were strong and fast, wild beasts hardly broken. The horse Vukašin picked leaned against the stall wall when he tried to put the saddle on until he growled at the horse. The big, pretty brown eye took him in and rolled before relenting.

After dinner, the seven of them packed their horses with supplies for the trail. It must be nice for them not to have to herd the cattle constantly as they rode. He imagined how he would like a life like Martin and Rhodes's.

By nightfall. The Western slopes of the Rocky Mountains glowed orange and purple on the horizon. Ilíc leaned against his saddle on the ground. His new horse craned its neck to reach the rough needles of the tree it was tied to, completely ignoring the grass on the ground.

So this was life on the trail. He could imagine living this way, traveling from place to place, never needing to meet new people and working whatever jobs he wanted. Maybe after Berle is dead, he'd come back to this place and buy it, build a little house, and live off the land. But first, the Viper must die. Six more days.

Chapter 7

Andras looked out the window of the house. Still no Pa. He stopped scrubbing the black pan and listened. No approaching horse. This wasn't the first time Andras had been left at home alone. He wasn't a baby anymore. But he felt nervous.

He had removed the rifle from the mantle and leaned it against the door so that he could grab it if needed. He finished the dishes and opened up the Alice's Adventures book. He loved the whimsical illustrations and silly depictions. He looked at the English words, and tried to sound out what he knew but he was just making sounds.

He gathered the laundry from outside on the line, folded it, and placed it in the chest. Still no rider. Piotyr is slow, but unless he stopped to take a nap, they should be back by now. He added another log to the fire and shoved it with the heel of his boot so that it rolled on to the flames.

Still no rider. The sun had not yet fully disappeared behind the mountains, but the sky was already darkening. He sat on the front porch in the chair that Ed made him, and he rocked, the golden-bodied rifle across his lap.

A low rumble of hooves echoed, and the shadowy form of a lone rider, riding hard, appeared at the edge of his vision. He waited. The rider got closer and closer until he recognized his father. Something must be wrong. Where was Piotyr? And the wagon? Berle reached the house smiling, his eyes bright, his face red and sweaty, his hair asunder.

"Hey, Andi! No need to worry! Piotyr and the wagon are in town. The axle is getting fixed, and I bought us a proper horse!" He presented the horse like a magician.

"Meet Gourd! He was a racing horse that won too often, and then got fat and lazy. He's still only three." Gourd swung his head and flared his nostrils. Andras couldn't help but smile. He was worried and upset, but Gourd brought Pa home safely. He hoped Piotyr would be safe too.

He hugged his Pa, and Pa hugged him, scooping him up and lifting him onto his shoulder like a sack of oats. "Nie, tato! *No, dad!*" Andras twisted and giggled, trying to put his fingers in Pa's ears, because that was the only sure way he knew of escape. Pa twisted his head to avoid his son's probing fingers, and lowered him onto the dusty rug. Andras used the soft landing to recover his balance and attack his Pa's legs. Pa was always too fast and too smart, stepping one foot back to stay firmly planted. He dramatically fell to the ground, and Andras took advantage. Pa's fierce tickling claws were waiting for him. Pa relented and allowed him to twist away.

"I was worried, dad." Andras broke the moment's fun.

"I know, Andi. I rode back as fast as I could. I'm sorry, partner." Andras nodded in forgiveness and hugged his dad.

"Tomorrow we'll ride Gourd into town and you can try and drive Piotyr and the wagon home. How's that sound?" Andras had been practicing his riding and driving since he had turned seven. He was not a "natural" as his father insisted, but secretly consistent. Piotyr had been Andras's practice steed for weeks now. Andras nodded enthusiastically.

The two men got ready for bed. Pa read more from the book, and then they went to bed. Berle didn't remember putting his head on his pillow; he was so tired. Andras tossed and turned. He remembered how he felt when Pa didn't come home, the tightness in his chest and shoulders, how his mind was consumed with only thoughts of his father. What if he had not come back? Would Andras have just made dinner, and gone to bed? And how long could he sustain that? The tilled ground was just barely beginning to sprout with tiny green shoots. Could he nurture the crops to harvest and then sell them in town? How much did he keep for food and the next season? And what did he do if someone came to rob him? He had never shot anyone. He fell asleep with his mind full of snarling growling fangs, tearing skin, and Buck's shrieks of death.

Berle woke early, gently, peacefully. His eyes fluttered open on their own like a leaf succumbing to autumn. The sun was not quite up yet. He dressed and pulled on his oldest boots. It was time to muck a stall. Calling it a stall was generous. It was a shabby lean-to affixed to the side of the house. Andras thought it was convenient because Piotyr would scrape his rump against the wall by Andras's bedroom every morning, signaling his preparedness to be bribed into work.

The house was silent. The floor did not creak, and the windows did not pop and rattle as he walked. He ground two handfuls of coffee beans and sighed. His recent adoption of coffee into his diet had been a tedious adventure. Following Vaclav's instructions, he drank it with cream or milk when they had it. He drank it in his favorite tea cup in an effort to convince himself that he liked it, but there was no getting past the burnt flavor of brown on his tongue. But, goddammit, he loved the way it made him feel. He felt as if he could carry Piotyr to the field and till it himself. He's sure Piotyr would not mind, but he didn't want to set any precedents.

Berle pulled on a thick, flanneled shirt over his clothes. The early morning air had a bite before the sun could come and warm the plains. Lastly, he put his hat on and tugged the brim securely down. He opened the door to the house quietly and sipped his coffee. He didn't feel any urgency to begin working right away, so he sat down in his chair on the porch, sipped his coffee and rocked slowly.

He inhaled deeply; the kind of breath that goes in both nostrils, fills the chest and belly, and you want to hold that breath for a few moments before you release the peace of it. The world was silent save the animals that relished the early morning darkness and chill. Birds that occupied the trees near the Walenty home announced their victory over another night. Two gray squirrels chased each other near some bushes before one retreated into a hole in a fallen tree near the creek. A doe stepped timidly into view, her ears swiveling at the slightest sound. Berle stopped rocking. He exhaled.

He listened for Piotyr's rubbing against the house, his sign that he was awake, but he was still silent. Strange. That loyal, old mule is a grumpy riser, but he's usually grumpy earlier than this. Berle put down his cup and stood from his chair. The doe turned to look. Berle turned the corner of the house where Piotyr's stall was, and his heart skipped. Piotyr was gone.

The gate to the stall was not complex, but he could not have opened it on his own. On the ground, he saw fresh hoof prints in the dew-soft earth, maybe hours old. Dammit. He followed the hoof prints in vain, knowing he wouldn't see that mule again, and he would owe more to Josef come October. But who would steal an old mule from a little house in the middle of nowhere? He immediately thought of the free-grazers, and he seethed with anger. If those bastards were trying to sabotage him…

Next he thought of Naiche, the Indian who introduced himself a while back. He hadn't seen him since, but he knew that Naiche was keeping an unseen eye from afar. As he rounded the corner, he heard a frustrated voice and saw Piotyr just beyond the corral fence. They hadn't gotten very far. Berle disappeared back around the corner and listened to the thief.

"Come on, Piotyr! We're going to try one more time! Pa is going to wake up soon, and you need to get in your stall." Berle peeked around the corner and saw the thief and his accomplice.

Andras was brushing his pants off after apparently falling off of Piotyr. The mule stared at him and chewed, annoyed at the bit in his mouth. On the other side of the corral, Gourd chewed grass and watched Andras, wondering when his time would come to buck Andras onto the ground.

Andras rounded the mule, grabbed a handful of mane in one hand, and planted the other on Piotyr's rump. He kicked a leg up and pushed with his hand while he pulled the mane hard. He vaulted himself onto Piotyr's back and took hold of the reins, squeezing his knees together just as Berle had shown him. Andras scooted up on Piotyr's back and led him around the back of the house. Andras put Piotyr in his stall, removed and put away the bridle, and then slunk to his window on the side of the house.

Berle heard it open and then shut. He returned to his coffee and chair, smirking all the way. Minutes later, Andras emerged from his room in clean clothes, his hair askew as if he had just woken up. He poured himself some milk, darkened it with some coffee, and then joined his Pa on the porch in the other chair. The two sat in the silence of the morning for a moment, taking in the warmth of the first beams of sunlight.

"You get too warm last night?" Berle asked him. Andras looked at him, confused. "I heard your window close as you were getting up this morning. I figured you got too warm and opened it up last night." They stared at each other as Andras formulated his response. His ears were bright red, but his face betrayed no emotion. Suddenly, he smiled.

"Oh! That. No, I was letting out a moth," he lied. Damn, that was a good lie. Berle nodded knowingly. He could get him somehow. "How did you sleep? Have you been awake for a long time?" Andras deflected, turning the conversation to his Pa. This kid was good. Berle took a long, noisy sip of his coffee and stroked his growing whiskers.

"Slept great! Was thinking about getting an early start on the north field today, get Piotyr hooked up to that tiller, and get it ready for those potatoes, but my coffee was just too good." Berle rocked and took another sip. Andras got up.

"I'm gonna get some more!" he said before turning to walk inside.

"Can you bring the pot, Andi?"

"Sure, Dad!"

"Thanks, Son," Berle said, taking the warm pot from Andras. Andras sat back down next to him.

"You're welcome."

"And great job squeezing your knees together when you were riding. You looked great out there. Very confident." Berle took another long sip of coffee. Andras did not respond. After a long moment of excruciatingly loud birds calling, Andras got up from his chair again.

"I forgot my coffee inside," and he disappeared inside.

The next morning, Berle woke up early again and did not conceal himself as he watched Andras practice his riding. It became the morning routine for the two of them to wake up early in silence. Andras would take Piotyr into the corral and ride while Pa would make the coffee for them. Then, after coffee was drunk, the day would begin.

Life became pleasantly routine for the two of them in their home together. It was a safe place for them to exist and grow together. Their chores were filled with laughter, loud complaints, and bad singing. Meals were always an adventurous event. Berle's knowledge of cooking ended with potato pancakes and other more primitive recipes he learned in the army. Their riding became one of their favorite activities they could share.

Every other week, Andras and Berle would ride into town for the day to buy groceries, Berle on Gourd and Andras on Piotyr. They would tie their mounts to the post in front of the general store, and they would go in together. Pa would chat with Mr. St. James while Andras practiced his reading by finding the items Pa had put on a list. Andras was proud of himself for the speed he had begun to grasp English literacy. He could sound out most English words, and he had memorized many words by sight. By the time he completed the list, Pa and the clerk were boxing up the goods and saying their goodbyes.

Next, they would stop by the post office, mostly to see if Uncle Vaclav had sent any news ahead. They were still expecting a visit from him after the summer months, after the heat, but before the heavy snow. Josef was coming through in October to retrieve his mules. Well, just one actually. Andras did not like to think about saying goodbye to Piotyr. He had grown quite fond of the beast over the last few months, and he dreaded the thought of not waking up to his enthusiastic morning butt-scratches on his wall.

There was no mail or packages today, but Charlie was a talker. Charlie was the postmaster in Foothill, and he prided himself on knowing everyone he collected mail for. As they exited the post office, a collared reverend spoke to the sheriff. The sheriff patted him on the shoulder and walked away, tipping his hat to Berle as he passed. The reverend adjusted his bifocals on his nose, but Andras thought he looked too young to wear glasses. He was younger than Pa by almost a decade, and he had a kindly, familiar face and gentle eyes, but he hardly smiled. When he spotted Berle, he waved and approached, taking Pa's hand warmly.

"Hello! I haven't had the pleasure of meeting you yet. I'm Paul Becker, or Reverend Becker if it's Sunday." It was meant as a joke, but Pa only gave a half chuckle. He'd seen this man somewhere before.

"Mr. Becker, it's a pleasure. I'm Berle, and this is my boy, Andras. We live out of town and come in to buy groceries and visit a few times a month." Berle tousled Andras's hair, and Andras did not stop him as he continued to stare up at Reverend Becker with hair blocking one eye.

"That would explain why I haven't seen you on a Sunday. Are you a practicing man, Berle?" His tone was friendly and genuine, if a little stressed.

"Practicing?" Berle was unsure of the question. He practiced many things; shooting, his English, riding, cooking.

"Religion. Are you religious?" he clarified. Andras looked up at his Pa. He had not considered this since they had built their home and gotten settled. They'd not been to church since they arrived in Colorado. They had a bible in the house, and they would read it sometimes, but Andras couldn't remember the last time he had attended church. It was probably with his grandmother in Polska.

"Oh, um… Not very well. What I mean is that I've been religious in the past, and I read my bible. I do my best to help the orphans and widows and promote the good out there. But the good Lord and me disagree on many points, and I have a difficult time going to his house to share a supper, if you'll pardon the reference, Father."

"Please, just Paul. It sounds like you're doing just as much as any other bible-believing disciple ought to. What points do you and He disagree on, if you don't mind me asking?" Pa shifted uncomfortably on his feet and tousled Andras's hair again as he stared up at him.

"Mainly, we disagree on who deserves to die and when. We've also expressed differences in opinions on killing." Berle cleared his throat awkwardly and looked around at who else may be within earshot. The reverend nodded sympathetically.

"Since you are a family man, seemingly, with integrity and honor, may I assume you were a lawman or in the army?"

"Yes, I served in the army before coming out West."

"In what regiment did you serve? My father served up North."

"Oh, no, I'm very sorr– I did not mean– I served in *not* your civil war. I– my son and I, we are from Poland." Berle stumbled over his words, desperate to clarify. "The conflict I served in was much far from here. And we were fighting a *different* country." As he stammered, his accent became more noticeable, and his words became messier.

Andras didn't understand. Everything his father said sounded like an apology, but he was saying everything wrong and making things worse.

"No need to apologize, friend," the reverend finally smiled at Berle's genuineness, "I'm glad you and your son are here, and so far from Poland. Please, I hope you come to view the church, and myself, as a resource and benefit to you and your family. If ever you're in town on a Sunday, please, come join us for our afternoon luncheon located by the big shading-tree." Reverend Becker turned and pointed at a huge willow tree that swept the ground with long, drooping boughs.

"Sounds great, Reverend, thank you. We will make it a habit to stop and say hello to you whenever we come into town. I don't suppose you'd go into the cafe or saloon for a nip and a meal before we get back on the road?" Berle offered kindly. Pa glanced down at Andras who nodded in concurrence before smiling up at the reverend.

"I can never decline the breaking of bread in fellowship with such fine folks. As it so happens, my brother runs the cafe and works at the saloon at nights. I'd love to buy the three of us a meal!" The three of them crossed the dusty road to the cafe when Berle suddenly realized where he'd seen the man before. Standing behind the bar of the cafe was the Reverend Becker, but with shorter hair and an apron instead of a black habit.

Weeks ago, they had met the cafe owner, Pete, who has an identical twin who works for the Lord. The brothers exchanged pleasantries before Berle reacquainted himself with Pete and laughed at his shock at learning they were twins. The meal was a hearty stew with lots of soft potatoes, carrots, and lentils. The bread was thick, warm, and delicious, and Andras dipped every bite in the stew.

Paul and Berle talked about the area, who owns the biggest plots of land, businesses in the area, what crops grow best in what seasons, and then about cards. Andras had no interest in any of the topics of conversation and dedicated himself to fellowship with the bread he was breaking. Pete kept bringing more warm bread anytime Andras finished his, and he set aside a large, warm chunk wrapped in paper for them when they left. They exchanged goodbyes warmly and wished well upon each other, reaffirming their intent to reconnect when they saw each other again soon.

With their groceries and sacks secured to Piotyr, and Andras with his bread, they set back out on the long trail home with full bellies and faces tired from laughing and smiling. When they were less than a mile from town, Berle and Andras turned around at the sound of approaching galloping hooves. Berle's hand disappeared into his saddlebag. The talkative Postmaster Charlie was waving a note in his hand and bouncing in the saddle at full gallop. He pulled the reins of his thick, old nag and paused a moment to catch his breath. He held the note out to Berle and explained between gasps.

"I beg y'er pardons, Mr. Walentys. The good Lord strike me with cataracts, if I let y'all come through the post office without me passing along your mail. That, and the Ranger'll come for me for federal infringement." Berle assured him that no offense was taken as he looked at the forgotten letter. "It was just such a strange letter. It weren't no name like I seen before, but I saw your name on there, so I set it aside for you knowing you'd come through, but daggnabbit, I looked in your mailbox but forgot the whole thing."

It wasn't postmarked or sealed. It was a plain, yellowy piece of paper with slanted, heavy, penned writing. On the outside, it said, "*Adresovano: Zymoviy Hadyutsi a.d. Berle Walenty.*" Berle's hands trembled as he held it, feeling as if his fingers were numb and he might drop the paper. He fumbled and rumpled the note in clammy hands. When he opened it, he wiped away sweat from his brow.

"*Zavershyty rozpochate. – Hush*" He shut the note and closed his hand around it. Berle jumped off his horse and walked towards Charlie, his clenched fist raised. His mind was a fog of oblivious faces, each with a thin black cross, flashing through his adrenaline-addled brain. A loud flash and pink mist over and over, screams, smoke, fire, and so much blood.

"Khto tse zalyshyv?! Huh? Tell me, Charlie!" Berle shouted at Charlie whose smile disappeared, replaced by dumbfounded alarm. Andras jumped with a start, and he clutched Piotyr's reins tightly, ready to spur him to action. What had his Pa said? That wasn't Polish; was it Russian?

"Well, just settle down there, Berle!" Charlie struggled to get off his horse. He raised his hands placatingly and took the crumpled note from Berle's hand. He looked down his nose at the note, trying to glean some aspect of truth from its cryptic nature. "I'll be honest, Berle, the only words I can read on this paper are 'Berle' and 'Walenty'. I don't remember the feller what dropped this off for you. He was… he was…" Charlie squeezed his eyes shut and tapped his forehead with two fingers. "That's right! He was a tall feller! Wore all black like he was going to a funeral, and I remember I told him that, and then he told me that he indeed was, and that I should give this to you when next I saw you. He said he was an old friend. I couldn't make no sense of the note. It wasn't like any writing I'd seen before. He had a nasty scar and wore a big fur jacket. Oh, and he spoke only in whisper the whole time. Ringing any bells for you?" Berle listened and squeezed the bridge of his nose and tried to speak calmly. His voice sounded Polish.

"You don't remember another name? Please, Charlie, it's dire. The life of my son might be in danger." Berle grabbed Charlie's wrist, and Charlie patted his hand. Andras wheeled Piotyr, who yanked nervously.

"Dad? What's wrong?" He sounded like a child when he asked it. Pa pretended not to hear and pressed Charlie further.

"Anything. A symbol, an emblem, accent, or anything?"

"I remember thinking his name was fake. It was one word. Short like a moniker or stage name. I remember it was an English word though!"

"Hush," Berle answered, reading it from the note again. Ultimately, not that helpful. A person coming to kill someone in the States wouldn't use their real name or state their true intent to anyone who might come looking for them, especially their target. Charlie stopped pinching his nose and snapped his fingers.

"That's the one!"

"And he left no further instructions?" Pa asked.

"Afraid not. He dropped by last week only for a moment." Berle took the note back, pocketed it, and mounted Gourd again.

"Let's go home fast, Andras," was all Pa said, and he began trotting back down the path with Piotyr doing his best to keep pace. Pa had to stop and wait several times for Andras to catch up with Piotyr being laden with groceries. When the house was finally in view, Andras called out, out-of-breath and near-frightened.

"Pa! Pa! What's happening?" he called out desperately. Pa leapt off of Gourd, removed his saddle, and hung it on the corral fence as he closed the gate behind him. In a quick walk, Berle entered the house, not shutting the door behind him. Andras quickly followed suit, unloading the groceries and penning Piotyr.

He jogged into the house behind his dad, calling for him. "Pa! What's wrong? I'm scared!" Berle stopped and looked at his son. Andras looked so small standing in the doorway. He barely filled half the height of the door, and he clutched a big chunk of bread that made his hands look so tiny. Berle had both rifles on the dining table. He put down the shells and wadding and knelt on the ground, eye-level with Andras. He opened his arms and invited Andras in. He ran to his dad and buried his face in his shoulder, wrapping his arms around his neck. Berle squeezed his son, and Andras held on tight.

"Przepraszam, Synu…byłem przerażony. *I'm sorry, Son…I was frightened.*" Berle stroked his son's hair and kissed his head.

"Dlaczego, Ojcze? Co jest nie tak? *Why, Father? What's wrong?*" Andras could not stop the tears from wetting his Pa's shirt. When

Berle pulled Andras away to look him in the eye, Andras had two muddy streaks down his face from the trail dust.

"You remember when I was in the army in Poland, yes?"

"Yes." Andras nodded.

"I fought a lot of bad people, and a lot of people died. This note," he held out the note for Andras to see, "is from someone who wants to hurt me because of what I did." Andras took the note and looked at the strange words.

"Who?" he asked, looking at the words. He couldn't read them.

"I don't know, Son. I don't know who this *Hush* is. That's why I'm so scared. I hoped to leave all this behind in Europe."

"You think they'll come to shoot us?"

"Maybe. Or maybe they just want to scare us. But, listen to me, okay?" Berle poked his son's cheek playfully to look him in the eye. "I'm not going to let anybody hurt you, okay?"

"And I'm not going to let anybody hurt you, Dad." Andras hugged his dad tightly again. When he pulled away, he looked at the note, pondering the strange words. "What does this say, dad?" Berle looked down at it, and swallowed.

"It says, 'addressed for the Winter Viper, alias dictus, Berle Walenty."

"Alias dic–ditcus—"

"Alias dictus is Latin for 'also called'." Berle pointed at the strange letters and explained slowly, allowing Andras to process at his speed.

"For the Winter Viper, also called Berle Walenty," Andras repeated quietly. "That's you? Winter Viper?" Berle nodded.

"A long time ago, yes. It was what the soldiers called me during the uprising."

"Why?"

"Because I got famous for being dangerous and clever like a viper. And it was cold, I suppose. I didn't think the name up; the Russians did. Your Uncle Vaclav thought it was very fitting, and he liked it quite a bit." Berle remembered with a strained smile. Andras opened the note to find more words he couldn't read. There were two words written in heavy, slanted handwriting.

"You can read that? What is it?" Andras ran a finger along the words, feeling the indent where the pen left its mark.

"It is…Ukrainian."

"Ukranian?"

"Yes. From Ukraine."

"Why?"

"Because they know I can read Ukranian, or maybe they are Ukrainian…" Berle thought about any possible enemies he might have in Ukraine, but none stood out. Andras wondered how many languages Pa knew. He didn't know his pa knew Ukrainian. He'd heard him speak Russian, Hungarian, Polish, and English obviously, but never Ukrainian.

"What does it say?" Andras asked. He felt the fear building in his chest, getting bigger, making his chest feel tighter, drawing his shoulders up. Berle pointed out each word as he read them out-loud.

"Zavershyty. Rozpochate. 'Finish what was started.'"

"What does that mean? What was started?"

"I'm not sure, Andi. Maybe the uprising? A fight? Whatever it is, it's not meant to be friendly." Berle took the note back and folded it, stashing it in a pocket.

"What do we do now?"

"We're going to be cautious. We're going to keep our ears and eyes open, and we're going to be careful. If someone followed us all the way from Europe, they could be very dangerous. We'll tell the sheriff. We'll write Uncle Vaclav. Don't worry: we're going to live for a long time in our new home." Berle kissed his son's head again. Pa was scared, and that scared Andras. Andras sat down at the dining table and watched his dad inspect and load his guns. After the rifles were clean and loaded, he set the pistol down on the table.

"Andras, you remember everything I taught you about shooting the pistol, yes?" Andras squinted at the pistol and recalled all the lessons and tips he could remember, the most important rules, loading and firing, how to aim, how to take it apart, which pieces to clean, and which pieces to let dad fix. He nodded confidently at his father, his face as serious as he could make it. Berle nodded in approval and patted Andras's tiny knee.

"Tomorrow, we'll go into town and tell the sheriff and post a letter to Uncle Vaclav, alright?" Berle hugged his son goodnight, and Andras walked to his room and sat on his bed wondering about all the things that had changed today.

Chapter 8

Old wood hissed and popped in the small campfire as Rowe tossed another log on the fire, sending glowing embers skyward like fireflies dying as they tried to escape. Shadows of jagged, malformed, humanoid shapes flicker against high, rocky walls surrounding the sandy campsite where the cowboys sit. Road-weary horses sway and chew on dry desert shrubbery, more out of boredom than hunger. Streaked like spilt paint above them, the glow of the Milky Way shines brighter than the moon.

Rowe sounded like an old dog lying down as he flopped to the ground and leaned against his saddle to stare at the flames. He also smelled like an old dog. At first glance, Barnabus Rowe was a filthy mountain man, clothed in skins and furs fit for a trapper, not a trail-hand. At second glance, after confirming he was indeed filthy, you would observe that he was abnormally large. He stood a head taller than most men and was thick around as a man and a half. His beard and fur trapper hat gave the impression he was a massive hairy beast.

As the free-grazers led Vukašin through the old cattle paths Rhodes's grandpappy had mapped out before the army had built roads, he spoke to the men he was traveling alongside. It wasn't a matter of personal interest or social obligation. He was bored. He'd as soon talk to his horse, but he'd miss the pleasure of new ideas and the English language's sloppy handling of punchlines. There was something so…stupid about the clunky barbarian tongue of the spoiled colonists who thought they could build an empire.

Ilícs had been fighting in wars since before any of them could remember. His grandfather, Kryzstovic Ilíc, spent his long life fighting Ottomans, not even owning a gun until after he was married and a father. Vukašin's father, Ladislav Ilíc, also spent his life killing Ottomans. Vukašin Ilíc had begun his life killing deer and wolves before killing his first Turk when he turned ten.

Once, Vukašin imagined a life where he would mold another generation of Ilícs through a son, but he could not stand the weight of the energy expended maintaining an emotionally dependent structure. Raising and molding a son in his own likeness sounded like a chore. Plus, he wasn't sure how long he could convey love before he went insane.

The gunhand of the crew, Asher Milan, swaggered out of the darkness. He cradled a paper in one hand as he sprinkled tobacco into it with the other. He tugged the small bag shut with his teeth, pocketed it, and rolled a perfect cigarette. He struck a match against the rough stone wall of their campsite. The end of the cigarette glowed and revealed the sharp angles of his face. Smoke circled his head like a veil as he sighed the smoke out his nose. Even around the fire, he wore a gun on his hip. He leaned against the stone wall and bumped the first ashes from his cigarette.

"When we find your man, Hush, what's the play?" He was nervous, but not jittery. He still had his cool and collected air about him. Rhodes, curious as well, approached and sipped his water from a small cup.

"Anyone know the nearby town well?" Hush rasped, his voice like paper torn from a book. Both Martin and Rhodes raised hands and nodded. Hush nodded and pointed at them with his chin. "Go into town and figure out the law situation. Make sure we're not walking into the marshal's birthday party or something. Then, ask around the folks you know in town and see if anyone knows anything about him or is close to him. The more we can learn, the more power we have going in. Once we have learned all we can, we'll set a trap and wait. The Viper is as slippery as he is deadly. If we don't kill him at the right moment, he could slip away and kill each of you one by one. It's important you keep this in mind when dealing with him."

"He didn't seem so scary when we met," Rhodes said. Hush's eyes flashed to him, looked him up and down appraisingly, and then sneered derisively at the man. Jack turned and walked away from the escalating confrontation.

"Then he fooled you like he did me and half of the Russian officers in Eastern Poland," Hush hissed at Rhodes and then stood to his full height and pulled open the collar of his shirt so that his neck and upper chest glared bright white in the orange firelight. "Do you know how many times I shot at him? Hm? Eight times. From the moment he broke cover to the moment I lost sight of him, I fired eight rounds–

four of which," Hush's whisper rose to a raspy growl, "Should not have missed, *could* not have missed. Then he disappeared over a snowy hill. The next time I saw him, he was emerging from two days of snow drift while I lay on the ground, bleeding out like an idiot who thought he was hunting a farmer." Rhodes looked at the grotesque scars that lanced across his neck and face, and then he nodded.

"We'll follow your lead, Hush. You tell us what to do. We just want him gone." Rhodes removed his hat, wiped his forehead, and then sat down in the soft sand by the fire. Vukašin paced past the fire and surveyed the team before him.

"His weakness is his only source of hope: the boy with whom he travels, his son. He will not allow his son to be harmed. In this way, we can control him. And once he is powerless, I will kill him." Ilíc flexed the fingers of his right hand, audible pops emanating from his knobbed knuckles. His right hand flashed to the pistol on his hip; he drew it, pointed it at Sanderson, and then holstered it with a spinning flourish.

Sanderson swallowed nervously and shook his head, saying "I ain't interested in your banditry, Hush. Point your smoke-wagon elsewhere, compadre." Sanderson stood and walked away from the fire. He was a cowboy to his core, and not much else. He understood the saddle tramps who pushed cattle and mettled in petty crime on the side. Life in the wild tended to influence one in that direction.

Ben Sanderson was born on a ranch, raised by a rancher, taught how to ranch, and then chose to leave home to be a free-grazer when his father confessed to covering up the deaths of four Chinese workers to avoid paying the family their wages. Ben respected the honest simplicity of cattle. He understood them, and it showed in his riding. He would already be blocking a particularly tantalizing riverbed before a specific steer would consider making an attempt. He knew which cattle to push to speed up the herd, and which ones to let wander to relax them.

Ben had run the occasional scam with Rhodey and his crew when the money got tight, but he mostly tried to avoid the real criminal work. He recognized Hush for what he truly was from the moment he first met him. Hush was the real-deal. Asher might play like he was hot shit, but Hush had seen and done some fucked-up shit. Hush was an Old Worlde type of killer. Hush wouldn't be satisfied with just killing you: he'd go back to your home, burn and salt your crops, and then light a fire in your children's room.

Sanderson wanted no part of it. He was paying off a parcel of land of his own. He hadn't told Rhodey and Martin yet, but he didn't think now was the right time. Ben was ready to try his hand at ranching. He had bid on a spread in California that had a stream that allegedly flowed with gold flake, and his bid was accepted! This big push was his last one. Now he was riding shotgun for this pale rider. One last job. He kept reminding himself that this was his last job. One last job. Then, California awaited.

"What do you mean, the boy is his weakness? What do you intend to do to the boy?" Barnabus finally spoke up, and everyone turned to listen. Vukašin heard weakness in his voice, compassion. There was no room for it.

"Steel yourself, Barnabus Rowe. When killing a bear, don't you also kill the cubs? A mother bird who dies leaves behind her young to starve and be plucked up by the raven, correct?" His rousing speech had the hissing rasp of a blade on a whetstone. "The war may have ended in this country, but blood still flows where we come from. The Winter Viper is a monster who takes without remorse and will put a hole through you before you can pause to feel bad about it. The boy's death will be fast and clean. There's no need to punish the boy for the sins of the father. His blood will be on the Viper's hands, not yours, dear Rowe."

Vukašin slowly crossed the campsite as he explained, walking ever closer to Rowe. Barnabus shifted uncomfortably under Ilíc's gaze, glancing at the others for support. He stopped in front of Rowe, his boot inches from where he sat on the ground. Barnabus looked up at him, his disdain hidden under his heavy tangled beard. Hush turned on his heel and paced in the opposite direction.

"When they are apart, we will move on both of them. The Viper will not do anything to risk the child's life. If he knows that we have his son, he will do as we ask."

"How will we get them apart? If he loves the boy most of all, it's unlikely he'll separate willingly," Asher reasoned. He was right. Waiting for them to be apart could take weeks, and they didn't want to wait around for a chance encounter. They had to fabricate something.

"You're right. We'll have to convince him somehow that he needs to go somewhere desperately, but also, there's an inherent risk, so he would choose to leave his son at home. In that way, he would perceive leaving his son at home as the safe option. That's when we would move on the boy. It's important he remains unharmed. Should anything happen to the boy, the Viper may lash out."

"Ideally, but how? What are you going to do that scares him so badly, it convinces him to leave his son behind?" Jack's worries were warranted. They were betting a lot on a theoretical situation. Hush thought for a brief moment, running his finger absent-mindedly along the curved handle of his pistol.

"We need to somehow make Foothill seem dangerous. He wouldn't bring his son into town, knowing it was putting him at risk. And I have an idea how." Vukašin pulled a yellowy paper from his saddle bag and began to write with his tiny nub of a pencil. He folded the note and put it in his pocket.

Rhodes tossed the rest of his drink into the dirt and stowed his cup.

"What's the plan?"

"Tomorrow, when you and Martin go into town, I'll accompany you and plant the first seed of fear."

In the morning, Rhodey, Martin, and Hush saddled their horses and rode east towards Foothill. Hush dressed in all black; pants, shirt, and hat, all completed with the morbid wolf pelt coat he wore. Rhodes and Martin dressed in their normal attire, functional and comfortable with a day of riding in mind.

They rode for an hour before they spied Foothill from a high ledge. The town looked small and sleepy from up here, and Hush imagined the shootout that would unfold between the thin wooden walls of this frontier town. He could barely smell the smoke and stink of civilization from here, but he longed for the dark, greasy alleys of cities and darkened rooftops of unawares citizens.

Mountainous trees thinned to thick bushes and worn roads when, suddenly, they were in civilization. Wagons, carts, homes, and farmers dotted the road and countryside. The three riders trotted down the road casually, catching the occasional odd glance from a towny. Rhodes pointed out the main sites of interest; the cafe, the saloon, the post office, the general store, and the sheriff's office. To their relief, the sheriff's office looked sparsely populated.

Boom towns like Foothill appeared overnight, starting as a campsite or regular stop on the trail, and then, almost overnight, buildings and churches and businesses populated the wilderness and tattooed themselves upon the frontier forever.

Vukašin strode into the post office alone, allowing his eyes to adjust to the change in light. An older voice cleared its throat and announced affably, "Well, how d'ya do, stranger? Can I assist you?" An elderly man with thin hair smiled and inclined his hat when he introduced himself. "The name's Charlie. I'm postmaster of this here town." Vukašin approached the counter and rapped his knuckles on the top of it.

The postmaster's nose had been broken before, and he thought it would be easy to do it again. His teeth looked worn and brittle, and he thought about what they would feel like crushing under his elbow.

"I'm hoping to leave a note for a friend. He lives nearby, and I want to make sure he gets this." Ilíc put the yellowy note on the counter and waited. The postmaster licked his lips and cracked his knuckles. Charlie looked at the note and then looked Vukašin over.

"You look like you're going to a funeral, friend," Charlie said darkly.

"Indeed I am. That's why it's so important my friend gets this." Ilíc turned and left without another word, and Charlie sat there, dumbfounded, staring at a note covered in words he didn't even know how to start sounding out. He recognized one line of text, *Berle Walenty*, and he set the note aside, waiting for the next time he would see the Polish farmer.

Ilíc walked out of the post office and sighed a deep breath of satisfaction. He was in The Winter Viper's hometown again, but this time, Berle would die with them. He walked to the center of the street and turned in a full circle, looking at the surrounding crowded businesses and the people who frequented this part of town. Should this turn to a shootout, he planned to put Rowe and Sanderson on opposite roofs, Asher would stand in the street with Rhodes and himself, and Martin and Jackson would hold the boy. The sheriff wouldn't have the guts to show up alone, and if he did assemble some deputies, they could be gone before they showed up.

For the first time in years, Vukašin felt the electricity of excitement in his blood. Once again, no one would be deadlier than Hush. He'd grown very fond of the moniker he had created for his frontier persona, and he smirked at the idea of people flinching at the sound of his name.

He pulled his hat further down on his head to shield the sun from his eyes. He formulated the moment in his head. The smoke of his gun would clear, and the Winter Viper would fall dead, knowing who it was that killed him. Somewhere, a woman would scream, another would yell to get the sheriff. He would holster his gun and smirk, untouched. Then, they would take the body back to his house, and burn them both. For a moment, Vukašin felt…sad. No, not sad, disappointed and listless.

The thought of not having the Viper to hunt would make his life feel monotonous and purposeless. What would become of Hush after the Viper was dead? It was he that inspired his quest for revenge and he that led to Vukašin coming to the States. By all accounts, he had the Viper to thank for the advent of Hush. Perhaps Hush would endure, or perhaps Hush would die alongside the Winter Viper, burnt in the grave beside him. Both ideas were romantic enough to tantalize him. He decided he would choose in that moment. This town, darkened by the mountains separating the east from the west, was the perfect setting for a killing. He would want to go see the Viper's nest also before killing him. Perhaps that was the proper place to kill him, but he wouldn't know unless he could see it.

The seven of them rode out of town together, heading east to the wide-open prairie of eastern Colorado. When they were close, Rhodes stopped the posse on a hill overlooking a tree-spotted plain scribbled with glittering streams that watered the nearby groves.

"This here is what my pappy described as 'god's country,' being as it's so perfect and unsullied by mankind." He leaned forward over the horn of his saddle and knocked his hat back to get a proper view. Rowe nodded and lit his pipe with a match he struck on the bottom of his boot. Vukašin sucked his teeth, annoyed.

"Is this our final destination? I don't see a small house or a fence." He wheeled his horse and drew the long gun from its sheath on the saddle. He followed the winding stream with his scope.

"The parcel is right over that way about a league or so." Rhodes pointed towards a group of groves where a thin stream cut through. Ilíc immediately spurred his horse and rode in that direction without looking over his shoulder. The six free-grazers followed.

On a hill enshrouded by a wild patch of small trees, seven men looked down on the little house with the little fence. A small corral held a chubby horse that munched absently at yellow grass. A little boy carried a little saddle to a little shed and guided out a sleepy mule. The boy hopped up on the mule's back and rode the mule back and forth across the corral. Vukašin brought his rifle up to his shoulder and tracked the boy. He heard Rhodes beside him gasp quietly.

"Hush…" he began.

"Hush yourself," Ilíc hissed back with airy words. The child was wildly unremarkable. He looked like dozens of other waifs he had seen in the last twelve hours. He had messy, lightish hair, he was small, and clearly, he was an inexperienced rider.

After several moments, a second body appeared from around the house. Ilíc inhaled sharply and instinctively held his breath as his finger caressed down the trigger guard to rest on the trigger. His elbow quavered. This was not the right moment. He needed to calm himself before the moment came at last. He continued to watch the pair through the scope, fingering the trigger all the while.

"Behold, the hunter's quarry," he whispered to himself. Soon. Not yet. He would wait until the Viper was alert and ready for him. Then he would kill him. Soon.

Chapter 9

Berle awoke early, his eyes wide open, mind aware and listening. He hadn't slept much, choosing instead to sleep in brief, sporadic shifts. His boots were already on his feet. Berle crept noiselessly to Andras's room and opened the door as slowly and quietly as possible. He was still sleeping, blanket pulled up to his chin. He breathed slowly and steadily, his mouth slightly open. His straw-colored hair was getting a little long. It hung across his forehead like a curtain, blocking one of his eyes. Berle leaned against the doorframe and watched his son sleep for several breaths before he pulled the door shut silently.

On the table was the yellowy note written in Ukrainian. Charlie had given it to him as they were riding home, and it had put a shiver in his heart that he had not felt since before Andras was born. He had read it and looked it over, back and front, what felt like a million times.

Last night, he slept with a gun. He had sworn to never sleep with a gun in his own home. He had sworn it to Clara during the secret wedding ceremony in the wine cellar below the French restaurant. He promised that, for as long as they shared a home, he would not sleep with a gun in their bed. He wanted to put the violence and the killing behind him, leave it in Poland with the Winter Viper, dead in the snow.

But he didn't share this home with his wife. And the violence followed him here all the same. Maybe the Winter Viper wasn't dead after all. Somehow, it had slithered across the ocean, over Clara's floating corpse, and back into the darkest parts of himself. Berle crossed the room to the desk, removed paper and pencil, and wrote to Vaclav,

Dearest Vaclav,

Colorado is beautiful, but it's been getting colder. It's starting to feel like it did before. That business from back home has set up shop in a town nearby, and I expect we'll be seeing lots of familiar faces soon. Come quickly! Winter is approaching, and it wouldn't be Christmas without you. Kyrylo will be here when you arrive, and he's bringing gifts.

Stay safe,

Zimowa Żmija

~P.S. My English is getting pretty good, yes?

Berle folded the letter and left it on the table to bring into town. He returned the pencil to the desk and carried his rifle outside to the porch. He lowered himself into his rocking chair and surveyed the horizon. As anxious as he felt, it was a beautiful morning.

The cold bite in the morning air helped wash away the grogginess of his fatigue. It had been a long time since he had kept watch overnight, sleeping one hour and staying awake for one over and over until the sun came up. Those last few hours before first light, every noise, every shadow sounded like Russians sneaking on their bellies or wolves creeping into camp. He dropped his shoulders noticeably as he took long, slow, purposeful breaths of the clean morning air.

Birds were just beginning their sunrise songs, and he could almost feel the air getting warmer. White clouds capped the Rockies this morning, almost as though they were sleeping atop the mountains, waiting to be roused by first light. He watched a small herd of deer gently emerge from a patchy rise of trees, their ears spinning and turning at each noise. There was something divinely beautiful and peaceful about watching a doe and her fawns feed on the morning dewed grass in the mists that hung to the shadows. They walked gracefully as they crossed the shady plain when they suddenly stopped, listened, and then bolted towards the nearest patch of trees, and then, hearing or smelling something else, diverted and sprinted with all haste away from the wild patch of small trees.

They must have smelled a snake or cougar to send them running like that. Berle stared intently at the trees the deer fled from, feeling a pang of anxious paranoia that made him grip his rifle and stand to his feet. He lifted the scope to his eye, and his stomach dropped. Riders, five or more, were disappearing behind the trees, riding into the distance to avoid being spotted.

"Fuck," Berle cursed aloud, lowering the rifle. They needed to leave soon.

"That's a swear." Andras emerged from the front door, dressed and ready to take Piotyr for a ride. Berle blushed and regretted his lapse in awareness.

"Yeah, sorry, Andi. Hey, we're gonna have to skip riding practice this morning and head straight into town to talk to the sheriff and send that letter, okay?" Berle tried his best to disguise his alarm, but Andras compounded it.

"Who is Kyrylo?" Berle froze, his mouth open, stunned. Andras lifted the letter and rubbed his eye. "I saw this on the table for Uncle Vaclav about Christmas. Are you going to tell him about the note?" Berle finally took a breath, seeing the letter in Andras's hands.

"I did. Do not worry. I told him to come soon. He'll know what to do. He's lived here longer," Berle explained, and Andras nodded. Andras noticed he didn't answer his question, but he did not press the matter. He saw in his dad's eyes that he was afraid.

There's something deeply damaging about seeing terror in your own father's eyes.

Andras ran inside to get his hat and satchel bag while Berle saddled and bridled Gourd. Pa pulled Andras up into the saddle in front of him, and he spurred hard, pushing Gourd to remember how it felt to be a racehorse.

Every mile, Berle scanned the horizon for any riders following. There were. Two miles from home, two riders began keeping pace with them afar, not attempting to hide themselves. Andras felt his father's anxiety and the exhilaration of their speed, and he gripped Gourd's mane in white-knuckled hands. Pa tested the limits of Gourd's athletic accomplishment, urging him to push all the way to town. He knew there were more. The two following them were meant to do exactly that: follow and make sure he knew they were following. The others were waiting somewhere else, probably in town.

Just as he suspected, the two riders pulled off and slowed as they pulled into town. He assumed somebody else was following them now. He needed to get Andras to safety. Whether Andras was safer with him or far away from him, Berle didn't know.

He rode through the main avenues at speeds that drew attention and ire from the morning pedestrians. Berle pushed off the back of the horse and helped Andras get down from the saddle. Pa wrapped Gourd's reins around the hitching post in front of the sheriff's office and knocked on the door. Almost too quickly, the sheriff opened the door, not in uniform, flustered and out of breath. Seeing Berle, his eyes went wide with alarm.

"Mr. Walenty! You are in town very early today! I'm just on my way out, actually. Out of town, that is, to spend time with family." He walked out and locked the door behind him. The sheriff dabbed sweat from his brow, looked at Berle and Andras, and failed to say anything. He brushed past them quickly and began preparing his horse.

"You already know," Berle muttered, answering his own internalized question. Andras looked up at his dad.

"What's that?" the sheriff asked, pausing.

"You already know about the threat and the people coming for me, and they already got to you, didn't they?" Andras looked at the sheriff and then at his pa and then at the sheriff again. The sheriff said nothing, but a tear dropped from his eye and disappeared into his trembling mustache.

"They threatened my daughter, Berle. They said they would…Killing her would be kinder. I'm so sorry, Berle. Andras."

"They'll kill my boy," Berle whispered to him, "they'll kill my son." The sheriff tipped his hat at the two of them, and spurred his horse hard, not looking back once. They watched the sheriff ride away in a cloud of dust and hooves. The law had left.

"C'mon, Andras. We need to get to the post office and send this letter." Berle grabbed his son's hand and led him down the street. Andras did not need to be pulled. Nothing was going to convince him to leave his pa's side. Andras knew something was very, very wrong.

In the innate, ancient parts of his brain, the corners of his subconscious that still looked out for lions and cave bears, he felt the danger in the air. He felt like prey, and Pa was the most dangerous man he knew. He felt like an exposed nerve, responding to every sound and quick movement as if catching it in the act would save his life.

Walking past Gourd, Pa drew the repeating rifle from the saddle and slung it over his shoulder. They continued to the post office. Inside, Charlie was reading a book.

"Well, howdy, Ber–"

"The man who left this note," he held up the note and slapped it down on the marble counter, "has he come back?" Of course, Charlie remembered the note. He shook his head.

"I'd remember seeing him again."

"He just ran the sheriff out of town. I need you to send this letter as quickly as possible to this address."

Berle and Charlie arranged the postage over the counter. Andras stayed close to his Pa, watching the door. A large bearded man smoking a pipe walked past, nodded in greeting to him, and kept walking. Across the street, Pete Becker was sweeping off the walkway, preparing to open. Nobody else seemed alarmed.

The church bells rang loud and clear, and Berle remembered morning mist and sanctuary. It was Sunday. Charlie made sure to pack the letter to be shipped out on the train that morning. Pa grabbed his hand again, and they walked outside together. Andras gripped his dad's hand tightly, keeping an eye on his feet so he didn't trip and slow them down. Pa's other hand was on the handle of his pistol, making no attempt to hide his alarm. With the sheriff gone, and a mysterious threat following them, maintaining the public peace was not his top priority. Townies parted the way with surprised expressions as he bee-lined towards his retired racehorse, who sensed the tension in the air and tugged on his tethered reins when he saw Berle.

And then nothing happened. They left town together astride Gourd, who galloped with excitement towards home. Berle glanced over his shoulder every few seconds, but saw no one.

They weren't being followed: why didn't he feel any better? They chased off the sheriff, but then allowed them to leave town. He was missing something. Finally, he saw home before them. The glittering creek that cut through the shady trees greeted him with a sparkling warmth.

Chapter 10

Vukašin lay on the ground, his ear pressed against a lichen-crusted stone. A Pawnee native had shown him this trick, and he had not had a chance to use it yet. He smiled as the deep bass of hoof beats signaled an approaching rider. He opened his black eyes and nodded to Asher who crouched beside him. Hush rolled onto his belly and pressed his rifle against his shoulder. Keeping both eyes open, he tracked the rising plume of dust and saw two bodies riding one horse in a full gallop. Martin, Rowe, and Sanderson must have done a good job in spooking them back home. He inhaled and held his breath. *One.* He pulled the trigger.

It happened fast, so violently, and completely without warning.

Excited to finally be home, Andras watched both of Gourd's ears disappear as a bullet ripped through the top of his head, killing him instantly. The horse toppled forward mid-gallop, catapulting Andras and Berle yards away into the hard, stony ground.

Andras was crying before he remembered waking up. His hands were bleeding and raw from the gravel and dirt he collided with, and he could feel the grit and gravel in his mouth. His face hurt, and his shoulder hurt, and then someone was lifting him up onto their shoulder.

Berle rolled onto his back and coughed, dust coming off of him in great plumes. His hip throbbed, and his back ached like he'd just fallen from a tree. He could hear Andras crying nearby, but he couldn't feel him when he reached out. His face was so full of dust and gravel, he couldn't see yet. "Andras!" he tried to yell, but he could only cough. He blinked and sat up with a great groan. The accompanying pain made him wince and slow. *His gun.* His hand darted to his empty holster. *"Where is Andras? Where is my gun? Who shot Gourd? Oh, god, poor Gourd..."*

The dust had settled enough that he could see around him more clearly. Gourd lay dead several yards behind him where he fell. Beside Gourd was a tall, sun-warmed man with youthful eyes and a wide-brimmed hat that blocked the midmorning sun. White smoke gleamed in the sunlight, wreathing his head as he exhaled it.

"I told you I wasn't going to let you stay here. Damn, if you had only listened." He took another drag and knocked the ash from his cigarette. He picked up Berle's repeater, and checked to see if it was loaded.

Andras stopped squirming and only cried. He hurt so much, he was so scared, and he wanted his mom. The man who had picked him up was not Pa. He flung Andras over his shoulder and walked away several yards before setting him back down and holding tightly onto the front of his shirt so that his toes barely touched the ground. He pinned Andras tightly against him and held a gun in the other hand. Andras clawed and tugged at the strange man's hand who shook him once and growled quietly to him from behind.

"Stop your squirming, and you might survive today. You keep your mouth shut, and you do what I say, okay?" Andras began to bawl again, and he nodded with muddy, bloodshot eyes and open wailing mouth.

"Pa!" was the only word that he could muster, and the rest was unintelligible sobs.

"Andras!" Berle called out at hearing his son's pleas. He turned to stand, but was greeted with his own rifle, cracking him in the side of the head. A flash of white, and he was on the ground, his head throbbing. There was no blood when he checked, and he spit at the cowboy who held his gun.

"You stay right there, Viper, or I'll hit you hard next." Berle froze.

"What did you call me?" The cowboy didn't answer, "My zustrichalysya? *Have we met?*" Berle studied his face, but he remembered nothing. The beating of hooves called his attention to the approaching riders. Two men, one forgettable, the other, like a vision of death.

Clad all in black astride a pale cream charger. His eyes were the void, the bottomless pit where Cocytus would bind the devil forever. Like lightning sprouting from his collar, an ugly, knotted scar of healed gnawed flesh ran up his neck and onto his face. He carried an old rifle, a pistol on each hip, and his coat was made from wolf pelts. He crouched down in front of Berle and studied him.

"Przekleństwo. Wyglądasz jak wieśniak... *Dammit. You do look like a peasant...*" His voice was a hissing whisper that gurgled with phlegm like a clogged pipe.

"Uwolnij mojego syna. Natychmiast. Proszę... *Release my son. Right now. Please...*"

"Zimowa Żmijo, nie możesz stawiać żądań. *Winter Viper, you are in no position to make demands.*"

"Zakładam, że tak Hush. *I assume you are Hush,*" he had recalled from the note. Berle spit a gob of bloody spit and grit on the ground between them. Vukašin gazed down at it for a moment before his hand darted forward with lightning speed and slapped Berle across the face with a stiff, hard strike. He nearly fell over from the hit, but stayed kneeling. This time, the bloody spit dripped out of his mouth and onto his own shirt.

"Sprawię, że będziesz mnie szanował. I zanim cię zabiję, przeprosisz. *I will teach you to respect me. And before I kill you, you will apologize.*" Vukašin stood and dropped something heavy into the dirt before him, turned, and walked away. A pistol lay between them.

"Zabraty yoho, Kyrylo. *Pick it up, Kyrylo.*" he called over his shoulder as he continued to walk. Berle stared down at the pistol and then around him.

There were seven of them and six bullets. Hopefully, six bullets. Two stood in front of him, two behind him by Gourd's corpse, and two with Andras. One of the men held Andras tightly from behind, his eyes red with terror and tears. He reached out and grabbed the gun slowly, feeling the warm metal on his fingertips. He opened the loading gate and peeked: six bullets.

While the others held guns, only Hush seemed intent on using his. The man holding Andras looked sick to his stomach. Berle wondered, if he killed Hush first, would the others bolt? Would they hurt Andras? That settled it. He would shoot Hush, then the one holding Andras. He would then need to immediately push towards him and kill the other, take his gun–

"Do you remember me, Winter Viper?" Hush called out. He was about ten paces away now. Berle stood on his feet, nursing his battered and busted body, and stood to his full height slowly. He held the pistol, his thumb on the hammer.

"Someone I should have killed long ago, apparently," Berle responded, his voice loud enough for all to hear.

"I hunted you for months before I found you. Then, as luck would have it, I was attacked by wolves, and you saw your chance to take the shot." The story he had told so many times. The face he had never seen up close. Vukašin leaned his shoulder toward Berle, showing the hole in the wolf's head.

"The…Serbian Demon…" he said, at last, the slow realization dawning on him like nausea. That encounter was the closest both he and Vaclav had ever been to dying, and it was a pure stroke of luck that the wolves attacked him.

"Damn, I think I like that better than 'Hush,'" Ilíc lamented. "I swore to myself as I lay dying in the snow, that if I survived, I would use the rest of the life in me to murder you. Not for money, not for justice, but because I'm better than you, and you're going to admit that."

"Fine!" Berle began, "You're better than me! I admit it; please let my son go, Hush!"

"No– NO!" Hush burst out, the loudest anyone had heard him yet. He gripped his throat painfully and lowered his voice to a hushed whisper again. "That's not genuine. You're scared and desperate, and that's not the same Winter Viper who killed half the Russian officers in Poland and more in Hungary, Serbia, and Ukraine. Is he still in there, I wonder."

Berle's thumb flexed to draw back the hammer, and Vukašin drew and fired the pistol. The speed of Hush's hands amazed him. Berle's pistol dropped to the ground, and blood dripped onto the white dust. He looked at his hand, a fleshy hole punched clean through. The pain came gushing in, and he nearly vomited and fainted. He clutched his useless hand and fell to a knee.

"On your knees again. Fuck, Winter, I am so disappointed. I may have overestimated you…" Vukašin removed the spent shell and replaced it. He approached slowly and casually. He picked up the gun from the ground and handed it back to Berle. "Take this gun, and pull the trigger, you fucking peasant, or apologize." He jabbed the gun at Berle. Berle took the pistol in a slippery, quivering left hand, his teeth gritted. He was looking at Andras. Andras was watching silently with wet eyes, two muddy trails down his face.

"Don't look, kid," Sanderson whispered to Andras. "Close your eyes." Andras squeezed his eyes shut, and Ben covered his eyes with a rough, calloused hand.

Berle's hand felt sticky from the blood. He pulled the hammer back awkwardly with a pale thumb and began to lift it. Vukašin, again, cleared his holster and fired before Berle could get a bead on him. Hush fanned his fingers across the hammer as he held the trigger, firing four times into Berle's chest.

Cold washed over Berle, and he collapsed forward. He felt a heavy, suffocating pressure in his chest, and he watched his own blood pouring from the four holes onto the dry, thirsty dust below. Hush leaned him upward again, so he was looking him in the eye. He leaned closely towards Berle's face so that they alone could hear.

"Vybachytysya," Hush cupped an ear and waited. Berle gasped and sucked mouthfuls of air. His head felt heavy, and he could hardly focus his eyes. He could feel air sucking into his chest, crushing his lungs like a sharp, aching ripping inside him. His lips moved noiselessly, and then he began again, expelling his final breath,

"Id...Idy do b-b-bisa, vovche layno." And he coughed blood onto Hush's cheek.

Hush propped the barrel of his gun under Berle's chin and pulled the trigger. Andras whimpered. When Vukašin stood, he was spattered with blood. Hush shoved the dead body of Berle over with a limp slump. He pointed at Sanderson, who held Andras's eyes shut.

"Now, the boy. Do it." His voice was glowing iron in water. Sanderson loosened his grip on Andras's shirt and whispered to him.

"Don't look. Just run. Run!" He shoved Andras away from him, and Andras began to sprint. Immediately, his toe caught a root, and he fell forward onto the ground, sprawling over a spiky bramble. He scrambled to his feet as a crack of gunfire whizz-snapped above his head.

"That was pathetic, Ben! Shoot him!" Andras heard one of the cowboys yell. A second gunshot, and Andras felt a heavy thud, then a stabbing, ripping pain through his right leg. The impact swept his feet out from under him, and he collided with the ground in another teeth-clattering crash.

He moaned and coughed out one choked sob, sat up, looked at his leg and yowled at the bloody hole in the top of his thigh. He didn't want to touch it, but he couldn't move. He sat there in the dirt in agonizing pain, staring at the bullet hole in his thigh.

A snap of a dried twig grabbed his attention, and he turned his head to see the cowboy who had grabbed him and covered his eyes, approaching with his gun in hand. Andras gazed up at him, tears still rolling down stained cheeks. The cowboy raised a booted foot and shoved him roughly onto his back. He pointed the pistol at his face and pulled back the hammer with a quick clicking snap.

"Close your eyes, son. Lay still. Don't you move." Andras's body was wracked by a horrified, agonized, helpless sob, and he squeezed his eyes shut and covered his ears. "I'm sorry, son. I hope you can find peace." The explosion from the barrel of the pistol was loud and hot, a great rush of hot air, gusting, popping, shredding. He felt the heavy thud of the bullet hit, and he lay still.

Andras didn't move. He laid still as he was told. This was death? Strange, he thought it would be…brighter. Colder. Softer. His leg throbbed again, but he dared not move. His ears rang in a high, tinny pitch, and his head pounded like the drum of a losing army. He heard the low scraping of dirt on boots as the cowboy turned and walked away. His right leg trembled terribly and ached sharply.

"Let's get the fuck out of here," Sanderson said, holstering his pistol and mounting his horse.

The other five free-grazers looked at him differently now, but he didn't look them in the eye to notice it. Vukašin looked up at Ben appraisingly from the ground. He patted Ben's horse on the neck and whispered in that wet scrape of a voice,

"I was wrong about you, Benjamin." Ben didn't look at him. He adjusted his hat and grabbed higher on the reins.

"'That so?"

"I was. I thought you to be a coward. I didn't think you had…" he snapped his fingers to recall, "*koja je fraza*— blood in your eye. Do you feel different now? I remember the first time I shot a child–"

"I feel like making tracks before someone comes sniffing around after all the shooting you did." Ben finally met Vukašin's eye, and a cold, dead shiver ran up his neck and down one arm. His tar-black eyes were so full of mad, maniacal vigor that he thought that Hush might leap up at him and sink his teeth into his neck like a demon. Blood and bits still clung to Hush, one side of his face messier than the other. Hush nodded and withdrew to his own horse.

Rhode's horse whinnied and reared as he blasted the hanging oil lantern off the porch hook with a well-aimed shot. He flicked his cigarette at the shattered mess, and blue flames twisted to orange as the wood began to char.

The seven cowboys rode away with their blood and plunder, leaving two dead bodies and Andras alone in the Colorado countryside beside a roaring tornado of orange and black. Rhodes studied his new lever-action rifle that gleamed brightly in the late-morning sun. Rowe had the long, heavy shape of the Winter Viper's old Whitworth forty-five Rifle. Hush had replaced one of his pistols with Berle's pistol, and he wore it proudly. Behind them, a mule brayed as it jogged around the corral in panic.

When the pillar of smoke was far enough away to shade the riders, Vukašin stopped and produced small bags of portioned-out coins that he tossed to each of them.

"Your cut, gentlemen. I hope you don't mind if I pay in silver." Jack's eyes went wide as he opened up the bag quickly and confirmed that it was, indeed, full of silver. Flat, pressed coins of some distant ruler or aristocrat. Silver was silver. Rhodes pocketed his pay and tipped his hat to Hush.

"It's been a real pleasure watching you work, Mister Hush. I hope you're not offended when I say I hope I never see you again." Martin, Rowe, Jackson, Rhodes, Milan, and Sanderson all turned and rode away towards Foothill.

Vukašin watched them ride away and wondered where the trail would take them next. He was a force of destiny. Nobody came into contact with Vukašin Ilíc, who wasn't forever changed.

Perhaps he would retreat to the great American wilderness for some time to ponder the next stage of his life. Killing the Winter Viper restored his honor and reputation to him. He would always be a predator, claiming the lives of his prey, but in what form was still to be determined.

He rode north. He knew not what lay north, but he knew not what lay ahead. What better way to illuminate the unknown than by charging into it, torch ablaze? For several hours, he led his horse up a shallow stream at a slow saunter, partially to obscure any trail he may have laid but also for the pleasurable pace at which he could experience the untouched beauty of Colorado. He paused and listened to new bird calls, stopped to pluck strange plants, and sat silently while a small herd of big-horned sheep crossed the stream in front of him and his horse.

When evening came, he made camp for the night, singing all the while to himself an old tune he learned as a child. His second-hand horse grazed calmly nearby as he unrolled his bedroll in his tiny tent. He reclined on it and stared at the warm, crackling fire that slowly became the main light source as the mountains to the west eclipsed the sun's radiance. The bird songs gave way to the waltz of crickets and baritone of nearby toads.

Trees that chattered and swayed in the day's breeze now whispered in reverence to the stars' gentle advent. Vukašin rolled a cigarette and lit it with a small burning twig from the fire. He pried open a can of peaches with his knife and slurped down his simple dinner with sticky fingers. By the light of the fire, Vukašin brushed down his horse and sang to it quietly. The quiet peace of the forest he was surrounded by warmed parts of his mind that had been cold for months.

"I think I'll call you *Zimowa*. How's that sound, hm?" He patted the horse's neck and tilted his head to gauge the horse's reaction. The horse did not react but only blinked and nudged his elbow. "Don't worry, Zimowa; I think you'll do the name more justice." After he bedded down Zimowa, he sat at the entrance of his tent, staring at the fire, chain-smoking cigarettes.

As he sat, he held Berle's pistol in his hand, engaging and releasing the hammer over and over like the mechanical clicking of a lethal clock, counting down the seconds of the next victim's life. But who was that next victim? What was a predator without prey, a hunter without a quarry, a spider without its fly? *Starving* was the answer.

Without the taste of blood, the tiger does not thrive. The average man needed food, water, shelter, maybe a good woman, and a job. Vukašin was not average, and he was not merely a man. He needed the taste of blood on his fangs, and the smell of fear in his nostrils. Perhaps he would try bounty hunting. He'd already been accused as such.

Nature assigned roles to all her children. Some were to be the predators, the rulers and masters of nature. Some were designed to be prey, the peasants and targets of nature. The rest of humanity were merely sentient vertebrates waiting for their mortal coils to slacken them to oblivion so that their bodies might dissolve to feed the prey. It was not evil or wrong to understand life this way. Nature did not make rules; she merely enforced the rules that her children created.

Vukašin was at a crossroads. Either he could find new prey, or he would change his nature and become something new altogether.

Chapter 11

Andras opened his eyes with heavy lids. His face was sore and stiff, and the cuts and knicks on his face had scabbed over. He felt the skin on his lips cracking apart as he opened his mouth, a refreshing wetness on them. The sun was unbearably hot and bright, and he could feel the weight of its radiance on his face like iron.

He moved to sit up, and groaned under the achy, sore creaks of his whole body. He felt like it took an hour to sit up, but when he finally did, he almost fell back over backwards. Crouched in front of him was a brown-skinned man with a stern, strong, unmoving face like it was carved from a mountain. His hair fell past his shoulders and was held back by a red patterned cloth tied around his head. He had a dark blue military coat over a linen shirt. If he wore trousers, they were very short and hidden beneath his shirt. He had a rifle across his knees, and he had his elbows propped on the rifle so that he crouched rather comfortably while Andras stirred from death.

"Hola, otra vez. *Hello, again,*" said the crouched man. "Cálmate... shhh. Estas seguro. *Easy there... shhh. You're safe.*" He raised his empty hands as Andras's eyes went wide with alarm.

"Please, help me," were the first words that came out of Andras's mouth. His words were sloppy and clumsy, tumbling out of a dry, bleeding cottonmouth. The man nodded slowly and placed the rifle behind him, holding out the gourd of water he had used to revive him instead. Andras looked at it strangely until the stranger uncorked it and handed it to him. The stranger pressed his hand against his chest and spoke English slowly and intentionally.

"I am Naiche. Do you remember me?" Andras coughed and choked on his first swallow of water and then continued to drink.

"You're the Indian who rode his horse real fancy and introduced himself." Andras struggled to speak. His lips felt huge and clumsy. His throat felt like shards of glass. The water helped.

As he moved to sit up, a red-hot surge of pain exploded from his leg, making him cry out, and tears began to form. Naiche moved quickly and covered up Andras's cry with a gentle hand. Naiche made eye contact with Andras and held his hand over Andras's wounded leg. He winced in anticipation at the closeness of Naiche's hand and saw the clean bandaging on his leg.

"We saw the smoke from far away, and we came to see what had happened. You're hurt, and we were unsure if you were still alive, but you have a stubborn spirit. I bandaged you, but you need to go slow, comprende?" Naiche held out a hand in assistance, and Andras took it readily. It hurt to even grip his hand. Naiche scooped him up in strong, gentle hands, and carried him to his horse.

"This is Kipi. She's a good horse. She's only mean to me." Niache's voice was gentle and low. He spoke both strongly and quietly. The horse flared its nostrils and chomped its long teeth in his direction. "She's a good partner. Don't worry. You just rest and stay quiet. We need to leave soon." As Andras settled onto Kipi's back, she moved slowly and gently, feeling his leaning and tipping. She carried him safely and slowly without rein or lead. Several times, Andras lifted his head to look at the strange quiet to see the same thing: five horsemen, men and women, without uniform or standard, riding and walking in silence. Andras saw pieces of his life in bags and being worn by the others. Naiche walked beside Kipi and kept a close eye on him, making sure he didn't topple off in his sleep.

Andras woke up shortly before sunrise on the second day. His head bobbed, and he opened his eyes to the mane and neck of a horse and a warm body behind him, Naiche's. Niache's voice rumbled through his chest, and Andras was very aware of how warm and heavy his hands felt. He struggled to focus his eyes. He reflexively reached for his hurt leg with slow, sluggish hands. Naiche grabbed his wrist firmly and returned it to his lap limply.

"*Tolguacha.* Thorn apple. It stops the pus and the pain." Andras did not fight or insist. What else could he do? Andras nodded with a bobbing lull.

"Fear not, young Walenty. You'll be okay once we get you to *Tavibo.*"

"W–w–where is To–Tavbi– Where is that?" Andras's words felt like trying to scoop warm preserves with a knife.

"*He* is not far from here. He lives further up in the mountains east of here." Naiche nodded up the ascending hills and mountains that bisected the sky.

They snaked up the mountain along paths that seemed to appear beneath their feet as they navigated up the cut-backs and weaved between boulders. The horses seemed confidently independent of their riders, who almost seemed to play the role of helper rather than rider or controller.

Andras slipped in and out of shallow, uneasy sleep. The medicine on his leg, the "thorn apple", seemed to be making him sleepy and weak. Or perhaps he was weak because of other extenuating circumstances.

He woke up feeling himself tipping off of the horse. He reached for a handhold but saw Naiche was lowering him down with the assistance of a woman who had been riding with them the past few days. She had Pa's boots in a bag on her horse, along with other items that caught her eye that weren't consumed in the flames. They had stopped at a humble cabin nestled in the shadow of the Rockies. A fire circle in front of the house smoldered from the evening before. Naiche held Andras in his arms while the woman knocked. She waited for a long moment and then knocked again. She turned and looked at him with an impatient glare.

"Fine, Liluye, just go in," Naiche finally conceded.

She shoved open the door and kicked over a chair, being as loud as humanly possible. A noise like a bear waking up rumbled from deep in the house. Liluye waved them in and crossed her arms casually. Someone– or something– was stirring in the back room, groaning and growling as it went. A thick, wrinkled man with dark brown skin emerged from the bedroom. He rubbed sleep from his eyes and waved them in sleepily. He had long black hair that hung straight and loose down his back. He wore a plaid patterned shirt and pants made from scavenged dungarees. He relit and puffed on a pipe and waved a lazy arm at them, inviting them to sit. Inside, the cabin was made to look like a wickiup or a teepee. The smell of herbs and skins swirled throughout the room and Tavibo dropped himself down into his chair at the table, a finely made chair, but not well cared-for.

The walls were covered in strange, alien adornments, drawings of animals and nature and geometric patterns were displayed on hides and drums, talismans dangled on ancient bone armor decorated with colorful beads. A long spear was hung on a wall, suspending a collection of brunette, black, red, and blonde tufts of hide. The tobacco smelled strange as it snaked across the room.

Naiche put Andras down on the table, and Tavibo rushed forward and saved his drink from being knocked over. Andras was still only half-conscious, but he was transfixed by all the smells and strange sights. The old Indian man put a rough, leathery hand on his shoulder and asked in a deep voice,

"Do you speak English?" Andras nodded. He nodded, then turned to Naiche and Liluye and spoke to them in their own tongue. Naiche pointed to a place on his own thigh and explained how the bullet passed all the way through, but not in any language he recognized. Andras's hands and legs began to tremble, and he felt very cold. Naiche nodded and left with Liluye, leaving Andras alone with

Tavibo. He did not speak to Andras as he closed the door, crossed the room, put another log in his stove, and then took several bundles of dried leaves and sprigs from the wall and various baskets. "You're going to be okay," he finally spoke, breaking the strange, irritated silence. Andras nodded noiselessly. "Who shot you?" Andras didn't know. He didn't know his name, though he knew his face.

He knew the face of the handsome cowboy, the hairy bearded one from up north, the young, antsy one, the dark-haired one from Mexico, the skinny one with the gun, the old man, and the pale rider in black with the scar.

Andras shook his head. He only responded with a gruff "Hm." Tavibo cleaned and dried his hands in a basin and then proceeded to cut open the leg of Andras's trousers, starting at the boot. He was careful with the sheep shears he used to snip them open slowly. When he finally exposed the wound, Andras felt the rush of cold air wash over it and the sharp ripping pain of the pants that stuck to his dried blood. He winced silently. Tavibo inspected it without touching it, leaning to see the other side where the bullet entered.

"You got lucky, little gunfighter. If that bullet hadn't gone all the way through, we'd be digging it out of the leg right now. We need to make sure you don't catch a fever, and we get it cleaned and bandaged. I'm going to mix up some herbs for the leg, and then some for you to chew on, okay?" Andras nodded quickly. Sweat began to bead on his forehead the closer they got to treating the gunshot. Tavibo meandered around his kitchen, sipping on his cup and gathering materials lazily.

"Are you a...a witch doctor?" Andras asked with weak words. Tavibo turned at his voice and rolled up his sleeves.

"No. I learned how to care for the People when I was very young. Just regular medicine."

"Who are the people?" Andras propped up on his elbow, conflicted between his curiosity about this native American and the hole in his leg that was about to be treated.

"*My* people, my tribe. They're far away now." His voice was level and unwavering. He didn't inflect expressively like most of the people he had met. Instead, Tavibo's eyes and shoulders told the truth of his heart. Andras knew not to ask more.

"Mine too." Andras looked at his angry, red, throbbing leg. At least the bleeding had stopped. Tavibo nodded and handed him a spoon with a strip of leather wrapped around the handle. He smeared a greenish paste on the leather and held it out for Andras to bite down on.

"Don't worry. It's only medicine. I'm not gonna waste leather and my good spoon on poisonin' you. Bite down. You can cry, but don't kick and thrash too much. I'm not gonna be trying to hurt you, but it might hurt, okay? I'm helping you, *hua*?" Andras nodded as tears swelled in his eyes.

He bit down on the leather-wrapped spoon. The paste on the spoon made his tongue tingle and tasted like bad potatoes and grass. He hated the flavor and wanted to spit out the spoon, but a blinding, red-hot pain jolted up his leg as Tavibo cinched down a strap on Andras's ankle around the table leg. The pain subsided for a moment, but the man began to study, prod, and lance out foreign objects. Andras clenched down on the spoon and squeezed his eyes shut.

It felt like all he had done for days was cry. His eyes felt tired and hot. He cried over the pain and for his Pa, he cried for Gourd, for his bed, for Buck, for his saddle, for his Ma. He cried until his hands went limp, and his head bounced onto the table.

"Rest easy, *shik'isn*," he said to the unconscious boy, and he completed his work as best he could with a pounding hangover and old supplies.

He woke up, and he was sure he wasn't dead this time. He was too sore, and he could smell the musty, stale aroma of wet leather and old wood. There was a repetitive, rhythmic *creak-a-squeak, creak-a-squeak* coming from somewhere nearby. When he opened his eyes, they seemed heavy and sore. His vision was blurry, and his head throbbed and seemed to pulse in time with his heart. The little light coming in from the window across the room seemed to beam straight into his eyes. He sat up in a slow twisting of his body and maneuvered his legs over the side of the saggy bed. He tested his feet on the ground lightly, pressing his toes against the ground.

Pain began to lance through his leg, and he winced loudly and backed off the pressure. His right thigh was wrapped in clean cloths that had been changed recently. There was an old crate of used cloths beside the stove. Many of them had turned brown after being bled through, but the ones on top had hardly any blood at all.

The creaking stopped, and floorboards groaned as Tavibo moved along the porch and opened the front door as slowly and as quietly as he could. Dusty beams of sunlight cleaved the room in twain as he moved inside.

"Hey there, pard'ner. How are you feeling?" His voice was low and flat, but sincere. Andras blinked away the sunlight and nodded.

"Good," he lied. Comparatively, he felt better than he thought he would. Each time he woke up or felt a twinge of pain shiver up his leg, he realized that his brain was not splattered on the Colorado prairie like Gourd's. And his father's. His whole body hurt, but his whole body worked. Even with the hole through his thigh, he could still wiggle his toes, and that seemed like good news. "Wh–Where are the men who killed my Pa?" Andras's throat cracked with thirst and heartbreak. Tavibo did not look at him. He shook his head, his long hair dancing in raven waves.

"I don't know. I didn't ask. When Naiche and Liluye brought you here, I did not ask any questions." Andras nodded and continued to wiggle his toes and flex his foot, testing the pain points. The old Indian crossed the room and leaned an old crutch against the bed.

Calling it a "crutch" was generous. It was a crooked stick with padding bound to the top with baling wire. "Use this until you can run without limping. Don't try to run until you can walk without limping. Do you understand?"

"No limping." Andras nodded and tested the new crutch with his hurt leg. It was awkward, and he tried holding the stick a few different ways before shaking his head and sitting back down on the saggy bed. Tavibo nodded slowly.

"You'll figure it out." He stood and retrieved his cup from the table, emptying it with one tilt. "There's some food for you here on the table." He knocked on the table with his knuckle and proceeded out the door again. After a moment, the *creak-a-squeak, creak-a-squeak* commenced.

Andras craned his neck to look at the table. As promised, a plate of food sat patiently beside an identical cup, awaiting his eventual hobbled arrival. He held the crutch out in front of him like a broom and leaned on it as it gripped the ancient floorboards. He smiled and let a warm chuckle bounce out of his chest as he wavered on the makeshift crutch. He hobbled over to the table and dropped himself into one of the chairs.

An electric jolt of red-hot lightning seared up his leg and snatched the breath out of his lungs. He gripped his leg and felt the table bump on his forehead as he tried to breathe through the receding pain. He wished he knew more English swear words. He knew some of the dirty words, some of the rude terms and gestures, but most of the *real* bad ones had eluded him so far. By the time the pain had subsided, he had abandoned his quest for swears and focused on the plate of food before him. Wet beans stuck to the side of a soaked piece of crooked-cut bread. A cut of pinkish-gray meat lay rigor mortis beside it, unawares of the flaccid greens that threatened to moisten its gray crust. It was one of the best-looking plates of food Andras had ever seen. Not a morsel of edible material could be found on his plate minutes later. It was only after he was chewing on the last piece of gristle from the meat did he find the spoon. It was under the napkin that he also had neglected to utilize.

When he finally leaned back from his meal, he was out of breath. He felt like he had just eaten for the first time in days. He guzzled down the cup of water and began to notice the details of the room around him. Since he had woken up, he hadn't taken the time to appreciate his surroundings.

What might look like the messy den of a lonely, sad, beaten, old drunk, was a museum of the life of a legendary warrior to Andras. He moved shakily to the spear hung on the wall. The rusted, dinged head of the spear was ancient. He could tell that much just by looking at it. The shaft of the spear was just as detailed and intricate as the rest of the house. Beaded strings, dyed cloth, and strips of finely-crafted leather adorned the handle. Near the middle, small tufts of hide with the fur still attached dangled side-by-side from laces of leather.

Andras touched the soft fur with his fingers, feeling the different textures of each one. He touched and turned one to inspect when a very human ear rotated to the front. Andras froze, the human scalp still in his fingertips. He could feel his food churning in his guts, and a visceral shiver ran through him. He covered the scalp so that the ear was hidden, and he turned away from the spear. The image of the severed human ear still attached to its scalp remained in his head.

On a small chifferobe, reddish photos sat in frames, capturing moments of wide smiles and levity. Shirtless young men on unsaddled horses and long, beautiful hair. They wore patterned headbands and carried rifles. Andras wasn't sure why, but he felt sad looking at these pictures. Seeing Tavibo alone and broken, not with the people anymore, it seemed wrong, like finding a fish in a tree or a hawk underground.

He dared not open any drawers or cupboards, but he was content to look at everything worth seeing. There was a small leather-bound notebook of pencil sketches and lists. He found pressed plants in some of the pages, and pages torn from other books to be stored in this one. The letters looked familiar to him, but they weren't in any language he knew.

"Put that down," came a deep, flat voice, not angry, but stern. Andras immediately put it down and almost fell over, trying not to put weight on his leg. He winced and turned. Tavibo had entered the house again, and he was gathering his things. He pressed his hat down onto his head and tossed Andras's pants to him that he had been mending on the porch. The sewing was strong and well done, but the pants fit strangely now, and the dark blood stain and holes remained. Pulling them on was an affair all its own, but after several minutes and several tears, Andras was dressed and lifted onto a smaller wagon than the one… than others he had ridden in before. The cart was pulled by one ox, who swung his head side to side slowly as it waited.

Several miles down the trail, Andras's curiosity finally broke the silence.

"Where are we going?"

"Foothill." Andras nodded.

"Do you have a horse?" Andras stared up at him. Tavibo did not seem irritated or annoyed. In fact, he didn't seem like anything at all.

"I once had a horse partner, but he died in battle long ago."

"Your horse was a warrior like you?"

"Yes, he was. Like me."

"What was his name?"

"Waupecony." The name sounded reverent as it came from his mouth. He sighed deeply and continued down the trail, not glancing at Andras once.

"Thank you for healing my leg." Andras felt strange thanking him. It seemed so… pedantic to thank Tavibo for saving his life with words. It felt cheap and insignificant.

"You've got a long path ahead of you, friend. What more can we do but help people on their paths?"

"Are you going to go home to the people now?" Tavibo sighed again and shook his head once.

"No, I don't think I will. I like living here. This is my home."

"Did something happen?" Andras immediately felt as though he had asked one question too many.

"Many things happened. A lot of people died. Some people betrayed others. In the end, there was nowhere else to go. We were fighting wars against people who spread across the land like locusts. It's impossible to live in peaceful coexistence with a predator unless you constantly feed it. We have nothing left to feed the monster, so now it eats us." Andras felt sad for him. Tavibo did not seem like a savage killer as some of the other settlers would paint him to be. He seemed like a man with no strength left to fight an enemy that wanted to take everything from him. It's true, the settlers were conquering this land. It was apparent in those who lived in the land. Andras recognized that hopeless, repressed aggression he saw in Tavibo's eye. He had grown up seeing that look in the eyes of the old men and then again in the eyes of the young men.

"What are we going to do in town?"

"I know some folks there who can help you. They're kind people."

"What will you do?"

"Go home."

"What will I do?"

"Whatever you will. You should be with your people."

"But Foothill isn't my people."

"No? Where are your people?"

"Polska."

"I don't know where that is."

"It's across the ocean."

"Hm. You can't stay with me." Tavibo's words felt final. Andras wasn't sure how he knew, but he stayed quiet.

Andras still felt lost, caught in a hurricane, spinning under a wave, being pulled out to sea. He was afraid to fall asleep again tonight, fearing that he might wake up somewhere new once more. He hadn't had the time to process all the events of the last few days. He had only begun feeling sad for Gourd, and he wasn't sure he was ready to feel sad for Pa yet.

Foothill came sooner than expected, and they approached town from the north. Tavibo kept his eyes low, letting his hat shade his face as they rolled into town. Andras noticed the glances from the townspeople. They would wrinkle their noses, look away, or even twist their mouths in disapproval at the very sight of him. When they saw Andras sitting beside him, they were twice as perplexed.

Andras's mended pants felt more uncomfortable than before as the people stared and glared at them. Andras shrunk away from the gazes and wondered to himself why they were so angry. He certainly looked a disaster, bloodied and ruined pants, ripped and stained shirt still dusty from being unhorsed, and he was covered in swollen bruises and cuts.

Tavibo looked far less battle-worn. His hat was sun-bleached and sagged in places, and his long black hair hung loosely and swayed with the cart and the breeze, silver, wily strands sparkling like a brook. His shirt was simple and comfortable, stained from age, not carelessness. His boots seemed older than he was but well cared-for and waxed over the decades. He didn't wear any weapons except for a beautiful knife with a carved antler handle. It was sheathed in ornately decorated buckskin, turquoise, beads, and small symbols. He had smacked Andras on the back of the hand when he reached to inspect it.

"I am not clean enough to be in town," Andras said quietly to Tavibo. He grunted in acknowledgement.

"Hm." Andras waited for him to say more. He did not.

Through the ambling bumble of townies, Andras spied a familiar face, and his heart quickened. He hadn't realized how desperately he had longed for the comfort of familiarity. The face he recognized belonged to a matching pair, the Becker twins, Peter and Paul.

Reverend Paul was a kindly young man who ran the local church and "preached a damned fine benediction" each Sunday, according to the local man outside Pete Becker's cafe. Tavibo stopped the ox cart in back of Pete's cafe. He rounded the cart, scooped Andras up in his arms gently, and carried him to a back door. With Andras twisting the knob, they pushed inside together.

Inside a dark, dry storeroom was a hammock, crates and sacks of grains and groceries, cans, bundles, and books. Andras was lowered onto a large crate so that his feet dangled against the side. Tavibo looked around the room and then looked at Andras sitting on the crate, bumping his left heel rhythmically against the crate absentmindedly.

The poor little white boy looked so small. Tavibo selected a corked bottle of water from a crate and opened it with a pleasing pop. Andras took it with both hands and drank deeply from it, dribbling all down his front. He was so small. This little settler was not an enemy. He was a victim of his people's desperation to buy, take, and have.

Tavibo had fought in many battles over his life. Before he was born, in the days of his grandfathers' fathers, when the first Europeans appeared from the South, the white men were explorers. As a young boy, Tavibo remembered hearing the stories told by his great-grandmother, how she marveled the first time she saw a horse. His grandfather spoke of endless seas of buffalo that would carve the land with their great stampedes. Then, the stories changed.

"Stay away from them" was the advice they heard. Suddenly, annual migrations were disrupted by settlements, forts, and company operations. More and more land needed to be used for mining, building, and farming. Wars and conflicts stained the land and sowed hatred on both sides. His father told him to beware of white-skinned natives. Some of the settlers would murder and steal the clothes of the people and ambush the army convoys in hopes of inciting a conflict that would eradicate the local tribes. Grandfather told stories about the French fur trappers who first started collecting Mohawk scalps for gold. In retaliation, they began collecting scalps as well. By then, it was too late. Too much blood had soured the water, and all would suffer.

Andras sniffed like small children do. He wiped his nose on the back of his sleeve and stared down at his repaired, blood-stained trousers. The bottle looked so big in his hands. This little boy was born in bloodshed. His family was taken from him, and now he was alone in the world without a people. Maybe they were alike in one way.

Tavibo grunted and exited through the other door into the kitchen. Andras sat alone in the dark, dry storeroom, his left heel bouncing against the crate rhythmically. His leg hurt, but it was more of a hot, tight ache now. His right leg was noticeably bigger than his left, but Tavibo didn't look concerned when he checked it earlier that morning.

Andras spied his favorite combination of letters in the English language on a large sealed can and wondered if he could reach it from here. Just then, the door opened again, and the same familiar face he spotted outside appeared through the door.

"Good god, you weren't exaggerating," he muttered to Tavibo over his shoulder. The big Indian followed him in. Pete knelt in front of Andras and looked him over, pausing to look at some cuts on his elbows and chin. "I'm so glad you're okay, Andras." Andras nodded.

"Thank you." He wasn't sure how to respond to that. He didn't feel okay. Yes, he was alive, but there was a moment when he woke up on Naiche's horse, and he was disappointed that he was still alive. It would have been so much less painful to have been killed with Pa and Gourd.

"We need to get you into some clean clothes and clean up some of these smaller cuts too," Pete said to Andras. He called over his shoulder to Tavibo. "When Naiche and Lil' came through, they told me what they found."

"You can still see the smoke from the East," Tavibo responded.

"Lil' pointed it out to me. I bought a few of the pieces she brought in." Peter unlaced Andras's shoes and measured the bottoms with his hand for reference.

"They belong to him," Tavibo muttered to Pete. Pete glanced over his shoulder at him and then at Andras again. Pete gathered a bundle of clean clothes and handed them to Tavibo.

"My brother can clean him up at the parsonage. I'll go for him after I close up." Pete tousled Andras's hair, releasing dust and trapped gravel that fell to the ground. "I can't imagine what you've been through, Andras. My brother and I are going to get you all fixed up, alright?" Pete's voice was gentle and fatherly. Andras nodded.

Somewhere new again. Tavibo scooped him up, loaded him into the cart again, and drove the ox to the church on the hill. Around the back of the church, a small house was built attached to the wall. Little more than bathing and sleeping space, Tavibo brought Andras inside and lowered him into a chair.

"I will go find Reverend Paul. Stay right here. *Yaa' ta' sai'*, Andras."

Paul Becker entered the small room, alarmed and concerned, but Tavibo did not accompany him. When Paul knelt down in front of Andras to inspect some of the other cuts on his elbows and chin, he heard Tavibo's cart bumping away down the road.

"Let's get you out of these ruined clothes and get you cleaned up a bit. I'll run the bath and get some clean bandages for your leg, alright? Lord, have mercy…" Paul rolled up the sleeves of his black habit and folded his spectacles into his shirt pocket.

As Paul removed the bandages around his leg, he did not cry. When he removed grit from a deep cut in his chin, Andras flinched, but he did not weep and pull away. When his elbows began to bleed again in the bath, and the water ran pink and brown, Andras did not whine and panic. Andras cleaned himself. He washed his feet and his hair, he scrubbed behind his ears and all the hard-to-reach-places, and he even scrubbed his nails. He washed in a way that would make Ma proud.

When he had to sit still to have his leg bandaged again, he cried, but he didn't make a sound.

He was so tired of crying. He felt like all he had done for days was cry and get carted around. He had no say in where he went, who he was with, what he drank, ate, wore, or even where he slept. He didn't feel very alive. But the pain in his leg, his elbows, his chin, his knees, his back, his shoulder, his neck, his f– all the pain reminded him that he didn't die at home with his Pa with a bullet in his head.

Andras was clean, dressed, fed, and his shoes were tied. Beneath his trousers, his wound was still angry and sore, only days old. Nevertheless, he no longer looked like the dead risen from the grave. Angry cuts and gashes spotted his face, and his hands and knees were as much scabs as skin.

He leaned on the crutch Tavibo had made for him and studied the painting on the wall before him. It was a large painting depicting a crowd of people exhibiting different levels of apathy toward the subject of the painting, a bloodied and suffering man, carrying lumber down a dusty road. Some of the people wept with their eyes raised to heaven, while some looked away, disinterested. Some were captured mid-shout, their eyes and fingers pointed accusingly. Andras felt bad for the man. All those people, and none of them helped. They must have hated him.

"How do you feel?" Paul broke the silence from behind Andras. He turned slowly, using the crutch carefully.

"Good, thank you, sir," Andras lied. Relatively, he felt better, but he was in agony. "Who is that?" Andras pointed at the painting.

"That," he began, approaching Andras and the painting, "is Jesus Christ of Nazareth." Paul studied the picture as well, taking in the details.

"I've heard of him. My Baba used to take me to church." Andras looked up at Paul, who looked down at him and gave a tight-lipped smile. The doors of the church sounded with a knock and opened immediately after.

"Reverend?" called the guest, "I stopped by because some folk said there was a big in'jun feller creeping around, and I wanted to check in." Wearing a shiny star and clean boots, the sheriff entered the church and tipped back his hat. "Hope'n the Lord's not offended by my wearin' a hat."

"Not at all, sheriff. Please come in. Jim stopped by earlier to drop off my friend here for some care." Paul smiled at the sheriff and motioned to Andras, battered and alive. The swaggering strut transformed into an anxious amble. He stammered, and sweat beaded his temples.

"Wha–Walenty? You're alive!" The sheriff stared aghast at him. Andras nodded. "I thought the– I mean when your Pa– How did–" He paused to collect himself.

"Well, how about that? Ain't that something," the sheriff celebrated. He was already turning away. "Good to hear! Praying for healing, son. Lots to do." He opened the door and made to leave.

"Did you catch them?" Paul called after the sheriff before he could slip out the door. The sheriff stopped and half-turned.

"Beg your pardon?"

"I asked if you caught them, the men who shot Berle Walenty." Paul's voice did not waver. It held a hidden contempt, a knowing bile that he could do all but hold in.

"No, unfortunately not, I'm afraid. I was out of town the day it all occurred. I came back and saw the smoke in the distance. Drifters, I heard, free-grazers maybe. Truly a catastrophe. And in our county? The investigation continues," he spoke quickly, stepping out of the door all the while and closing it on himself.

"Pa and I talked to the sheriff the same morning they killed him. He was packing up and leaving, and Pa asked him for help, but I could tell he was too scared." Andras stared at the door as he talked, expecting it to open again. Reverend Becker shook his head and sat down on a pew nearby. He smoothed his hair and exhaled loudly.

"Sheriff Leonard is a coward. The only public he serves is himself. When he's not taking bribes, he's too drunk or afraid to uphold the law. That star on his chest is more qualified to protect this town than he is– Listen to me, gossip, libel; please forgive me, Andras."

"Don't worry, sir. I won't tell him what you said. I think he is a coward. If he had been there– Maybe if he could..." All possible outcomes he could imagine with the sheriff present were still bleak. That lazy coward didn't have the sand to look Hush in the eye, or more, pull a gun on him. No, the sheriff's presence would not have saved his dad's life. If the sheriff could not defend his own home and people, then he was lost. "Maybe the city could get a new sheriff?"

"Unlikely, but we should pray for it. The Lord provides all that we need, and He'll see us through this dark valley." Paul smiled warmly at the wounded child and wondered. Andras pondered what he meant by "dark valley" and what it had to do with his dad. Andras nodded.

Later that day, Paul took Andras to his brother's cafe for the day while he visited some sick folks a ways out of town. Andras liked Pete. He wasn't as quiet or gentle as his brother, but he had a loud laugh, told crass jokes that mostly went over Andras's head, and he called him "Andi," just like Ma and Pa used to.

The first week of working at Pete's was difficult with his limited mobility. The gunshot wound had begun to heal and mend, and Pete and Paul kept a close watch on it. Andras's job was simple: count items in the store room and make sure the numbers matched his invoices, and then he wrote items that needed to be made or bought on a black board in the kitchen.

Andras's reading and numbers were better than they were a year ago, but he still was no scholar. Hours of frustration and focus finally began to culminate into a quick fluency that sped up his tasks, finishing inventory in the storeroom before breakfast was finished being made. He found that, while he was working hard, focusing, counting, or carrying, his mind did not wander to memories of screaming mules, burning pain, and Pa's body, its head splayed open.

During the day, he thought of sacks of flour, tins of lard, jars of butter, carrots, potatoes, beef. But at night, when he lay on the cot in Reverend Paul's house, he could not quiet his mind enough to allow it to sleep. Insomnia, to a seven-year-old, felt like solitary confinement.

It didn't take much snooping to find books, some old and leatherbound, others massive and dusty. He chose one and began to read. *Critical Commentary on the Apocryphal Texts of Scripture.* "Texts" was a word he knew. The other ones were just a smart-sounding series of letter-sounds he knew. He read on his cot by the light of a single candle until he began to read the same line over and over, he read on his cot by the light of a single candle until he began to read the same line over and over, he read on his cot by the light of a single candle until he began to read the same line over and over, and he drifted off to sleep on page two.

Foothill was home now. It wasn't where his family lived, not the place he fought to protect, and not where he was happiest. The smoke from his house had been visible for a week. Each time he looked up at it, he was transfixed for a moment, a black memorial pillar erected for his father and the life he had planned for them. And then, one day, it was gone.

It's not that Andras forgot what had happened or that he had accepted the events and how they transpired, but when he thought about it, it was just... something that happened to him. Each day was a day he was further removed from it. He woke up thinking of his Ma and Pa, and he fell asleep remembering what happened that day.

His leg hurt less and less each day, and the townsfolk didn't look at him as a cursed pariah anymore, but merely a burden they could not afford. Pete and Paul Becker were his connection to Foothill, and seemingly the only people who noticed him. The sheriff had avoided the cafe and church like a malaria ward, and he never seemed to be looking in Andras's direction.

Besides the cafe and church, Andras did not see much of the city, and he did not venture off the path between the two. Each morning, the people of Foothill would see Andras limping from the church on the hill to the back door of the cafe, and then he would limp back at night. He worked for his meals in the cafe and helped Pete clean up. After services on Sunday, Andras would hold the door for the congregants and sweep the floors.

The people of Foothill did not hate Andras, but they were inconvenienced by him. The sheriff's aloof apathy, mixed with his helpless state did not create an appealing candidate for an impromptu adoption. People saw him on the street as hardly better than a vagrant or a stray. Yes, he was a contributing member of Foothill, but the circumstances surrounding the murder of his father and the razing of his homestead gave cause for everyone to think twice before involving him in their lives. That suited Andras just fine. He didn't want to talk to them either. The Becker brothers were the only people to extend any kindness to him, and Andras was going to return in kind.

It was still early morning, and the cafe wasn't serving breakfast quite yet. Andras had finished his morning count and came out front to set up the dining room. Pete was behind the bar polishing the last of the morning's plates for breakfast. Charlie came bounding into the cafe out of breath, not desperately, but excitedly. Spotting Andras immediately, he called out.

"Son! Andras, my boy! A letter!" Charlie held up a small envelope, waving it. Andras stopped wiping the table and clutched the rag with white-knuckles. He'd never received postage before. Who would be sending him a letter? Pete Becker emerged from behind the bar and intercepted the kind old man.

"Easy there, Charlie. What's this about?" Andras approached from behind Pete and tried to see the letter in Charlie's hand.

"The boy's got a letter, Peter. He didn't have a mailbox, so I brought it over here as soon as I found it." He showed it to Pete. "Officially, it's for his pa, but since he's…well, since he's not able to receive it, it goes to his next of kin." Pete lowered his voice.

"It's only been a few weeks, Charlie. Do you think a seven-year-old boy needs whatever this might be?" Pete reasoned calmly and logically, but Charlie grew defensive over his role. His mustache quivered, and he raised a finger.

"Now, you listen here, Peter Becker. I broke your daddy's nose twice, and if you think you're gonna stop me from my duties as postmaster, well then, a crooked nose won't make you so identical no more." Pete laughed loudly at the crotchety threat and stepped aside. Charlie held the letter out to Andras. He took it and turned it over in his hands. It was addressed to Berle Walenty. A rush of hot, messy emotions washed over Andras, and for a moment, he wanted to hand it back to Charlie and run away. Pete lifted Andras under his arms and placed him in a chair and then pulled out a chair facing his.

"Andi, you alright?" When Pete spoke gently to Andras, his voice got gravelly and raspy, from the tobacco probably. Andras nodded. Andras never had a brother, but he liked to imagine that Pete and Paul were his older brothers. They were twenty three and both unmarried, so they didn't feel like adults completely yet. He opened the letter:

Dearest Zimowa,

I'm truly impressed by your English, but your handwriting still looks like a donkey wrote it, holding a pen in its teeth. New York is still the same as ever; loud, lively, and beautiful, with just a touch of stench.

I'm surprised to hear about the old business starting back up, but I'd love to come out and see for myself soon.

I wouldn't miss Christmas for the world. I'll have already bought the tickets before you read this. We'll see each other soon. Give all the family love from me. I'll bring gifts for the kids as well!

Stay safe,

Vaclav Sarna

~P.S. Mary and I are to be married! I moved into Helen's spare bedroom after Vernon died. Mary is excited to visit as well. Helen is sending a box of preserves soon.

Uncle Vaclav's response left him feeling a complicated mix of urgency and despair with just a twinge of foolish hope. Peter craned his neck to look at the letter that had bled the color from Andras's face. He looked like he was going to throw up. He flipped it and checked the back, then the front again in case he had missed anything. He must have missed something. None of the words had magically changed or rearranged, and he double-checked his reading.

"Andi, who is Zimowa?" Pete asked, turning his head to read over Andras's shoulder. Zimowa. *Winter.* Andras shrugged. He'd heard Vaclav and Hush both call Pa that before, but he assumed it was a nickname from his army days.

"A name for my father, I think. My Uncle Vaclav called him that, and sometimes just 'Zimo.' In Polish, it means Winter." Andras handed Pete the letter. "He didn't mention anything about Hush or the other cowboys or anything." Charlie stroked his beard thoughtfully and "*hmmmmm*"ed as he pondered deeply.

"Anything else, Charlie?" Pete prompted the old postman. The old postmaster snapped out of his brainstorm and waved a hand at Pete as if he were a pest.

"Fine! Shoo me away like an ol' dog, and see if I come waggin' my tail next time you whistle at me. Just trying to apply my expertise and worldliness to this international conundrum is all!" He exited the cafe, ranting and complaining all the way back across the street until he closed the door behind him. Pete shook his head and chuckled after the raving postmaster.

He turned back to Andras and nudged his boot with his. Andras was rereading the letter again, his face contorted in vexation.

"What are you thinking, boss?" Andras shrugged. He really didn't know what to think. Opening the letter, he was ready to be comforted by his Uncle Vaclav's promises of safety and help sooner than Christmas. Christmas was still months away. The trees hadn't even begun to turn yet.

"Christmas. I guess." He looked pleadingly up at Pete. Pete nodded and smiled.

"Guess we'll have to get you a coat then, huh?" Pete and Paul had talked about Andras dozens of times, at least weekly, but never did they discuss what was next for him. Andras wasn't sure himself. Vaclav was the closest thing to a family he had left. Poor Uncle Vaclav: he had no clue that his best friend was dead, his head blown open and left in the dirt to rot or burn. He needed to write him back as soon as possible.

"Can you teach me how to send a letter?" Andras asked hopefully. Pete stood and led him to the front door of the cafe, snatching the rag from Andras's hands.

"No, I cannot, but that ornery old crocodile at the post office should be able to point you in the right direction." He knelt down to Andras's height and handed him half a silver coin.

"I need to open up the cafe. Take this for Charlie. It's old silver, but he still takes it. Do you feel good about going to the post office and then straight back here?" He looked out into the street. It was still early, so the morning traffic hadn't begun to buffet the walkways with hungover miners and women with gaggles of children in tow. Andras nodded. He snatched the coin out of his hand, and Pete poked him in the forehead with a thick finger. "Straight back!"

"Straight back!" he echoed in reply.

Andras skip-limped down the walkway, favoring his leg more out of habit than pain. He jogged across the road, not stopping to wave or chat with passing folks or peruse the morning goods. Andras kept his eyes low to avoid meeting anyone's gaze and stopped for a passing pony carrying a block of ice. He entered the post office and double-checked the coin in his hand. Charlie was bent over a ledger that he was scribbling intensely.

"Mr. Charlie?" Andras's voice made both of them jump with a start.

"Well, hello, Mr. Walenty! Didn't I just see you?" Andras nodded. "Well then, what can I do for you?"

"I need your help sending a letter to my Uncle Vaclav. I brought money. Pete said you like old silver." He held up the halved silver coin, and Charlie appraised it with his spectacles just like an old man would. Charlie welcomed him behind the counter and gave him a chair to sit. Charlie gave him a paper and a beautiful fountain pen and sat beside him.

"I'm not very good with writing, Mr. Charlie. Could you help?" Charlie's face scrunched into wrinkles as he smiled and nodded.

"Suppose you told me what you wanted to say, and I transcribe it for you; how's that?" Andras nodded. Charlie adjusted his spectacles on his nose and dabbed the nub of the pen on his bottom lip like a scribe capturing the word of his lord. He held pen to paper and nodded to Andras with soft eyes that sparkled with a kindness only an old man could convey.

"'Dear, Uncle Vaclav…'"

"Very good start, son, keep going."

"Dear Uncle Vaclav, Pa is dead. A killer named Hush shot him. I'm okay. Please come soon and get me." He stifled a stuttering breath and sniffed, wiping his nose on his cuff. Charlie finished transcribing, and looked at Andras over the top of his spectacles.

"I'll send it out right now, son. And don't you worry about the fee. This is a special occasion." Andras pocketed the coin and nodded. He went straight back to the cafe.

Chapter 12

Vaclav forgot how much he hated trains. He had forgotten the swaying rhythm, the repetitive clack-clacking of the wheels, and the oppressive crush of being put into the cramped cars. But this train ride was different from the last train he had ridden.

The last train he was on was a military convoy train. His battalion and he had crammed into the train cars and ridden kilometers through cold and wet only to be slaughtered on some muddy hill. As he remembered, he could almost smell the bile, piss, and sweat.

A soft, warm hand on his wrist yanked him back to the present. What a beautiful anchor Mary was. She made him want to be wherever she was. He wanted to nurture and protect that glow she had that gave him hope. Mary was his American dream. His destiny manifest was found on the pillow beside him each morning, not on some distant coastline. Vaclav had found his fortune before ever he crossed the Appalachians. She was smiling at him. He was smiling back.

"Is everything alright?" Her voice was low and only for him. He nodded and placed his hand over hers and squeezed it once, holding it against his cheek. She kept it there.

"Everything." They stared at each other for a shared moment, letting their eyes say what their lips had already promised. Vaclav's smile melted to a concerned grimace as his mind drifted to the note in his pocket, and the gun in his carpet bag beneath his chair. "I'm just…

worried." Her smile melted too, and she brought her other hand to cup his other cheek. She studied his eyes.

"Whatever happens, we'll do it together." She meant it to bring him peace and comfort, but it only quickened his heart.

"That's exactly what I'm afraid of, Mary. If Berle is in trouble, it could be dangerous for you. If anything happened to you..."

"Nothing is going to happen to me." She patted him on the cheek hard with one of her pretty hands. It stung a little. "My Polish freedom fighter will keep me safe." He smiled and nodded, and he kissed one of her hands.

"You're right. They're fine. We'll be fine." Vaclav told himself as much as he said it to Mary. He looked out the window again.

"I'm feeling rather excited to see the West. I've never seen the plains before! The way Vernon used to talk about them, they sound like oceans the color of sunsets. And we'll see Andras again! I can't imagine how much he's grown." Mary's excitement was infectious. Vaclav couldn't very well brood around Mary's unshakable hope and love for life. Even after Vernon's death, Mary cared for and supported Helen. Now, Vaclav and Mary cared for Helen as if she was their own family. "Oh goodness, imagine if we find gold or oil while we're there! We could build a house right next to Berle's, and we could all live out West together. Helen would love it out here." She leaned across Vaclav's lap to better look out the window.

Vaclav looked at Mary, the curve of her jaw to her neck, the loose hair that curled into a ringlet by her cheek, the smooth, unscarred skin of her warm cheek.

"It certainly is beautiful," he agreed.

But his mind drifted to darkness again, and he removed the letter from his pocket. Mary noticed and looked down at it, rereading it again. *"Colorado is beautiful, but it's been getting colder. It's starting to feel like it did before."* Vaclav could read between the lines of Berle's vague letter. It wasn't a secret code to be cracked. "Getting colder" and "like it did before" both made him think that the business from back home was old war business. *"Seeing lots of familiar faces"* was troubling as well, because, all the people he could remember from the war, he'd rather not see again. The reference to Christmas must be a ruse to throw any interceptors off the trail, but it does imply an urgency and importance. The reference to Kyrylo was most troubling.

"Who is that?" Mary asked, pointing to the strange name. Vaclav shook his head.

"I don't know why he would have written that. It can't be good, though." Vaclav felt the urgency to reach Colorado quickly building in his chest and his shoulders.

"Everything is going to be okay. If things were worse, I think Berle would have sent another letter or said the danger more explicitly." Mary's logic was sound, but it didn't bring the peace she expected. "Besides, if he is half as incredible as you have told me, then he'll be fine until we get there." She rested a hand on his knee. He stopped bouncing his leg when she touched him.

"You're right. I know you're right." He exhaled and patted her leg beside his. "I love you, Mary."

"And I love you, Vaclav." She rested her head on his shoulder and closed her eyes with a peaceful smile. "Nie martw się, potężny wojowniku. Ochronię cię. *Don't worry, mighty warrior. I will protect you.*"

After a moment, her head began to feel heavy, and he dared not move for fear of disturbing her peace. He gently folded the letter and returned it to his pocket again. He decided to allow the rhythmic swaying and clacking to lull him to sleep instead of driving him insane. It was easier to fall asleep beside Mary.

The conductor's shouts roused Mary and him from their short nap on the train. The hot sun beamed through the window, warming them, making it hard to wake up. Outside the window, steam and dust billowed below the train. People milled to and fro, leaving and boarding trains, waiting and searching for their next ride.

They gathered their bags and stepped onto the train platform. Vaclav was riveted by the alien atmosphere of this new world. Before him was a beautiful long building with a clock tower with the words **UNION STATION** in large white letters. Rocky outcroppings and spires dotted the distance. Red brick buildings and telegraph wires stretched for miles. People wore wide-brimmed hats and boots, sturdy fabrics of light colors and utilitarian accessories. While still fashionable, the people of the west dressed ready to brave the frontier.

Mary's excitement was palatable. She had secured her hat to her head and tied the ribbon beneath her chin. He offered his elbow to her, and she took it with a giddy smile. She looked beautiful. She truly did deserve to live in a place with horizons and trees.

Inside the station, marble, chandeliers, steel, gold, cravats, and waistcoats. He was entranced. Mary marveled at the beauty and crossed the marble floor to the ticket depot for their connecting train. Vaclav wandered. He was pleasantly surprised to find a small bar where they served drinks, beer, and sandwiches. It was sparsely populated, so he took a seat at the bar. One other man sat there. The bartender poured him a beer and Vaclav took a moment to relish in the beauty of the train station.

"Where' you heading?" said the man at the bar. He was older than Vaclav by a decade, at least, no more than twenty, and he had the tan, rough exterior of someone who grew up on a saddle. His hands were calloused and knobby, probably from years of breaking them and hard, precise labor.

"Visiting my brother." Vaclav partially lied.

"He sick?" The cowboy asked.

"He might be, yeah."

"My condolences. I'm heading out West myself."

"What's waiting out West?"

"I got a sweet little spread in California. I bought it now that the Mexicans left."

"Here's to you," Vaclav said, raising his glass, "May your fields be fruitful." He took a drink of his beer.

"Cheers." the stranger joined in the drink.

"My fianceé and I are heading to Colorado to pick up my nephew. My brother has been having a hard time."

"It's unkind out there. Lots of suffering and death everywhere you go. Out here, evil is like mud. It's impossible to get through it without getting some on you and taking it with you." The cowboy stared at his drink ruefully before he downed it in one tip. He turned to face Vaclav and held out a rough hand in greeting.

"Benjamin." Vaclav took the offered hand and gave it a strong shake.

"Sarna." He smiled at him.

"What kind of business you in, Sarna?" He motioned to the bartender, who poured another glass of brown liquid.

"I work a stable back East. Boarding horses and things of that nature."

"That's good, honest work. I'd go back to working stables if my knees and back weren't as old as they are." Ben chuckled and patted one of his knees.

"I enjoy it. I love working with the horses. What about you? What do you do for money?" Vaclav adjusted on his stool and settled deeper. Benjamin winced as he thought how to answer.

"Up until recently, I ran cattle. I've been free-grazing with the same couple of cowboys for a good long while. A little while back, I decided to finally settle down somewhere and make roots. I've been in the saddle for too long, I think."

"What makes you say that?" Vaclav asked with genuine interest. He sipped his cold beer. The cowboy made a low, grumbling growl as he pondered his answer.

"Answer me this, Sarna," he began with a new vigor. He pointed a finger at him. "Have you ever done something that you were afraid might ruin you forever?" Vaclav's eyes darted to Mary instinctually and then back at Benjamin.

"What do you mean?"

"Ever done something so vile or detestable, you were worried that you might never be able to pray away your stains? Something wrong that changes you. You know what I'm talking about?"

"Yes. I do." Vaclav's voice dropped as his mind wandered to younger days, snow, the burn of vodka, and the chill of mud.

"That's why." Benjamin slapped his bad knee again, emphasizing his point. "I ain't who I thought I was gonna be, and now I'm looking back at my life, hoping no one finds out the person I've become. I feel like I'm hiding everywhere I go. So, I had to get out before the last of me was gone for good." Benjamin was tipsy and emotional, and Vaclav was glad to be able to be present for this old cowboy's new life direction.

"I do know exactly what you mean," Vaclav assured him. Mary approached from behind and lay a hand on Vaclav's shoulder. He took her hand and stood, putting a hand on her waist and looking at her. "This is my fianceé, Mary. She and I will be boarding our train to Colorado shortly." The old cowboy turned to Mary who extended a small, confident hand in greeting. He gingerly took her hand in his rough, jagged hand and squeezed gently, careful not to break her.

"Colorado is beautiful country. Kindest wishes to you both." He managed a tight smile and a nod. Mary's eyes glittered as she beheld this picturesque cowboy, this conqueror of the high plains. Each wrinkle in his dark skin told the story of a year under the stars. She smiled kindly and inclined her head politely.

"You are so kind, sir. Have you ever been to Foothill? That's where we are headed now." The tan complexion of the old cowboy washed pale, and his eyes darted between the two of them. Benjamin turned in his seat and finished his drink with a trembling hand before tilting his head into his hat and standing, leaving a silver coin on the bar.

"I am so, so sorry. I need to leave. I beg your pardon. Ma'am." He stood and left the train station in a slightly swaggered beeline. The coin continued to dance on the counter, slowing to a noisy spin.

Vaclav watched after the anxious man as he exited the building before he slapped a hand down on the coin to stop its spinning.

"That was peculiar. Did I say something wrong?" Mary fidgeted with the pendant on her necklace and turned to Vaclav. He lifted his hand and looked down at the coin.

"That's a strange coin. Is it silver?" Mary asked. Vaclav lifted the coin and studied it with a dark expression. He returned the coin to the bar for the bartender to retrieve and stood, the muscle in his jaw tense. He picked up their luggage, grabbed her hand and walked quickly towards the door. He leaned in close to her and whispered,

"It's Russian."

Chapter 13

A procession of bonnets and Sunday hats paraded out the front doors of the chapel, low murmurs blended together. Talcum powder and parasols, bibles and boot polish, trimmed mustaches and pinned buns, Andras watched from his branch in the big shady willow. He swung his legs underneath him lazily and waited for them all to file out so he could start sweeping.

He enjoyed this perch very much ever since he discovered it. While climbing up the small belfry above the entrance, he noticed a thick branch that had sagged low enough for him to hop onto with a long step. He could see above most of the buildings nearby, and nobody ever saw him. He felt like an Indian, a ghost of the prairie stalking among the settlers, unwelcome, deadly. He imagined sometimes that he was spying on different people in the neighborhood, watching them when they thought they were in secret.

The din of the congregants waned, and Andras walked carefully across the branch, crossed over to the roof, and climbed down the ladder in the belfry.

"I was wondering if you were up there again," Paul chided him churlishly with a smirk. Andras smiled, knowing he'd been caught.

"I promised I wouldn't ever fall out of the tree until after your final benediction," Andras responded matter-of-factly.

"It's true. I can't have your yowling disturbing the Good Word." Paul made a mock-stern face and nodded him inside. Andras bounded down the center aisle of the pews and snatched the remainder of the communion loaf from the stand in front of the lectern. He plucked out the soft insides before starting to gnaw on the crispy crust. Paul brought a broom over and had to wrestle the last of the bread away from Andras who was trying to eat it all so he wouldn't have to share. Andras laughed like a goblin and rolled away from Paul, who nibbled contentedly at his small liberated morsel of eucharist.

Paul was oddly quiet as he straightened the hymnals and shuttered the windows. Both he and Andras felt the strange silence, and it made Andras feel anxious, as if he had done something wrong. When Andras had finished sweeping between the pews, Paul cleared his throat loudly.

"Hey, Andras, come on over here. I need to talk to you about something. You're not in trouble. Promise." He sat down on the low dais where the lectern was elevated. Andras jogged to the front and jumped behind the lectern and yammered mockingly with a goofy face. They shared a moment of silliness, and Paul imagined for a moment what it would be like to be a father. Eventually, Andras settled for Paul to get serious enough to broach the topic he was dreading.

"Andi, I'm going to ask you some questions about the day your dad… and I'm only asking because… because I care about you, friend. I've really enjoyed getting to know you since you've been staying with

Pete and I. I've never pressed you about it, and you never felt the need to air it out." Andras nodded and glanced at the wood grain of the pew seat beneath him. He felt very sad very suddenly as if he wanted to start crying right then. "I've always respected it. You're very tough for a man your age and size." Paul leaned towards him. Andras could almost hear the physical combat inside his brain, wrestling with the words.

"It's coming time o'the year when the free-grazers come back through. And there's a good chance some of those cowboys will stop by here to water their horses and spend the night before they return home for the winter." Andras's eyes flicked up to meet Paul's, and a chill slithered down his spine. The boy's eyes flashed with such intense distilled hatred, he feared for his life for a moment. But just as soon as that fiery wrath razed, it was extinguished by a deluge of hot tears. Paul believed the bitterness in those tears would poison him.

"I'm saying this because I want to know what you think. I'm not your pa: I'm not going to tell you what to do, but I am going to do my best to keep you safe and living." Andras sniffed and nodded. "With all that being said, what do you feel? What are you thinking?" Paul fell silent and waited.

Andras kicked his feet and shrugged.

"Angry." It wasn't the right word, but he didn't know how to articulate the crippling inability to act upon the visceral urge to enact fatal violence upon someone. Andras was a child, but he wasn't a fool.

He knew there were no circumstances in which he would emerge victorious in a physical confrontation with any of the men who murdered Pa, least so, Hush.

"Angry…" Paul repeated back. From behind them, Pete Becker came into the chapel, out of breath.

"Sorry! I missed service. Did you tell him?" Pete's voice was like a shout compared to Andras and Paul's hushed tones. Paul waved a hand at him to shush, and Pete came to sit next to Andras. "Sorry."

"Tell me what?" Andras looked up at Pete. Pete shoved his head playfully.

"We're trying to figure out what to do next, Wally." Andras liked Pete's nicknames, and he also liked how polite Paul was.

"I don't want to run away. This is my home now." Andras spoke with such firm confidence, Pete almost agreed right then.

"We're not saying we have to run away. Pete and I just want to make sure you're safe and, if you want to, we can go and stay out of town a few days 'til the cowboys blow home. What do you think?" This was clearly the preferred course of action, and it was clearly the safest.

The Beckers were not soldiers or gunfighters, and Andras was a seven-year-old and a little small for his age. The safest course of action was to remove yourself from the enemy's line of sight, but those are the rules for an offensive, not an escape plan. Andras shook his head. Pete and Paul looked at each other.

"I want to kill them." Though his face felt hot, Andras did not cry. He looked at the Beckers, and he tried to convey to them with all of the maturity he could muster that he was not speaking as an emotional child, but with pure intent of vengeful retribution.

There was something inside Andras that had unreeled, become unbound, and no matter how he knotted and twisted and reasoned, it would never be the same. Something in him had broken, snapped off from a moment of sudden rending stress, and no amount of tinkering would be able to return it to its original form. But from that twisted, broken mass emerged jagged edges, serrated, masticated shapes, hurting anyone foolish enough to touch. Somewhere inside Andras, the tissue of who he might have been was knitting back together, torn, scarred, ugly, tough. At night, when he woke up gripping his leg in silent agony, as he clawed at the cramping, healing leg muscles, he thought only of the faces of the men who were there that day.

And he remembered the face of the man who was not there. Andras's ire built daily for the cowardly sheriff whose badge protected him like a spoiled child. What use were jagged, sharp pieces if not to be used as a weapon or destroyed to create something else?

"Andras, the sheriff isn't liable to do something like that." Pete's mouth twisted with disappointment.

"I know that. I said *I* want to kill them. The sheriff is a coward who preys upon his own people and doesn't protect his home. In Polska, we had different rules. Mr. Gremchen taught me all about that." The rage that bubbled and simmered in Andras made him feel sick. He imagined himself shooting the sheriff, and it frightened him. He stopped himself, and put his hand against his own chest. His heart thudded behind his ribs like a dog pulling at a chain.

"Andras, I can see how angry you are, and rightfully so. You've been wronged. Your father was stolen from you, and your life changed forever. But our scripture tells us that vengeance belongs to the Lord. God will enact vengeance for you. To seek out revenge, to lash out in vengeance, well, that's trespassing on God's Country." Andras felt Pete's hand on his shoulder, heavy and comforting. The fire did not subside inside him, though he took note to hide it better in the future. Andras nodded.

"Do you still want to stay?" Pete asked him. Andras realized that this was his decision, and the weight of it impressed upon him for a moment. He felt it on his chest.

"I want to stay. If Uncle Vaclav comes, and I'm not here… I don't want to miss him." He looked at the brothers, gauging their responses. Pete looked troubled, but Paul seemed stumped. "You said it was my decision," Andras reminded them.

"Fair enough. That settles it, then. We'll lay low until they pass through, if they come through at all. We'll wait for your Uncle Vaclav. Until then, it's business as usual."

Business as usual became an anxious waiting game as more cowboys trickled in and out of town. Andras studied each of their faces as they trotted past down the stamped-flat streets. They patronized the cafe and paid their dues with only several drunken brawls occurring. Sheriff Leonard lamented his increased workload, citing the higher traffic of visitors for his fatigue and time spent in the saloon.

Each morning, he strutted to the sheriff's office, disturbing sleeping drunks, throwing rocks at stray dogs, and shouting at any unattended child. Andras had taken to visiting that street each morning, sitting on a doorstep or haunting the sheriff's peripherals. For some reason, Andras never seemed to be on the receiving end of his poison.

Andras knew that it was only a matter of time before either Uncle Vaclav arrived to take him away, or the cowboys came back to finish the job. Either way, he needed to be ready. Perhaps Uncle Vaclav would be able to help him with the killers, too, once he got there, but Christmas was a long time away. Andras shook his head to rattle the thought from consideration. Uncle Vaclav would never approve of him killing, much less carrying a weapon. He would just have to do it before Christmas. Maybe he could steal a gun from Sheriff Leonard or swipe one from the gunshop across town.

Andras knew that Pete and Paul each owned a gun, but he didn't want to steal from the Beckers after everything they'd done for him. Stealing from your family and neighbors is wrong. The Becker brothers and Uncle Vaclav were the only family he had left.

This morning, Andras sat on his perch in the sagging willow by the church, his legs dangling freely beneath him. Pete wasn't awake yet, so he didn't feel any need to rush to the cafe. He noticed that most of the cowboys and free-grazers arrived in the early morning, and they usually made their way to the cafe, and then the saloon, eventually before turning in for the night with whatever deprived comfort they found that evening.

Today would be an important day. Today, Andras was going to steal a gun. A loaded gun, hopefully, but one step at a time. Nearby roosters shouted hoarsely their morning greetings. It was nearly time for him to plant himself somewhere along the sheriff's morning commute. A chill breeze swept down from the mountains and chilled his exposed ankles. Standing carefully, Andras shimmied to the church roof, into the belfry, and down the ladder, barreling down the green hill with the speed and momentum that only a seven-year-old could muster in the morning. When his feet finally hit the creaky, splintering planks of the town sidewalk, he was panting, and his ears shone bright red.

The smell of the morning's bread was wafting down the street like morning glory, and the cocks crowed again as the morning sun painted the Rockies above. The streets were still sparsely populated. An older woman donned her bonnet and set off at a lively pace somewhere urgent. A carpenter nailed roof tiles to a new bank beside the sheriff's office. Andras chose a painted wooden railing to lean against, resting his chin atop his crossed arms. Like a cat, he waited. Lazily, maliciously, he waited for the sheriff, knowing the psychological tension it inflicted upon him.

Today, he would wait for the sheriff to go in and then come out again for his morning whiskey at the saloon. Like a cowardly, useless clock, the sheriff appeared around the corner, his bow-legged swagger jingling the spurs that sparkled on his heels. Andras didn't move. He didn't call out or attract attention to himself at all. Sheriff Leonard's eyes swept the street, his eyes squinted from the early sun. He spat a glob of chaw on to the street and sniffed loudly, tipping his hat at a lady across the street from Andras.

The sheriff seemed to tense for a moment, and then continued on his way. Andras smirked. The sheriff must have spotted him in his peripherals and then tried to pretend not to notice. Stupid coward. The idea of a big adult sheriff being scared of a seven-year-old boy was hilarious to Andras. Of all the shittiness in his life, knowing he could spook the sheriff was one of the few joys he relished.

The sheriff emerged again from his office, his brass star gleaming like gold. The curved handle of his pistol sat near the front of his pants, a dark-brown stained leather cross-draw holster on display. He turned down a different street, and Andras waited until he couldn't see him anymore before crossing the muddy road.

The front of the sheriff's office was small; one barred window, a door, and a wooden sign with the eight-pointed star of the law. The street was still relatively empty, and there was nothing overtly suspicious about a local urchin seeking out the sheriff's assistance. He turned the knob and held his breath. To his relief, the moron did not lock it before leaving to get his morning drink. He closed the door behind him silently and scanned the room quickly.

An old, peeling desk sat to his right, cluttered with papers, junk, and personal effects. Further back, three cells lined one wall. A soft snore and a sleepy sniff hinted at a guest in the jail overnight. Andras froze and held his breath as the sleeping form shifted and turned on its side. He waited ten more seconds before taking another step forward. On the wall opposite the desk was a wooden gun rack, displaying two long guns. There's no way he could sneak out of the sheriff's office with a rifle without drawing a lot of attention to himself.

Another loud snort from the prisoner made him pause and suck in his breath in a gasp. He shifted again and cleared his throat. Hanging on a hook across from the center cell was a gun belt lined with thick, stubby cartridges. A dark-gray felt hat hung atop it. The curved wooden handle of a pistol could be spied from where he crouched. Andras's heart pounded blood through his ears, and he wondered for a moment if his heart was loud enough to rouse the sleeper.

He padded softly across the small jail to the hook on the wall. He extended to his full height to lift the hat from the hook, and then gently lifted the belt. It was heavier than he expected, and the pistol shifted slightly in the holster. Reaching up to return the hat, the pistol slid from its leather sheath and clattered to the hollow wooden floor with a loud, bouncing thud.

Andras dove to the ground, failing to catch it and choosing instead to grab it as quickly as possible. He grabbed the loose pistol in one hand and the gray hat in the other when a hoarse whisper made him spin on the spot, holding the hat against his chest, hiding the pistol in his other hand.

"*Psssst!* Hey, kid!" The prisoner was lying on his side on the cot, propping himself up on an elbow. "Grab the keys, and let me out. I'm a good guy! I go to church and send my ma money an' everything. C'mon, par'ner." He glanced at the door nervously and sat upright on the cot.

Andras hadn't moved. He felt the wall bump against his back as he leaned away from one of the men who had killed Pa. His fingers tightened around the handle of the pistol, and his trembling thumb found the hammer. Andras noticed that his teeth hurt from how hard he was clenching his jaw, and he forced himself to take a full breath.

The prisoner was a thin and bony young man, maybe a year or two older than the Beckers, and he brushed his greasy hair behind his ears. He had ridden up beside Hush while the other held him tight. His hair was longer, and he was filthier, but Andras was sure of it. The moment felt like minutes.

"D-d-do you know me?" Andras's voice wavered like a scared child's. The prisoner squinted and cocked his head slightly, studying the strange boy closely.

"No, I don't recall ever knowing anybody from here. I've only been here one other time. You got my hat there, kid, give it here." He extended his hand through the bars and waited expectantly. Andras held out the hat, revealing the pistol in his other hand. He did not take the hat, but instead withdrew his hand, unsure. "You uh… got my gun there too, pal. I can take it from ya'. Hand it over real careful-like." He reached through the bars again, slowly this time, palm upturned. He pressed himself against the bars and crouched, reaching as close to Andras as he could. "Give it here, boy, or that lawman is gonna come back here and irrigate both of us with that scatter gun o'er there, 'kay?" The pistol quivered in his hand. Andras looked down at the blued metal and wooden scales on the handle.

In a single smooth motion, he pulled back the hammer and rested his finger against the trigger. The prisoner's eyes went wide, and he backed away from the bars quickly and put his back against the opposite wall.

"Whoa, whoa, take it easy, son—"

"You can't call me that."

"Alright, I'm sorry, alright?" He held up his hands placatingly and slid down the wall so he was eye-level with Andras. "You don't want to shoot anybody, kid. You don't wanna be a murderer. Besides, everyone will hear, and then what?" Andras slowly turned the pistol towards the kneeling man and glanced at the door.

"Do you wanna know why you can't call me 'son?'" Andras's voice was cold and emotionless as steel. The prisoner held up his hands.

"Oh god, please, don't kill me. I'm helpless. I'm on my knees. I'm begging you please." His voice shook and his bottom lip quivered.

"Do you know who you remind me of right now? My dad. When he died. He was kneeling on the ground, helpless, begging." Andras lined up the rear sights with the front and gripped the handle tightly, wrapping his other hand around to brace it. The prisoner blubbered and a bubble of snot shrank back into his left nostril as he sobbed once.

"I know I done wrong, I know, I know, please, god, don't kill me!" He cried and dripped and bowed prostrate on the ground, begging the floor for mercy. Andras's stomach churned. His hands began to tremble just like his knees were. This awful, pathetic piece of shit that someone gave a name made Andras sick. He felt like he needed to vomit, but he wasn't sure if it was from fear or disgust.

"Look at me." Each word was spat through gritted teeth. The infantile squirmings of the pathetic display before him muddled the childish timbre of his voice. Inside, his heart thrashed about in mad rhythms, his stomach rolled in flips, and his bones vibrated.

As Asher Milan looked up at Andras, his puffy, tear-stained, snotty, stupid face, Andras's bones settled. His heart slowed, and he saw in Asher Milan's eyes what he knew without a doubt was dehumanizing, animalistic fear, and Andras knew he had nothing to fear from him anymore. When before, the weight of the gun made his hands shake, now he realized the weight was not from the metal and wood.

He squeezed the thin trigger and felt the sharp kick of the pistol in his hand. The explosion from the gun still rang in his ears like the final chime of a church's tolling.

When his hearing fully returned, all he heard was the loud banging of the hammer next door. The smoke shone white like fog through sheets of sunlight from the windows. Andras coughed and waved his hand back and forth in front of him to clear the plume. The prisoner was silent. Andras crouched low as the smoke cleared and inspected what he had done.

He lay face down on the cell floor, his knees still under him. His hands were lying on the floor in front of him, and the fingers seemed oddly crumpled in a way that Andras's eyes lingered on. A glimmering halo of black-red expanded away from his obscured forehead. His greasy hair lay in the expanding puddle like drying kelp on the beach. The back of his hair glimmered wet, and Andras didn't have to lean in close to see the recess in the back of his skull where the bullet exited. His body was unsettlingly still with its dead-spider hands.

As the smell of the gunpowder dissipated, he smelled the sharp brown odor of feces and urine. Andras's hands started shaking again, and he felt the rising bile in his stomach. He coughed violently once and vomited on the floor. Andras stood, sniffed, wiped his mouth on his sleeve, and returned the pistol to its holster. He slung the gun belt over his head like a bandolier and pulled on what he assumed was the prisoner's coat over the belt and holster.

Lastly, Andras picked up the dark gray hat and put it on his head. Surprisingly, it was only slightly too large for him. He had some butcher's paper in the back of the cafe that he could use to pad the band until he got bigger. He took one last look at Asher Milan before he exited the sheriff's office.

"I'm nobody's son now," and he walked out the front door.

Chapter 14

Andras wished the sheriff's office had a back door. He kept imagining a posse of tin-starred lawmen ready to enact swift, righteous judgment upon this newly-christened killer, charging around every corner. Every opening door was an accusing witness, ready to confront him for his recent conversion to murder. Every barking dog knew what he had done, and it hated him for it now. As he faded away down the sidewalk, Andras kept his eyes low, his face obscured by his new-old hat. He squeezed his arm against his side and felt the pistol's handle under his new coat. Just in case.

He took the long way back to the cafe and slipped through the back door. Not until he had placed the gun belt in an opened crate and covered it with his folded coat and hat did he start breathing heavily, like he had held his breath the whole way here. Andras pushed his wet-straw-colored hair to the side, off of his forehead, and sat down in the swinging hammock, allowing his brain to catch up to his body. His body was catching its breath in a cool storeroom on a soft, swinging hammock, but his mind was wiping vomit from its chin, watching the expanding puddle of blood and brains seep into the deep grooves of the knotted floorboards.

The storeroom door opened, and Andras nearly toppled out of the hammock, barely saving himself by snagging his heel on a shelf.

"Morning!" Pete said, chuckling as he watched Andras untangle himself from the hammock and regain his footing. "Why are you so sweaty?" Pete asked him. Andras shrugged.

"I was running," was his explanation. Pete's attention shifted down to the opened crate beside the hammock. Andras's sweat ran cold. Pete crouched down and reached into the box.

"Where did you get this?" Pete asked, producing the dark gray felt hat. He held it by the fold and studied it admiringly.

"I found it… with some garbage," Andras replied quickly, "along with a coat." As soon as he said it, he wanted to bite off his tongue and throw it away for such a fatal betrayal. Pete looked down, reached into the crate again, and stroked the coat, feeling the warm wool exterior.

"That's a lucky find. And that jacket will be perfect for when the snows come." Pete returned the hat to the open crate and smiled, his fists on his hips. "Ready to open up for the day?" Andras nodded. Pete plucked his heavy canvas apron off the hook on the wall and left him alone in the storeroom.

Andras took the opportunity to fully catch his breath, wash the vomit from his mouth and nose, and get back to work like nothing had happened. Before he left the room, he loosely placed a lid on the opened crate, barring any other bargain-hunters from his stash.

The breakfast crowd was another wave of dusty cowboys and saddle-tramps, traveling west before the first snows of Autumn. The regulars hugged the bar, lamenting their favorite tables and typical quiet atmosphere. Andras was busy this morning, carrying stacks of bowls and plates to the kitchen constantly. He didn't even finish his daily count until near lunchtime. By the time the morning-shift's dishwashers cleared out of the back, Andras was stacking the last of the lunch dishes on the tall shelves that still made his right thigh tug painfully when he stood on his tip-toes to push the bowls to the back.

He flopped down onto a sack of oats and groaned upon finding out it was mostly empty. He had put in an order for more oats this morning. His mind had been going faster than he could keep track. When he remembered killing that prisoner, it felt so long ago. It wasn't until he pulled on his new felt hat and saw the pistol and belt waiting for him below that he remembered the order of the day's events. Again, he hid his second-hand gun belt beneath his new coat in the box and covered it with a lid. He rubbed his sore rump as he walked out the front of the cafe.

"I'm off to the general store to pick up those oats we bought. Mr. Christianson won't deliver them until late, and we need them for the morning," he called over his shoulder. Pete smacked himself in the forehead with the heel of his palm and replied back as the door swung shut.

"Thank god for you, Andi. I completely forgot!"

He breathed in the fresh outside air and smiled as the sun warmed and squinted his eyes. He'd been cooped inside all day with anxious, teeth-chattering energy, and now that he was outside, his legs wanted to run and sprint and jump all the way to the general store. His wild, wired sprint wasn't the kind of joyful vigor a youthful boy might feel on a beautiful day like this. It was the kind of desperate energy a caged animal feels when it sees the door open just a crack...

The general store wasn't too far from the saloon, and he could hear the clangy timbre of the ancient piano within. Andras had only set foot inside the saloon once. It wasn't the proper place for a child to be. Besides the drinking and gambling, Andras had learned plenty of other references to experiences one could have within the saloon, but he wasn't sure exactly what they were describing. The evening had begun for many of the saloon patrons already. From across the street, he heard the dull rumble of many conversations being had over loud music and the clatter of many people in one place.

Often, Andras wondered how many of the men inside bore darker secrets than his. Since he had left Polska, America had taken everything from him. He could barely imagine the extent of suffering and loss of those who were born here. Of the hundreds of times he had heard this land referred to as "the land of opportunity" or "the land of plenty", he never once considered that the opportunities were pried from the blood-stained, dead-spider hands of another victim of opportunity. Every dead rancher was an available plot, every slaughtered tribe was better nearby hunting, every skinned, rotting bison was three dollars in the pocket of an American.

Andras pushed open the general store door to the sound of a pleasant tinkling bell. The hunched Mr. Christianson looked up from under his long, bushy eyebrows. The twinkle of his wet, friendly eyes were a kind reprieve from the irritated glares he got from most whose paths he darkened. He smiled, showing his unbelievably perfect ivory dentures, and he shuffled around the counter with the hunch of a man who had suffered under honest labor his whole life.

"By the wig of Washington, if it isn't the youngest Becker boy. What can I help you with today, son?" He was a silly, unpredictable old man who shared ownership of the general store. Andras tried to imagine Mr. Christianson as a young man, but it was impossible to picture him without the ubiquitous wrinkles and wisps of white hair that floated above his head like morning mountain mist.

"I'm here to pick up the oats for the cafe." Andras smiled at him politely and waited with his hands behind his back. On the counter beside the cash register was a stack of small paper boxes of pistol cartridges.

"Ah! Saves me the effort. Let me fetch it for you." The old man turned to a door to the back room and emerged with a sack of oats. Andras hugged the sack and nodded goodbye to the old man. The shopkeeper muttered to himself quietly about Andras being such a fine young man. Andras left the store, clutching the box of bullets in his pocket. He tasted the sour bile of shame in his mouth, and didn't look back over his shoulder. Across the street, the saloon had fallen silent. The jangling of discordant keys had stopped, and the laughing had ceased.

Holding his sack of oats across the street from the saloon, Andras listened and tried to understand the cause of the disturbance. A small group of men slipped out, and hurried off down the street, some to wagons to race home or towards the edge of town.

In a flailing stumble of arms and shouting, Sheriff Leonard burst out of the saloon, staggering to one side, stuttering in cowardly placation. Andras bolted down the alley to his right, turned the corner around the back and scaled the crates on the back of the general store, leaving his sack of oats at the base of the stack. He pulled himself onto the roof of the general store, and crouched low, sidling up to the edge of the slanted roof so that he could see down into the street.

The sheriff had regained his footing, and was walking backwards away from the saloon into the street. Throngs of patrons filed out the back, and the ones sly enough to slip out the front did so silently and quickly. Nobody had drawn guns yet, but the scent of murder was in the air.

Emerging from the entrance of the saloon with a smoldering expression of building wrath, Hank Rhodes stepped out of the saloon flanked by two other paralyzingly familiar faces. Andras ducked down behind the short awning of the roof and held his breath, hoping they didn't see him, panicking about what to do. After seeing Asher Milan in the jail, it only made sense the others would be here as well.

From the street below, muffled talking could hardly be heard, sharp, hard words; accusations? He heard the stupid whine of the sheriff's voice,

"You got it all wrong, Rhodes! I ain't–" he sputtered. Rhodes pointed a knobbed finger at him and spat his words like poison.

"You ain't done shit, you gutless ass, and now my boy's got his melon splatted all over your goddamned jail!" Andras couldn't bear to just lay there and listen. He removed his hat and peeked the top of his head over the edge.

More saloon patrons poured out from behind the three cowboys. The biggest hairy one had Pa's old rifle slung across his back. For a long moment, Andras didn't hear anything but the rising, piercing ring as his pulse quickened, and he remembered watching Gourd's ears disappear in a hot burst of pink before flying through the air. A door slammed directly below him as Mr. Christianson closed and locked his shop door before the situation outside escalated any further. Andras's attention snapped back to the present, and he noticed the expanding crowd. Down the street, folks in wagons watched tentatively. Some leaned on railings, chewing apples, while some mounted their horse and rode home before the bullshit ensued.

"Listen now, all three of you's," the sheriff began with a found sense of fight in his tone, "turn back around, and go inside 'afore I bring you in for public nuisance." His right hand lowered to the handle of his pistol while he pointed at the door of the saloon with his left. All three of the free-grazers tensed.

Barnabus Rowe took a half step back and showed his palms to the skittish lawman. Martin Xochitl-Tlajuillakan took a step to the right, his hand dropping to his own pistol, a similar vibrant rage in his eye. Hank Rhodes froze, his eyes flicking down to the cross-draw holster, then back to the sheriff's eyes. He squinted and spit a thick gob of something vile on the ground between them. His expression twisted into one of disgust and provocation.

"Sure you don't wanna straighten up in the jail before you invite us over, Sheriff? Or is that where all your deputies are, cleaning up your mess?" Rhodes relaxed his shoulders dismissively and turned his back on the sweaty lawman. Martin seemed to loosen like a bowstring as well, slowly and carefully so as not to cause further harm. Rowe visibly exhaled and adjusted the rifle sling on his shoulder. But the sheriff wasn't leaving it be without the final word, not in his own goddamned city.

"Hey!" He shouted like someone trying to start a fight, "Henry Rhodes Jr., I have half a mind to run you in for accessorizing to murder!" Rhodes stopped and turned back around. Martin looked to his boss. Rowe took another step back, placing a full horse trough between the sheriff and him. Rowe leaned over and untethered a horse that nickered and pulled nervously at the hitching post, and it trotted away down the lane.

"The fuck you saying, Leonard? You got something you wanna articulate?" Rhodes kicked dirt and took two sideways steps at the sheriff, who pulled out his pistol and brandished it in the air threateningly. Surrounding townsfolk gasped, ducked, and cried out. Martin pulled out his gun and dropped low. Barnabus crouched down low behind the trough and unslung Pa's rifle.

Hank saw the flash of the sheriff's steel, and he dove forward, reaching for the gun in the sheriff's hand. Leonard swung down with the pistol, intending to club Hank with the barrel, but instead struck him somewhere in the back. Rhodes collided with the sheriff, and the two landed on the soft earth of the street. There was a great scrambling flailing of arms and boots before Martin charged forward with gun-in-hand and put boots to the sheriff. A pistol fired, and a woman shrieked as a window shattered and dropped great slabs of crystalline blades. Martin careened away from the melee, ducking and waving his pistol behind him.

The sheriff and boss separated, and Hank lay on the ground pointing at the sheriff, yelling at Martin to, "Shoot him!" Leonard rose to one knee and drew back the hammer of his pistol, waving it between Hank on the ground, and the fleeing Martin. Martin ducked into a recessed doorway, most of his body hidden. The sheriff fired again, and the blue wall beside Martin exploded into splinters. Martin fired back, and the ground behind the sheriff splattered into a new crater. Hank drew his own pistol, not five paces away from the sheriff and fired high. The bullet whizzed above, and Andras remembered the sound of war.

A great, low, baritone clap of thunder gave way to a rolling white cloud from behind the horse trough, and the sheriff went barreling backwards, a wet, red crater where his brass star used to hang pinned, buried deep by the two-hundred-fifty-grain lead bullet in his chest. Martin emerged from his cover and fired another shot at the collapsing man. The bullet passed into his hip, and he fell over strangely, dead.

Rowe stood from his fatal vantage point and nodded at Martin and Hank. They all exchanged appraising glances for a moment before they removed their spent shells and replaced them with fresh cartridges. Rowe didn't bother. He shouldered the rifle again and nodded West. A local spoke up as she reopened her shop,

"Y'all just shot the law. Better clear out before the marshal comes sniffing." Rhodes tipped his hat in thanks and clapped Rowe on the shoulder. Together, the three men jogged West up the road, infiltrating the resuming traffic of ignorant passersby. The surrounding witnesses began to disperse, either fearfully or from boredom. Nobody rushed to the sheriff's side. His wake would have leftovers.

Andras rose from his belly and carefully jumped down the crates, hefting his sack of oats as he ran westward along the backside of the buildings, parallel to the retreating cowboys. His right thigh ached from the strain, lances of electricity and hot stabs, but he endured. When the road turned right, Andras's parallel path became a perpendicular alley, crossing the three killers' path. He crouched low and counted down when he thought they'd be passing by. Andras held out his finger and thumb like a pistol and looked down the barrel like his Pa taught him. *Three, two, one,* he thought to himself. Barnabus Rowe passed by. *Pshew* went the finger gun. Hank Rhodes followed. *Pshew* went the finger gun. Martin passed last, his face far paler than his usual rich brown. *Pshew* went the finger gun. "*Mudak,*" Andras cursed at them, blowing invisible smoke from the end of his forefinger.

It wasn't until he reached the backdoor of the cafe did he feel sick to his stomach. The sack of oats flopped to the floor, and a tiny paper box was stashed away.

"Andras?" Pete's voice sounded frightened, and a moment later, the storeroom door opened. Pete knelt in front of Andras, and he took him by the shoulders. Pete's grip was not hard, or unkind, but he held him tightly like something valuable or fragile. Pete scanned him for injuries.

"I got the oats, Pete. I'm okay." Andras reassured him, but his voice cracked as Pete's caring concern softened his shell.

"Of course you did, of course you are. Look at you," Pete said, brushing his straw-colored hair off his forehead, "how are you so damn tough?" Andras smirked and shrugged. The smile quelled the tears that threatened to loose, but he didn't want Pete to leave yet. "I heard the shooting down the street, and I saw people leaving, and I got scared something might'a happened. Good god, that was a lot of shooting! Were you close?" Pete let go of Andras's shoulders and adjusted the loose lid of a nearby crate so he could sit on top of it. Andras's eyes darted to the crate for a moment before he hoisted himself onto the hammock, sitting on it like a swing.

"Real close. Saw it well enough. Happened right in front of Mr. Christianson's store. They gunned down the sheriff!" Andras leaned forward as he spoke, the load of what had happened over the last twenty minutes beginning to unpack in his mind.

"The sheriff? Sheriff Leonard?" Pete's hand flew to his forehead like it did when he was very upset.

"Yeah! Three of them. They came out of the saloon across the way–"

"Who did, Andras?"

"The sheriff and the cowboys!"

"The cowb- What cowboys?" he asked, confused. It dawned on him. "*Those* cowboys? *The* cowboys?" he emphasized.

"Yes! The same ones who killed my pa and shot me, but not all of them were there. I found one of them in the jail, and three were in the saloon when–" Pete held up a hand, his other on his forehead.

"You found one? How?" Andras held his gaze for a moment, backtracking what he had said. His sweat ran cold, and his mouth felt dry.

"I...found *out*...one was in jail," Andras clarified, adding a tinge of Polish accent to the end of his sentence. Pete nodded.

"Got it, then what?"

"I didn't know where the others were, but then I saw three of them come out of the saloon, and they were yelling with the sheriff."

"What were they yelling about?" Pete's hand immigrated from his forehead to his mouth as he listened. Andras thought very quickly how to order his words.

"They found out someone shot him in jail."

"Holy sh–bible, who shot him?"

"They don't know! And the sheriff didn't know neither, and they were real mad, calling names, but then the sheriff–"

"What'd they call him?"

"Let me tell you the story!" Andras urged him, shoving his shoulder. Pete nodded quickly and leaned forward. "So, they were yelling, see, and the sheriff got mad, and reached for his gun, and said he would bring them in for murder. The boss, Rhodes, the one who came to our house before it was built, he got so mad that he tackled the sheriff to the ground. The other one ran up and started kicking the sheriff, but then the sheriff's gun went off, and it turned into a battle. They were shooting back and forth and missing a lot, but then the other one who stole my pa's old rifle shot him in the chest. The book lady by the general store told them that they should run because the marshal would come sniffing. Then I ran back here." He gasped and paused to catch his breath, realizing that he hadn't taken a breath during the entirety of his retelling. Pete blinked, stunned.

"The sheriff is dead? Jesus Christ…"

"Pete, what if the marshal doesn't get here for a long time? Can someone stop them?"

"Rhodes? Henry Rhodes? You said Rhodes was the man fighting with the sheriff?" Andras nodded. "That cruel, dirty, sheep-mountin–" Pete bit his tongue and started again. "Henry Rhodes Jr., son of 'Big Hank' Rhodes. Everyone 'round here was scared of the name Rhodes since *Big* Hank's daddy, Clay Rhodes, came down out of the mountains with a pack full of furs and helped put Foothill on the map. Mind you, there was a whole load of folk who made Foothill what it is now, but Clay was a mean, enterprising son-of-a-bitch who started trading in furs and then skinned his way through a whole herd of buffalo and owned damn-near half the town. Now, with all that money and all those people in his pocket, what do you think happened to anyone who tried to stake on his claim, hm?" Andras held up his thumb and forefinger like a pistol.

"*Pshew.*"

"Bingo. Big Hank is a big mean bastard too, and he got all his daddy's money. Later on, he goes cripple of some pecker-fever, leaving his tiny prick of a namesake son and all this money waiting for him up North once his pa finally kicks it. The Rhodes you know has been pushing cattle for years, waiting for his daddy to die. It seems like every year he gets more and more hateful, and now he's a damned murdering son-of-a-bitch to boot. He's got so much hatred for his bastard daddy; he's started beatin' on other people so he doesn't ruin his inheritance."

"Does his daddy know that his son's a… uh, what he's been up to?" Andras tried to conceive of an adult parental relationship and the strange dynamics that were created when money and business were thrown into the mix.

Already, Andras knew the difference between working-Pete and relaxing-Pete. Relaxing-Pete called him "Andi", teased him, laughed loudly, and drank whiskey. Working-Pete, on the other hand, usually addressed him as "Mr. Walenty" or plainly, "Andras". He didn't tease Andras in front of the customers and expected Andras to reflect that same professionalism.

"I would not assume to know the mind of Big Hank, but I would guess no. And if he did know, he probably wouldn't care unless it meddled in his affairs. I'm guessing that's why Hank Jr. chooses to stay so far away. He's biding his time until he can claim the title of 'Big' for himself. Pff," Pete chuckled in disbelief and pulled a small flask from his boot. He tipped some into his mouth and did not return it to his boot. "I'm sorry, Andi, sorry that your pa got mixed up in this, sorry that you got tangled in it, and now, it's still hurting you. It ain't fair. If I was you, Andi– hey, listen to me." Pete nudged Andras's knee with his hand to regain his childish attention. Andras looked at him, fully attentive. "If I was you, and I know I ain't, but if I *was* you, I'd get the hell away from Foothill, away Rhodes and Hush and all that shit from Poland, and start all new. When your uncle gets here, you should leave with him." Andras's eyes dropped to the floor. He swung his feet anxiously.

Pete didn't say that he didn't like Andras and wanted him to go away, but the advice to leave felt the same. Pete and Paul had been his family since Pa died, and he was left for dead all alone. When Andras looked back up and met Pete's gaze, it did not look like the same child who was swinging his feet innocently in a hammock a moment ago. Andras shook his head.

"No, Pete, I can't go. When Uncle Vaclav gets here, he's going to help me kill the men who killed Pa. If it happened the other way around, and my dad lived and I didn't, that's what he would do. He would find every single one of them who hurt his family and burned his home, and he'd take everything from them no matter how long it took." Andras thought about not getting to say goodbye to his mother, the brutal ambush and murder of his father, the sheriff who'd been gunned down in the street, and it didn't make sense. Rhodes, Hush, and the rest of the cowboys, all deserved to die. There was no amount of recompense or repentance that could wash away what was taken from him. Money could not buy who he would have become, growing up in a home with his father, a horse, and a future. Pete scooted closer to the hammock and spoke low.

"Andras, listen to me. What you're talking about is crazy. You are still a child! Men like that will not hesitate because you are little. They will kill you just because you're in the way. This isn't a chance to get back at them; it's a chance to start over and make a life for yourself."

"But I don't know what my life is supposed to be now! This is the only life I can think to do! I don't want to go to an orphanage or church-school. I just want to be with Pa…" Pete's eyes studied him anew, and he did something that he had never done before. Pete crossed the small room towards him, and pulled him into a tight hug. Andras wrapped his arms around Pete and squeezed as hard as he could.

"This isn't fair to you, Andras. I wish you could stay here with me. You are always welcome with me, alright?" Pete's voice was muffled by the twisted shirts and pressed ears, but Andras nodded in response to his question.

Maybe Uncle Vaclav wasn't the only family he had left.

Chapter 15

Vaclav and Mary were to be married. Mary wanted very much to be wed in October or late September because she loved wearing coats and loved to watch the changing leaves dance in the wind, struggling to break free of their arboreal captivity to dance several moments before resting forever. It was in that brief moment of perfect, terminal freedom that Mary was inspired.

Vaclav dreamed of a big, loud affair filled with exotic European foods and dancing late into the night. Mary's dream was simpler. She wanted to be wed on the porch of Helen's house with only several of her closest friends and family. It would be intimate and quiet. Vaclav would always play offended when she suggested a more modest ceremony, saying,

"You would shade the brightness with which my love for you burns?" She would roll her eyes, and he would giggle at her. The wedding was mere weeks away now.

The stage coach to Foothill was arduous and unexciting. Mary spent her time reading and looking out the window, pointing out her favorite sights to her fiancé. Vaclav only brought two pieces of luggage; a small bag with clothes and provisions for a day, and a long leather sheath that housed his rifle. It had been a long time since he had held a human in its sights, and he was hoping he wouldn't have to.

Mary and he had packed and bought tickets the day they received Berle's strange letter in the mail. Mary was concerned and confused, but when she pressed him, he only said, "My brother needs help, and I'm not going to wait." She started packing her clothes as well. He wasn't sure what he did to deserve a woman like Mary in his life, but he wouldn't question it.

When they arrived, their first goal was to find Berle and Andras. Vaclav had never seen the parcel of land, and he was wondering what sort of house a no-nonsense soldier like Berle would construct for his son. The land was several miles east of the town proper, and they would stop in town to freshen up before meeting Berle.

The coach driver was a thick-foreheaded man with the jawline of a more primitive time. He did not speak, but merely grunted, sometimes humming recognizable songs to himself. Around his neck hung a small blackboard that he used to communicate vaguely sometimes, but mostly, he just drove. They hadn't caught his name when they bought passage on the wagon, and he had barely looked them in the eye since then.

Weaving through the harrowing cliff-paths and rockslide dangers, they finally arrived on the other side of the Rocky Mountains. Mary gasped as she beheld the stretching landscape of hilly horizons, trees that reached for the heavens, and greenery that begged to be enjoyed. Below them, a sprawled town lay in the shadow of the mountains.

The city center was a densely-packed nexus of commerce and public life, while the homes and roads grew to become more and more scarce the further they moved away. Foothill was the frontier town that Mary always fantasized about. The stage came to a squeaky, shifting halt as the driver applied the brake and opened the door for Mary. She tied her bonnet beneath her chin and stepped out of the coach.

Colorado sunshine was hot and beat down on her bonnet like heavy rain. She inhaled the smell of mud, horse shit, baked bread, cooking meat, and something sour. When her feet met the ground, the heels of her shoes immediately sunk into the earth prompting Vaclav to catch her as she swayed. She giggled and finished the trek to the security of the sidewalk. Vaclav paid the driver a little extra and shook his hand awkwardly. The driver nodded and carried a huge sack of mail into the post office and disappeared. Vaclav and Mary began down the road of this new frontier city filled with the bravest and most ingenuitive of Americans. Men wore sturdy shoes and pants with wide hats and waistcoats. The women were still elegantly dressed, but in lighter, simpler forms. Their hair was tied up in buns, and some women even wore ladies' boots beneath their skirts.

Vaclav was not enamored with the place as Mary was. As soon as he stepped out of the coach, he could smell the bitter, sour note of anxious fear and chaos. It had been a long time since he had smelled it, but it was unmistakable. Smelled like home. Mary touched his arm gently and indicated to a livery stable down the lane, saying,

"I'll go get us some horses for today." Vaclav nodded and pointed at the saloon across the street from the general store.

"I'll head in there and see if anyone knows Berle and Andras. Be careful, Mary. Somewhere around here are dangerous people." She looked him in the eye and cocked her head.

"I'm just going to get horses. Don't worry! I'll meet you back here." Mary turned and set off, taking in the sights as she did. Vaclav watched her for a while before pushing open the saloon doors with a great squeak.

Within, the air was cool and hazy with tobacco smoke. As his eyes adjusted to the darkness, every head in the bar was turned to look at him. After a moment, they went about their business. Vaclav threw a leg over a stool at the bar and knocked twice on the wooden counter. A bartender glanced up, poured a drink into a short glass and then slid it down the bar towards him. He deftly caught it and glanced at the foggy drink. He had expected a brown or golden liquor, not a cloudy whitish cup of what smelled like…limes? He sipped it, and cringed for a moment before relaxing and submitting to the taste. It was sour and sweet, and the tequila was cooler than expected. He took another sip and nodded. The bartender finally made his way to Vaclav and leaned against the bar, draping his towel over his shoulder.

"What'll you have?"

"What is this?" Vaclav held up the glass for reference.

"Tequila, limes, and honey. An old caballero taught me, and I made a few adjustments of my own. He was telling me they would put it in their water long, long ago while they were riding the trails. I mostly enjoy it as it is." Vaclav nodded again and took another drink.

"I'll have another, and I'm also looking for someone." The bartender poured him another from a great ceramic pitcher and then poured himself one.

"You picked a strange time to just show up, friend."

"Strange how?"

"It's been a violent time in Foothill as of late. Lots of killin' and stealing going 'round. Just a few days ago, our sheriff was shot not thirty feet from where you sit now."

"By who?"

"Some group of free-grazers that come through. They got in a nasty way in here and took it outside. I heard a hell's worth o' shooting, and when I went out to check, the sheriff was dead in the street."

"And what about the free-grazers?"

"They're still here in town! They considered running before the marshal arrived, but they haven't left yet. Figured they got time, I s'pose. They stay at the inn and drink here." He shrugged apathetically, "They pay, and nobody's crying over ol' Leo."

"Is that why they all…" Vaclav mimicked turning in his chair to look at the door anxiously. The bartender chuckled low.

"Pretty much. Hopefully, you're not looking for one of them, are you?"

"Fortunately not. I'm looking for a friend of mine, Berle Walenty. Know him?" The bartender wiped the bar with the towel from his shoulder.

"Sounds familiar, but I'm not placing a face to the name. You know where he lives?"

"Eastward is where his property is. Maybe I'll just head out there." A young boy scampered up to Vaclav and tugged his sleeve. The boy could not be more than five years old.

"Your missus is waiting outside with horses, sir!" He patted the kid on the head, and paid for his drinks.

Outside, Mary was sitting properly sidesaddle, her skirt draped over the side. She adjusted the laces of her bonnet and smiled regally atop her palomino mount, shining like sunlight through water. The other horse, a female bay, nodded her white-spotted head and trotted sideways as Mary held her reins. Vaclav smiled up at his fianceé. She blushed under his gaze, and brushed a lone curl behind her ear.

"What?" she asked with a smile and red ears. His smile split into a silly grin, and he shook his head.

"It's nothing. I was just thinking that you really do look like you belong out here. Even sitting on that horse, you look…"

"Nervous and terrified this golden-boy is going to buck me into a cactus? Because that's how I feel. Now mount up, 'partner,'" she winked and handed him the reins. Vaclav stepped into the stirrup and swung a leg over.

"Remember to keep your heels down, and take it slow. We've got plenty of daylight left, and we're here. We made it." His confidence warmed her, and her shoulders lowered noticeably. He kicked lightly, and set off on a trot with his fianceé in tow.

Leaving town, the muddy roads and avenues gave way to wide, dusty, beaten paths dotted with the occasional persistent flora. The late summer flowers were waving goodbye to the dwindling warmth in the cool breeze. Splashing through a shallow stream that cut across the path, Vaclav brought out the small map of the area surrounding Foothill and traced his finger along the stream.

"If this is the stream I think it is, it eventually cuts across Berle's property. What do you say, we just stick to the stream? We can stop and water the horses, if need be, and I fancy the shade of these trees." He turned in his saddle, and she was smiling at him, her perfect riding posture almost looking comfortable and natural. They splashed down the stream for nearly an hour before the sparse patches of shady trees gave way to wide-stretching prairie and rolling hills. From their elevated vantage point, they could see the winding glittering path of the stream and the distinct shape of a fenced property around the home. They exchanged smiles once more and Mary nodded.

"You were right. We made it. I'm so happy to sleep in a bed and eat food made in a proper kitchen." She kicked her horse and started down the hill towards the Walenty home. Vaclav followed close behind.

"Don't get too excited about the proper kitchen. Berle only knows how to make potato pancakes. Everything else he tries to make just ends up tasting like somebody ruined potato pancakes." She laughed at his jab and then slowed her horse, pulling the reins slowly to her chin. The smile had melted away, and in its place was a slack-jawed expression of alarmed confusion.

"Vaclav…what's… Look." She pointed at the house. From this distance, it was clear that the house was not shadowed, but scorched and leaning to one side. The porch had collapsed down on itself, and part of the corral fence had fallen over after catching aflame. Vaclav kicked his horse hard and slapped its flank with a loud "hya!" The bay mare dropped its head and galloped down the hill. Mary followed moments later, her lips praying silently.

Vaclav arrived at the corral fence, slid off the back of his horse, and mantled over the fence, breaking into a quick run toward the house. He could see the extent of the damage now. The roof was in carbonized chunks all over the ground, the panes that still sat in their frames were warped and stretched, and the whole house seemed to lean to one side as if daring the wind to shove it a bit harder. Vaclav stopped at the back door and turned the knob with a sharp click. The twisted frame had jammed the door, so Vaclav put a boot beside the knob, and he shoved, unjamming the door, and prompting the rest of the wall to noisily fall to the ground in black swirls of ash and loud rending-snapping. As the dust cleared, Vaclav spied Mary around the front of the house. She had her nose and mouth hidden behind a folded handkerchief.

"Mary?" he called to her. She heard his quick steps and saw him appear around the corner.

"Vaclav, don't…"

"Mary, are you alright?" She didn't know how to tell the truth without wounding him deeply.

"Don't come over here, Vaclav." She took a step in front of him, blocking the view of the decomposing skeletal corpse.

The ground beneath them both was damp with something that used to be human. He turned away as a pungent, sour odor drew his attention to the larger, decomposing horse. Dangling shreds of flesh clung to the bones of the slain beast. It had been stopped with a single shot to the head. Vaclav looked at the horse and then scanned the horizon, spotting a small grouping of thick shrubs and trees. He looked down at the horse again and shook his head.

"Goddamn, that's a long shot."

Mary still blocked his view of the smaller body. "Which one is it? Is it Berle, or…" She nodded and stepped aside. The sight made him shiver and squeeze shut his eyes for a moment. When he crouched on the ground, he was looking directly into the top of the filthy skeletal head, bits of hair and tissue still clinging to it. The prairie had not been kind to Gourd and Berle's corpses. Much of the remains were scattered or missing due to scavengers and exposure. He walked to Berle and knelt beside his old friend.

"They shot him here, under the chin. He was helpless." Vaclav pinched the bridge of his nose and squeezed his eyes shut. "Fuck," he whispered to himself. "Odpocznij teraz, przyjacielu." Vaclav turned away from Berle's corpse and punched the ground. "Tak mi przykro. Powinienem był przyjechać wcześniej…"

Mary knelt beside him and placed a soft hand on his shoulder. She felt him flinch, tense, and then relax to her touch. She said nothing. She let him grieve. Mary couldn't imagine what he was feeling. She knew that she could never understand the bond between these two brother warriors. She would soon be his wife, but she had never killed to keep Vaclav safe. She had never guarded him from enemy fire as he ran for safety. She would never understand the depth of the wounds they shared.

And now he was gone. Suddenly, unexpectedly, horribly, he was gone. Not twenty-four hours ago, he was rereading Zimowa's note, anxious to see his old friend and his brave son again. Now he arrived to find that his best friend had been murdered weeks ago. There was no grave, no funeral, no monument to his service to the people of Poland, just a scattered pile of tissue-crusted bones and a greasy stain where his body decayed away, alone.

Mary held up the edge of her skirts as she navigated the perimeter of the burnt home. She stepped gingerly over the scorched lumber and unrecognizable refuse. The only audible sound was the quiet bereavement of her beloved and the call of a lone hawk circling above. Finally, she found what she had been searching for. Gently, reverently, she used a mostly unburnt stick to leverage a shelf off of a mostly-usable spade. It must have been hanging on the side of the house when the fire began. With determination in her eyes, she carried her spade to a lovely shady place beside the stream that crossed through their land.

Mary attempted to begin to dig, but the fabric bound around her elbows, and the skirt was blocking her view of the ground half the time. After several frustrating minutes of tight sleeves and frivolous buttoning, she carefully laid the bodice and outer skirts of her dress over an exposed oak root nearby. She began to dig, deliberately making a pile to fill the small grave back in. There wasn't much left of Berle to bury. The broken skull, most of the ribs, a femur, and assorted shards and bone pieces scattered the front of the burnt skeleton that once was the Walenty homestead.

A lone saddle blanket, dusty and sun-bleached, draped over the partially burnt fence. She covered her nose and mouth with her hand and shook the blanket out with the other. Months of exposure and drifting filth ruffled out of the blanket like a ghost disturbed from its sleep.

When Mary knelt beside her beloved, he had gathered the broken bones and small effects he could find nearby and collected them in his hat. It sat beside the rest of Berle's remains. She laid the faded saddle blanket beside Berle and reached for the nearest femur, masking her hesitation beneath her sadness. Vaclav reached out to stop her.

"No, please. He was my friend. Let me." He sniffed and wiped the end of the nose on his wrist. Mary took his hand in hers and gently touched his cheek.

"Please. He is our family. Let me help."

Together, they collected the bones of their fallen friend and folded them into the blanket before lowering it into the small grave that Mary had dug with the partially burnt spade under the shady oak by the creek that ran through the land that belonged to Berle Walenty, known by his enemies as "the Winter Viper," by his brother as "Zimo," and lastly and most importantly, as "Pa."

Chapter 16

Vaclav stood and wiped his nose again. Mary wrapped her arms around him, and he held her tightly. After a silent moment, he cleared his throat and brushed out the inside of his cap before returning it to his head and tugging down the brim, cocking it to the right. When he returned to his horse, it swung its head upward at him, irritated at his expedient dismount before. He withdrew an older, larger pistol from a saddlebag and inserted six stubby cartridges into it. He placed it into his main holster and checked his other pistol next, ensuring the six cartridges were ready for action.

"Vaclav, what are you doing?" Mary's voice was stern and concerned.

"Mary; Berle and Andras were murdered. Someone from our past came all the way here to kill him, and I'm going to make it right. Berle said in his letter that the familiar faces were seen around town, s–"

"Make it right, Vaclav? Killin' whoever did this isn't going to make it right. It's just going to replace one killer for another." Vaclav did not look at Mary. He could not look at her. He adjusted his gun belt, removed his coat, and busied himself so he didn't have to look into those eyes that could see the truth in his heart.

"I'm already a killer, Mary. For a long time now." He finally turned to look at her, and he was shocked at how small she seemed. She clutched the locket around her neck in two tiny, pale hands. Digging and a gentle wind had loosed some of those dark curls so that they tumbled across her forehead. Her shoulders were drawn up, and she looked up at him. He reached for her, offering his hand for her to take.

She stepped towards him, and bypassed his hand, pressing herself against him. Her forehead rested against his chest, and she could feel his heart behind his ribs, thrumming slowly and consistently. It was like a drum. His slow beats calmed her pounding heart. When he spoke to her, she felt his voice all around her.

"I have to do this, Mary. And I'll come back to you and marry you in the Autumn." Her forehead still pressed against his chest, she nodded. "I promise," he said finally. She felt his heartbeat quicken for a moment. She looked up into his big, brown eyes, and she took a moment to memorize them. The same eyes that had charmed her into a saddle had also melted her skeptical heart. They were the eyes of a man who had seen loss, evil, death, and defeat, and had emerged with room enough in his heart for love. He was not a sun-browned saddle tramp with twang in his voice and a swagger in his stride. He was a calloused, damaged immigrant who had fought every step of the way until he found his peace in something better than a home.

"I'll hold you to that, Vaclav Sarna." She unfastened her locket from her neck and pressed it into his palm. "Give this back when you come back to me." He closed his hand around it and lifted her chin to look down into her eyes. They kissed for a long moment, choosing to leave unsaid all their fears and doubts. This is what they would choose to remember as they parted ways for but a short while.

They rode back to town together, slowly and peacefully, enjoying the late morning warmth and awakened countryside. The birds rejoiced in the day's warmth. Soon, the leaves would change, the snow would come to block the mountain passes, and the rivers would freeze before the long nights consumed all their firewood. Today was a sweet memory of warm days fishing at the pond, of climbing trees, and stealing fruit from yards.

As the first signs of Foothill began to dot the beautiful Colorado countryside, Mary was reminded of what came next. Shortly, she would disembark on a coach and begin the arduous trek back to New York where Helen would be waiting. Poor Helen.

Vaclav was a glowing coal. He burned and radiated heat, threatening to ignite anything that might come too close. With his rifle on his back, his pistol on his hip, and his cocked hat, he did not look like a free-grazer looking to rest for the night. The coach departing East was already in front of the post office, and the funny old postmaster was yelling in piss-poor Spanish to a young man trying to secure the luggage.

Mary and Vaclav's goodbye was brief. They kissed and held each other briefly before she boarded the coach with her bag and rolled away in a cloud of dust and wooden squeaking. Vaclav returned Mary's horse to the stable and exchanged his for a strong, young horse that wouldn't be opposed to trails and hard running.

He hitched the new fidgety roan to the post in front of the saloon and paused to study the other horses hitched nearby. Many of them were laden with traveling supplies; tents, cooking implements, bedrolls, and the like. This time, when Vaclav entered the saloon, he allowed his silhouette to make the introduction all its own.

His tilted cap, the sharp lines of the rifle slung diagonally across his broad-shouldered, tapered body pronounced by the hand that rested atop the holstered pistol, an old world pistol that promised ancient conflict. He wore shorter ankle boots, unlike the high riding boots many of the frontiersmen wore. His hat was not the broad-brimmed hat of the West, designed to shield the wearer from the sun on the unforgiving trails. Vaclav's hat was old wool, bent wires, and cracked leather: a hat designed to protect the wearer from harsh, bitter cold that left its mark on one's skin like Winter's memory.

The springs in the saloon door groaned and popped when he stepped inside, and many eyes followed him to the bar. The barkeep nodded a silent hello and twisted the end of his long brown mustache that he always twisted when he was nervous. Recognizing the ceramic pitcher from last time, the shootist pointed at it, asking for a drink. The bartender poured it into a short glass tumbler and passed the glass to him. Vaclav gave a nod and turned to sip his drink and survey the room.

He knew exactly how he looked: he looked like trouble. Walking into a saloon with two loaded firearms and no silver star usually spelled it out with a capital T. He tugged the right side of his cap down and took a long sip, locking eyes with each patron as they went back to their drinks and hushed conversations.

The saloon was patronized by a dusty array of townies and cowboys making their way home before the snow. Waistcoat and watch chain gleaming, a banker guffawed at his friend's lewd joke. By the door, three men played cards, or they pretended to as they glanced over their shoulders at him and whispered. A bearded mountain man in a large furry coat sipped a mug of beer while his long rifle leaned against the wall behind him. Sitting closest to Vaclav was a man wearing a black hat with a brown vest and hair that poked out like it had not been cut in a long time.

"Somebody," Vaclav began loudly, almost yelling, his voice filling the room. The man with his back turned started nervously. "Killed my brother…and killed a little boy as well. The same men responsible for killing that little boy also gunned-down the sheriff." Vaclav scanned the room for reactions. Some stared at him intently, while others avoided eye contact completely, trying to mind their business. "I aim to find them. And kill 'em if need be. I know they been drinking in here since they murdered my brother and his boy. Anyone willing to tell me what they know will be safe from the hell I'm bringing." Eyes glanced around the room. Mostly, they looked at the door and down at their drinks. "Proszę. Był moim bratem…" Vaclav said the last words quieter, imploring anyone who would understand, *"Please. He was my brother…"*

To his right, a woman cleared her throat, prompting Vaclav to turn. She wore a dress that was too small that accentuated all of a man's favorite attributes. She had the appearance of one of the saloon's in-house entertainment. When she wasn't serving drinks, she was flirting the gold out of miners' pockets, and swindling the bills out of bankers' folds. Her knuckles were scarred, and her nails were long. Although her green eyes and pinned-up auburn hair flashed with bold promiscuity, the gnarled scar that stretched from the corner of her mouth to her jaw hinted at a woman who understood the way of the world.

She patted the seat besides hers and waited. Vaclav approached the woman and put his repeater on the bar in front of him. From this close, he could see the pulled skin where stitches had held her flesh together until it healed on its own, and the scars remained to tell the story. She looked him over once, appraisingly, and then the charming crooked smile returned.

"Stay awhile, handsome. It's rude to wear your hat indoors, ain't you heard?" Playfully, she bumped the brim of his cap with a ringed finger. Vaclav removed his hat and stuffed it in his pocket.

"I'm not looking for company for the night."

"Neither am I. You said you were looking for those boys that shot that rancher and ol' Leonard?"

"Is that the name of the sheriff they shot?" She nodded once slowly, and then swiped his glass and stole the last of his drink in a fluid, practiced movement. She wiped her mouth and set the glass down, bottom up, with a loud clack. Vaclav appraised her now, trying to derive a clue as to whether or not to trust her.

"Why would you tell me that? What do you gain?" he narrowed his eyes as he asked, studying her. She turned and ran a long fingernail along the jagged smile of a scar she had.

"Equity. Eye for an eye. Just like God intended," she cooed coldly. Vaclav nodded slowly in understanding. "My respects to your brother. I didn't know him well, but he seemed kind. He seemed a good father to the kid." She glanced down at the glass that she fiddled with nervously, and she stopped herself.

"Thank you. And my respects to your face. Nobody deserves…that. Now, please, what can you tell me about the murders?" He scooted closer to her as he quieted his voice. He could smell the tequila from her like a perfume. Clearly, his was not her first drink of the day.

"Lil' Henry Rhodes and his band of saddle-tramps are the ones you're looking for. They come through Foothill a'couple times a year, always pushing whatever livestock they can wrangle. Rumor has it, Henry has a rich daddy up North with all kinds of gold and oil, and when he goes the way of syphilis, guess who gets the keys to the kingdom." She raised her eyebrows at him and then winked one of her bloodshot emerald eyes.

"Lil' Hank always hangs around with that Mexican feller, Martin or some'ot. Then there's the greasy one who got his hat size adjusted a few days back. You needn't worry about 'im anymore. Then there's the old one, Ben Sanderson. He grew up in these parts and knew Big Hank back when he was just regular-sized Hank." She tallied the members of Rhodes's gang on her fingers when the name Benjamin triggered a memory of a drink shared in a train station. The man he had met was called Benjamin, was older than he was, panicked at the mention of Foothill, and paid with the Russian silver.

"*Mudak*," Vaclav cursed to himself. He punched his thigh hard enough to make himself flinch and rub his leg. "I just saw Benjamin at the train station in Ogden. He told me he was heading out West to California. Fuck, I should have followed him when he left!" Vaclav seethed at himself, nearly steaming. The saloon worker shushed him as he escalated and pulled him back to his seat.

"There's more, and if you don't keep your head, you won't keep your head, reckon?" He nodded and relaxed, glancing around the room quickly. "You're gonna have your chance real soon, okay, so just listen. There's also a new young kid who's always following one of the older ones around like a thirsty kitten, 'Stoney' I hear 'em call 'im. The other new guy is a giant bear of a man what came down from the mountain and damn near talks as much as a tree." Her eyes followed someone over his shoulder.

"What's his name?" Vaclav asked, beginning to notice her gaze. She slowly grabbed the glass off the bar and leaned over to place it safely behind the bar.

"His name is Barnabus Rowe, he wears a big fur coat, carries an old rifle, has had seven whiskies in the past hour, and he's walking out of the bar right now." She nodded at the giant wall of fur that teetered towards the swinging saloon doors. Vaclav returned his hat to his head and tugged the front-right corner down mechanically. He slung his rifle over his shoulder and slapped the Russian coin on the bar.

"Is there any standing law in this city as of today?" he asked, standing from his seat. Without turning to watch him walk away, she replied, "No, there is not."

Vaclav walked quickly and caught up to him in a few long strides. Rowe was not hurrying anywhere, and he seemed to impede the foot traffic of the passersby on the sidewalk around him. He hiccuped comically, and his coonskin hat went crooked. Vaclav followed him from ten paces behind and kept a hand on his pistol. He wouldn't shoot a man in the back, especially not surrounded by innocent folk. After walking nearly the length of the street, Rowe made a steeply banking left turn off the planked walkway and into the soft, dark street. Vaclav made the same left and walked parallel to his path.

"Barnabus Rowe!" Vaclav called out, his hand hovering over his pistol. The hairy man seemed to pause mid-step and turn to look at the stranger who had shouted his name from behind. When their eyes met, Rowe's eyes narrowed, and his mouth hung open, clearly confused. His hand fumbled to his hip like a freshly caught trout, and his pistol lifted from its holster, fired wildly somewhere into the ground in a great crack of thunder, and tumbled through the air, landing behind Rowe in the mud. He swung his arms wildly to catch the wayward weapon, and tumbled to the ground in a great crash of fur and flesh.

Children crossing the street disappeared down alleys, and one wise dog ducked into a barely-open doorway where someone peeked to see. He laid still. A single leg seemed to flop and struggle to gain traction before just giving up. Vaclav sniffed and drew a cigarette and match from his pouch, struck the match on his thumbnail, and inhaled a long drag. A crowd had gathered on the sidewalks, careful to stay out of the line-of-fire. "Is it the same gang?" "I can't believe there's another one." "Why isn't there a new sheriff yet? Can't the deputies do anything?" Vaclav walked slowly towards the supine man, casually, nonchalantly, exhaling a breath of smoke from his nostrils as he brushed the initial flaky ash from his cigarette.

Andras slowed his breathing as he closed his eyes, crouching on the slanted roof of the cafe. In his hands, he held the pistol that belonged to Asher Milan, now his pistol. His forefinger rested along the side of the trigger guard, and the hammer rested half-cocked.

While in the storeroom completing his final counts for the day, Andras heard a gunshot just outside in the street and the pounding of people hurrying on the boardwalk outside. He sat frozen for a moment, listening. Then, he bolted to action.

The gunbelt he had punched extra holes into fit him perfectly now. The leather loop he added kept the pistol from falling out while he climbed and ran. Behind the cafe was a stack of crates exactly like the one behind Mr. Christianson's shop that Andras had scrambled up just as deftly as he had this one. Now, concealed behind the slant of the roof, he waited and listened before finally creeping up to the edge to take a look.

In the street, Barnabus Rowe lay in the mud, seemingly unconscious. Approaching slowly and coolly was a stranger who looked as if he had come from the Northeast. He smoked a cigarette as he neared, seemingly unbothered by the murderer lying in the street. Was it already over? Did this stranger just shoot Rowe in the back? Maybe the marshal had arrived and was cleaning house.

He rounded the hairy man, careful to keep his distance. Even from where he hid, Andras heard a loud snorting snore from Rowe. "Jesus Christ," he heard the man say. Finally drawing his pistol, the stranger kicked him hard in the back, and Rowe shouted in pained surprise. From beneath the folds of his coat, Barnabus swung the pistol up toward where his attacker stood above him, but the stranger was ready for his ruse. Catching the swinging pistol with his free hand, he twisted it, jerking Barnabus's fingers into unnatural shapes. The pistol fired again, this time over the cafe, fragmenting with a wild sound. Andras ducked and drew his pistol to his chest, so he could aim over the roof.

The stranger did not relent of Rowe's mangled hand, and ripped the pistol free from its twisted members. Rowe shouted again, agony and hatred, and lunged up toward his assailant with a broad hunting knife.

The stranger took a quick step back on his left foot and, Rowe's stab arched into a slice that landed harmlessly in the mud. The same left foot slammed down on the blade of the knife, pinning it to the ground. Before Rowe could withdraw his hand, his face was splattered onto the muddy street in a smoky flash of explosive gunfire.

Barnabus's limp corpse flopped back down and didn't move. The stranger let his pistol swing forward on his finger into a forward roll, then he flipped it backwards, hooking the sight on the inside of his holster and letting the pistol follow it inside. When he turned away from the faceless corpse, Andras spied the flash of a scar on his face, and the distinct heroic jawline of his Uncle Vaclav.

"Stryjek!" Andras yelled, standing from his hiding place. "*Uncle!*" Vaclav's eyes snapped immediately to the young boy on the roof who had gotten the drop on him, and his voice cracked emotionally as he called back in their Mother-tongue.

"Moj bratanek! *The son of my brother! My nephew!*" he cried and ran towards the cafe. Andras flew down the slanted roof, barely touched the crates, and was swept off of his feet by the strong arms of his Uncle Vaclav. Andras clung to his uncle's shirt desperately, and he finally let out a wail that was the sound of all his accumulated, unspoken hurt that had been suppressed for two months.

His throat ached, and his vision blurred as he wept out the poisonous grief for his murdered father, the robbed moments with his mother, the home he would never create memories of Christmas within.

Vaclav cradled Andras's head and held him to his chest as every last bit of strength melted out of him. Andras wept so bitterly and so loudly that he did not know where he was when he stopped crying.

When Vaclav set him down on a small stool, Andras's eyes were sore, and his voice was hoarse. His chest quivered with involuntary sobs as he settled. His hands were hard to open from how hard he was gripping Vaclav's shirt and coat.

"Pozwól mi spojrzeć na ty," Vaclav said, brushing hair from his forehead, *"Let me take a look at you."* Andras felt fatigued and empty, like he had cried out every last drop of moisture in his body. Andras reached out with a limp hand and loosely pinched his uncle's cheek like a sleepy grandmother. He nodded and patted Vaclav's cheek.

"Musiałem się upewnić, że nie śpię. *I had to make sure I was awake.*"

"What do you mean?" Vaclav asked Andras. Tossed onto the bed was Andras's pistol, still half-cocked. Andras stood from the short stool by the hotel's vanity and walked to where the pistol lay. Using both hands, he holstered it clumsily. Vaclav watched, amazed at how a child so small and so young could have survived so much. He could not conceive it. Andras crossed back to the small stool and sat. His feet barely touched the ground. Vaclav studied him over, his eyes glinting with repressed tears.

"I dreamed a lot that you came and took me home with you. And every time I tried to reach out and touch you to see if it was real, I woke up. But not this time."

"Not this time, Andras. I'm really here. And I'm not going to leave you, okay? Your pa was my brother, and that makes you my family. We stick together, yeah?" Andras nodded. Vaclav opened his mouth to speak, but then paused, listening. Andras listened too: the sound of multiple people hurrying up the stairs made his skin prickle and hair stand on end.

"Pod łóżkiem," Vaclav hissed, and he stood, taking his place behind the door. Andras slid to the floor, but did not crawl under the bed. Instead, he concealed himself along the side of the bed, staying low against the floor. He kept his hand on the handle of his pistol. The boots stopped outside the door noisily. Andras held his breath. Vaclav held his pistol in one hand, and the doorknob in the other.

As soon as the knob jiggled, Vaclav yanked the door open and grabbed the wrist of the person holding it. He yanked hard and twisted the arm, causing the arm's owner to twist and roll into the room, his feet crashing into the bedside table with a pathetic mewl. As the second body charged into the room, Vaclav grabbed the collar of the man in black and yanked him backwards into a tight one-armed chokehold. The other arm held a pistol to his head. Laying on the floor, Andras pointed his gun at the first man who was slowly getting off the floor. He groaned, and two unfocused eyes noticed Andras.

"Pete?"

"Andi?"

"Pete kto?"

"Cafe-Pete!"

"Who?"

"Andras?"

"Paul *and* Pete!"

"Znasz ich?"

"Tak! Są dobrymi przyjaciółmi!" Andras shouted at Vaclav, holstering his pistol and shielding Pete, who had surrendered on the floor to Vaclav, who was holding Paul and pointing a gun at the prone Pete. Vaclav released Paul and spun him around. It was only then he noticed the reverend's collar. Vaclav's eyes widened with horror. He crossed himself quickly and took Paul's hand as if to kiss it. Before his lips reached the ringless hand of the reverend Becker, he relented.

"You're not Catholic."

"Sorry, no. Anabaptist." Paul withdrew his hand hesitantly from Vaclav's.

"It is I who should be sorry," Vaclav confessed apologetically. He extended a hand and helped Pete off the ground. Pete rotated his shoulder painfully and cringed as he tested his arm. "I hope I didn't hurt you. I wasn't expecting anyone else, and things were a little hot out there," Vaclav explained. Pete waved his good arm dismissively.

"Think nothing of it. I was just…surprised, that's all," Pete Becker explained. He turned to his brother. "Did you hear that? He wasn't expecting us." Paul straightened his collar and bent to pat Andras on the shoulder reassuringly.

"You're right, Peter. You really got the drop on him," Paul agreed sarcastically. Vaclav closed the door behind Pete and turned to address the room. It was only then they all realized how small the room was.

Pete closed the cafe after the day's latest killing and threatened to possibly reopen for dinner. Inside, Paul, Vaclav, and Andras sat at a table. Pete brought four glasses and a bottle to the table before he recounted and put one back. The three adults all took a long, noisy swig of their golden drink, and Andras waited while the three of them recovered. Andras began.

"Paul, Pete: this is my Uncle Vaclav. He fought in the war beside my pa back in Poland." He turned to Vaclav. "This is Peter and Paul Becker. They took me in after Pa died, and I had nowhere to go. They helped me to read better and count, and they taught me how to work in a kitchen and a church." Paul leaned over and squeezed Andras's shoulder warmly.

"Honestly, my brother and I don't know anything about caring for children. Our ma didn't survive birthing us, and Pa's getting too old for hard work. Andras is a fine young man, and it's been a real pleasure getting to know him." Andras smiled from the kindness of Paul's words and beamed at Uncle Vaclav. His face felt sore and strange like he had not used those muscles in a long time.

"I can never repay the kindness you have dealt to me and Berle's memory. I thought Andras dead and burned, but finding him here, alive and under the care of two upstanding gentlemen, I can hardly believe it myself. If there's anything I can do for either of you, please, just ask. I won't be in town for much longer, but while I'm here–"

"What do you mean?" Andras interrupted. The other three all turned to look at him. "What do you mean you won't be in town much longer?" Where are you going?" Vaclav squeezed Andras's shoulder like Paul had.

"Not just me. *We*. We're going back East together, back to New York. We'll live together with Mary and Helen. There's a schoolhouse nearby, a cafe just down the road, and we live close to other Polish folk, if you remember."

"You want to leave?" Andras asked him, confused.

"You want to stay?" Vaclav responded incredulously. Pete and Paul looked on, sipping their drinks as the two spoke.

"There's still four more! And Hush is still out there. We can't leave yet! It's not fair!"

"Andras, they will kill both of us if we stay. I just gunned one of them down in the street in broad daylight. I didn't come here to fight a war. I came here to bring you home."

"Będę chronić mój nowy dom! *I will protect my new home!*" Andras stood from his seat boldly, raising his voice slightly at his uncle. Vaclav leaned back in his chair and thought hard. Andras took a calming breath before he continued. "I need you to listen to me, not as a child, but as a person asking the only family he has left in the whole world to help me make it right. Those men murdered my Pa–your brother!–while he knelt on the ground and begged. They held me while they did it, too. Then, after he was dead, they set me loose and shot me too, right through my leg! They burned our house, stole Pa's guns, and shot our horse. And I don't know if Piotyr is alive or not."

At the mention of Pa's guns, Vaclav glanced over at the Whitworth forty-five that he took off of Barnabus Rowe's faceless corpse. He had leaned it against the table when he sat down. The rifle seemed to present itself as an argument in Andras's appeal. Vaclav exhaled loudly and ran his hands down his face, exasperated. He tipped back in his chair and thought for a long while. He rocked on two chairs legs and looked at Andras, then at the rifle, then at the Beckers, and then back at Andras.

"Fine. We kill Rhodes and Hush. But listen, Andras: we're going to do this my way. You're going to follow my lead."

"What if the others get in the way, too?" Andras asked hopefully.

"Then, we'll remove them as obstacles." Vaclav's voice was steel that made Paul's skin crawl. "Does anyone know where Hush and Rhodes might be?" Vaclav turned his attention to Pete and Paul. Pete spoke up first.

"Nobody has seen neither hide nor hair of that creepy fuck since Berle's death, but Rhodes was here in town a few days ago. Either he's still here nearby, or he just recently left. I imagine, once he hears that Rowe is dead, he and the rest of his boys will skip town and run home to Big Hank."

"Then we'll have to get to them first. If we miss our chance, we'll be waiting until next spring with the snows coming." Vaclav explained to Pete and Andras. Paul nodded gravely.

"What about the marshal? He should be here any day yet. What do we tell him?"

"The truth. Tell him Rhodes and others murdered Berle and the sheriff, and a few folks are going after them. If we could get their faces posted from here to San Francisco, that could slow them down, if they're avoiding towns." Vaclav's knowledge of tracking convoys and troop movement was beginning to stir again after years of disuse. Andras noticed the scar again on his face that caused one eye to squint ever so slightly more than the other.

"Or it could cause them to rush home from fear," Pete countered. Vaclav nodded in reasonable agreement.

"Either way, we need to make tracks soon, if we're going to follow them. They might have already left." Vaclav stood from the table and slung his rifle over his shoulder. He paused and looked down at Berle's rifle leaning against the table. Andras approached from beside Vaclav and took his wrist.

"Pa would want you to bring it," he said, and put the barrel of the heavy rifle into his hand. Vaclav lowered his rifle and handed it to Pete.

"Hold onto this for me? It's been through a lot," Vaclav asked. Pete nodded and hefted the weapon as Vaclav lifted the rifle of Zimowa Zmija, squeezing it against his shoulder, and then checking the scope. Pete looked Vaclav's rifle up-and-down and noticed the repaired woodworking in the rifle's body near where the shooter's cheek would rest.

"What happened here?" Pete asked, hoping for a good story. Vaclav smirked as he recalled the tale of his most harrowing near-death encounter with a Serbian sniper. Before Vaclav could begin the account he had relayed so many times, Andras was gripped by a sudden realization of a gap in Vaclav's knowledge. Andras's hand shot out and gripped Vaclav's sleeve, yanking him close.

"Boże mój! Uncle Vaclav! It's Hush! It's him! This whole time!" Andras's frantic appeal was falling upon confused ears. Vaclav knelt in front of Andras and took him by the shoulders.

"Andras, deep breaths. Start from the beginning." Vaclav modeled a slow, relaxed breath. He took a moment, nodded, and then finally blurted out,

"Hush is the Serbian demon! He came all the way here just to kill Pa! We always thought he was dead, but he wasn't! He's still alive, and he killed Pa!" Andras could feel the hot tears building in his chest, and he fought them down. Vaclav stared through him, and his hand drifted to the scar on his face.

Vaclav remembered that Winter well. It had almost been a year since the rebellion had begun, and the Russians had all but captured and quelled the resistance, but you would never know it seeing the rebels in action.

Like usual, both he and Berle had set out to make trouble for the Russians. While they sat on a hillside and waited for a passing convoy, they were ambushed, and Vaclav almost lost his head. For a moment, he thought he did. An impact like a falling boulder slammed into his rifle and breached the chamber, rendering it useless. The powder from his own shot had ignited and burned a mean scorch across his left eye.

By the time he knew what had happened, Berle was yanking him to his feet and running. He saw Berle's mouth moving, knew he was shouting, "uruchomić! Zajmę się tym! *Run! I got this,*" but he only heard the rushing of his own blood in his ears and a high ringing. Disoriented, Vaclav half ran, half stumbled through the snowy woods, bouncing off of trees and icy boulders like a twig careening down a shallow, fast-moving stream. He ran for what felt like miles, and when he finally stopped to breathe, he did not see Berle behind him.

The ringing in his ears had subsided mostly now, and he could only hear his heavy breaths and the twittering of some nearby birds. His rifle was fucked. Turning it over in his hands, he shook his head. He fingered the missing chunk of wood and twisted metal sadly before he slung it across his back. He drew the pistol from his hip and glanced out from behind the boulder he crouched behind. Still, no one was coming. Berle was still back there, and Vaclav wasn't going to leave him behind. He shoved off the boulder and moved low and quickly, weaving between the trees, following his path in the snow. Knowing the other sniper was still out there, still hunting, Vaclav knew he needed to be cautious.

He saw no sign of Berle besides messy, scattered prints when he was right behind as they retreated, and then his tracks split off to the right. He cursed to himself under his breath and knew he couldn't just follow Berle's tracks to where he was because that would not only ruin Berle's hiding place, burt there was a good chance the enemy sniper would see him coming and put one in his chest. Vaclav forged a new path through the snow, hoping to curve around and flank their attacker.

It was hours of silent, slow walking, pausing, listening, watching, laying down, standing up, and then moving again. The sun had nearly completed its journey for the day before Vaclav spied his first signs of movement. Among the trees, far ahead, a lone gray wolf sniffed the snow for tunneling rodents and nesting birds, its ribs sharply pronounced beneath its filthy fur. The wolf made no noise as it moved until it caught a whiff of Vaclav's scent. The wolf lifted its head and stared right at him, its yellow eyes meeting his. Through the lens of the scope of his useless rifle, he watched the wolf drop its head and lope towards him in a wide arch. The wolf stopped, sniffed the air, and then released a ghostly wail of a howl into the darkening sky that faded into a yelping as the wolf began to jog. Not far away, Vaclav heard the responses of its fellows. He cursed again, and altered his course, trying to avoid the pack. One sniper against a whole pack of wolves? No, thank you. He only had five shots in his pistol, and he wanted to save one for the bastard who shot his gun.

Behind him, he again heard the howls, and he swore he saw movement to his right, running parallel with him. His heart pounded as his mind raced, knowing he was being hunted not only by a pack of hungry winter wolves, but also by a rifleman somewhere in these woods. Again, he cursed and looked up at the tree he had stopped to lean against. He holstered his pistol, tucked the flap, and began to climb. His knife clunked against the tree each time he reached higher, making a metallic scraping. He stopped climbing and hugged the thin pine to rest a moment. He must have been at least twelve feet up when he saw his starving gray pursuer appear at the base of the tree, sniffing. The wolf looked up and let out a frustrated whine and a yelp that prompted a second wolf, lithe and black, to circle the base of the tree as well. Vaclav smirked and let loose a glob of phlegmy spit down onto the gray wolf.

"Ha," he whispered to the frustrated wolves, "nie będę dzisiaj wilczym gównem." Just then, the gray wolf rested its forepaws on the trunk and tried to jump. Vaclav's smile disappeared. Using his right hand, he jiggled the handle of his knife, trying to break loose the frost.

When he finally drew it, he roared and brandished the blade, swinging it threateningly at the predators. The wolves seemed unperturbed. Vaclav wondered what Zimo would say when he found him like this. He would probably make a coat from the pelts to remind Vaclav everyday how he got treed by a couple hungry pups. From deeper in the woods, another ghostly wail caused the wolves' ears to swivel, and they loped away, panting and huffing great clouds of steam.

"Zgadza się, uciekaj." Vaclav muttered as he carefully climbed down the tree. When he reached the ground with knife-in-hand, he drew his pistol and began to jog in the direction opposite of the wolves. Behind him, the trees moaned the echoes of a human shriek so animalistic and agonized, his whole body erupted with goosebumps. Then, there was a second scream, longer and drawn out, that ended with a sharp crack of gunfire. When the echoes of the gunshot faded to the hills, it was replaced by the responding howls of the arriving pack. They had found something to share.

It wasn't until later that Vaclav learned that the unfortunate victim was none other than the Serbian sniper who had been hunting them. When the wolves attacked, Berle put a bullet in his chest as an act of mercy. Thinking back on that day, he often wondered if he inadvertently shepherded the hungry wolves to the Serbian demon's location, but he thrust it from his mind.

Now, however, he couldn't avoid thinking about it. Knowing that Hush, the man who mercilessly murdered Berle Walenty, was the same man that Berle Walenty put down all those years ago made him want to finish the job all over again. He'd make sure he was all-the-way dead this time.

"How do you know that?" Vaclav asked the manic Andras.

"He said it. He told Pa when he killed him. He wears a coat made from the pelt of the wolf he found dead on top of him. He had a big scar on his face and his neck from where the wolves gnawed on him, and his hands are so fast, Uncle Vaclav. Do you think you can kill him?"

"Of course I can, just as easily as he could kill me. Surviving the wolves doesn't mean anything. He's still only a man. You put a bullet in him, and he'll die just like anyone else." Andras nodded.

"Then it's settled," Paul began, "the two of you will bring Henry Rhodes Jr. and the Serbian shootist to justice, and then you'll take Andras back home to New York to live with you and Mary." He looked at Pete, Vaclav, and lastly at Andras. Paul knelt before Andras and removed a chain from around his neck that held a silver cross pendant. He handed it to Andras.

"I want you to keep this. It was my grandmother's, and it's always protected me and brought me luck. God go with you, Andras." Andras looked at the cross pendant for a moment and then held it out for Paul to take back.

"I don't think God would like what we're off to go do. And besides, if we're trespassing on God's country, maybe I'll see him there." Paul pushed Andras's hand back towards him again.

"Then keep it as a gift, so you don't forget about us." Andras could agree to that. He surged forward and hugged Paul, who hugged him back warmly. Saying goodbye to Pete was more difficult than saying goodbye to Paul because Pete was crying. Pete made Vaclav promise to keep Andras safe, and that they must come say goodbye before leaving back East. Of course, Vaclav agreed and shook his hand warmly. In exchange, Vaclav made Pete promise to keep his rifle safe, and that he would absolutely be back to get it.

There was no final evening of laughs and relaxation before they headed out. Vaclav lifted Andras onto the horse and then mounted up behind him on the saddle. He spurred the roan mount, and it leapt forward. He turned its head north, and spurred again. This time, the horse nickered and surged forward, leaving flying bits of mud and gravel flying behind them. With his uncle behind him, his gun on his hip, and his hat on his head, Andras set out to catch Rhodes before he escaped to the security of his father's oil fields.

Chapter 17

When he was six years old, Henry Rhodes Jr. met his father. It was a bleak affair. His mother had dressed him in his Sunday finest and laced his shoes and made him wear a kerchief around his neck. It itched terribly, and he hated the way his pants felt.

When they were let into the tall, fancy office with the big window, Henry remembered feeling excited, nervous, and terribly afraid. His entire life, his mother had told him of his powerful and wealthy father who was always away on work and would return someday to be a proper family. As he grew older, he wondered if his mother actually believed it when she had told him that.

Sitting at the long desk covered in papers and bags of coins, ledgers and stacks of paper, topographical maps and a jar containing a rattlesnake preserved in some golden liquid. The office was silent save for the silent scratching of the fountain pen on the desk. They had driven two days to arrive at this remote nowhere, dotted with small cabins and workers building a town. In a few short years, this oil field would become a massive metropolis with millions of dollars flowing through it, until the oil ran out.

But today, it was a place of reunions and introductions. His mother took his small hand and led him into the room, stopping several steps in front of the desk. His mother cleared her soft voice and spoke.

"Hen–" a lone extended forefinger stopped her mid-syllable. He finished the line he was writing, set the pen down, and then finally looked up from his desk. There was no passionate reunion of once-estranged lovers, no hug full of silent longing, no prolonged glances brimming with unspoken endearment. He looked at her like he would a client or one of his employees.

"Please forgive me. It's been very busy. Can I help you?" he spoke as he would to a stranger, not the mother of his son.

"Mr. Rhodes, like I mentioned in my letters, this," she pushed him forward lightly, "is your son. He's six years old, very smart and very strong." His father finally spared him a look and stood from his desk. Big Hank was worthy of his namesake. He towered over his son and was a full head and shoulders taller than his mother. He buttoned his coat and rounded the desk to survey him as he would a mare. Henry smiled up at his father, but looked to the ground when the smile was not reciprocated.

"Do you read and write?" Big Hank asked him. His voice was a rumble like thunder or a falling boulder. Again, his mother spoke up.

"Yes, he can. Both. He's bee–" Big Hank held up a lazy hand again to silence her, and she immediately fell silent.

"Do you read and write?" he asked again. Hank Jr. nodded at the floor silently. Big Hank snapped thick sausage-fingers in front of his face. He noticed his mother flinch in the corner of his eye. "Speak up, boy. Look a man in his eye when you talk to him. Show him you're not afraid." He met his father's gaze and held it.

"Yes."

"Yes, what? Speak clearly, boy!"

"Yes, sir, I read and write very well." For the first time, he felt as if his long-estranged father saw him. Big Hank nodded slowly and pointed to the desk.

"Take that pen and write your name on a paper there. Show me." Henry Jr. began toward the desk, looking over his shoulder at his mother. He didn't know that would be the last time he would see her. He rounded the desk and picked up the shiny, expensive pen with the wood handle and nickel lever. As he held the pen, his hands trembled, but he wrote all the same. It wasn't his finest penmanship, but he was proud of what he had done. *Henry Earnest Rhodes Jr.* read the paper before him. Big Hank approached from behind and inspected the writing over his shoulder.

"We will practice more." He took the paper and crumpled it before tossing it in the fireplace to one side of the large office. "How much?" he finally said. Henry Jr. looked at his father, confused to see he was addressing his mother.

"I beg your pardon?" she replied.

"How much for the boy? I suspect you didn't come all this way just to introduce us." She stared at him, her eyes darting between the two Henrys.

"I just thought that maybe…" she began and then trailed off to silence.

"You thought, what? That you would come in here, and I would give you a ring and all the money you need for opium? How much for the boy?" Big Hank pulled a billfold out of his desk drawer and opened it.

"Fifty dollars," she blurted, seeing the billfold. He removed the bill, and she took it from his waiting hand. Without so much as a longing glance, his mother turned with her treasure and left with only the sound of echoing footsteps to mark her exit. Henry moved to follow her, but two large hands rested on his shoulders.

"Do not chase after her, boy. She traded you for opium." Big Hank turned him around and knelt on the ground, so his son would listen. "Do you know how to determine something's worth, son?"

"By its weight, sir?" Henry Jr. answered hesitantly.

"Incorrect. The best way to determine something's value is to sell it. A vein may yield carts of gold, but if there's no one to trade with, then it's just a pile of shiny rocks. How do you determine something's value? By whatever someone is willing to pay for it. Gold is valuable because people would kill for it, not because of any inherent value." Henry Jr. tried to understand, so he nodded in acknowledgement. "Right now, you are worth fifty dollars to me. That is not an investment. Do you understand me? Perhaps it was that opium-whore's poor haggling skills, but you are currently the lowest value asset I own. I need you to prove to me that you are worth more, do you understand?" Henry Jr. nodded again.

"Yes, sir."

"Good. Now get out. Go become worth something."

Hank Rhodes opened his eyes to the first glowing of the rising sun. Dark purple clouds skated slowly past each other, casting shadows that streamed with the glory of morning. The craggy boulder surroundings were only shadowy shapes, still chilled with the night's persistence.

This was the closest he'd been to home in nearly a decade. No wonder his dreams were so full of him, back when he was more than a fat, crazy, old man. There was a time when Hank looked up to his father for his unyielding tenacity and brutal business tactics. But then he learned that everything was business to Big Hank. Nothing valuable was meant to be kept. Value was attributed through transactions. So, when Hank Jr. was fourteen, he withdrew himself from his father's treasury, and vowed to return for the reading of the will, of which he was the main beneficiary due to his father's advanced mental decay. He never thought he would be returning while his father was living, especially to seek asylum.

Rhodes rubbed his eye and flicked away the crust that had formed at the corner. He scratched his hair and yawned, sitting up from his saddle headrest. Beside him, the night's fire had burned down to smoldering coals. Adding a small pile of twigs and dried grass, he bent with his head low to the ground and blew air across the coals. After a moment, the fire was revived. He tossed more kindling into the growing fire as it popped and hissed away the moisture inside the plants. Martin stirred next, turning over beneath his blanket. Hank tossed a pebble that landed on Martin's blanket so that he uncovered his head and looked around.

"Que? Es hora irse? *What? Time to go?*" Hank shook his head.

"Nah, not yet. We still have some time. Let Stoney sleep. He's been a mess since he heard about Rowe." Martin nodded in agreement and reached upward in a long stretch. He knocked his boots empty before he pulled them on and scratched his belly in a deep yawn. Hank unwrapped some bacon from his saddle and shared a turnip with his horse, who had wandered over at the sound of voices.

Jackson woke up quietly. He listened to the other two talk quietly over breakfast, discussing the plans for the day.

"If we push north all day, we should cross into Dakota territory by sunset. By then, no marshal is going to cross county lines. At least not to chase down the likes of us."

"Why don't we keep going north?" Martin indicated on the map. "It's a little extra time in the saddle, but at least we don't have to see your father."

"Because I don't want to run forever. I need this to be over with." Hank hissed.

"Over with what?" Jackson finally spoke up. Both turned to look at him. He repeated his question. "You need what to be over with?"

"Running. I'm tired of running. And that stranger in town who murdered Rowe, who knows if he's on our trail?" Hank explained, annoyed.

"Yeah, who was that? A bounty hunter?"

"I'd be inclined to believe it, if I knew there was a bounty out for us, but there ain't, see? Dammit, Stoney, use your brain," Hank barked at the nineteen-year-old. "Whoever he was, he weren't local."

"Did you get a look at him?" Stoney asked Martin.

"No, pero he did make a point to take Rowe's rifle. Do you think he knew the dead rancher?" Martin poured some coffee into his mug.

"Goddammit, that fucking rancher. We never should have partnered with that Serbian bastard. He was bad through-and-through, and look now! Where is he? Is *he* running?" Hank threw a stick he was fiddling with into the distance angrily.

"He didn't kill the sheriff," Stoney interjected quietly as he sipped his own coffee. Hank spun on his heel, his face contorted with anger and violence.

"God-fucking-dammit, Stoney, shut your gawdammed hole! If you want to run home to Illinois, then go! Nobody is keeping you here!" and he waved a dismissive hand in his direction. "I never should have brought you along to begin with. You're no–"

"No killer? You're goddamned right–"

"I was gonna say you're no cowboy! You're just a boy who learned to ride and thought he was ready for this."

"'Ready for this?' I was ready to push two-hundred head west and then go home! What are we doing out here? We're outlaws!" Jackson's voice continued to rise. Martin stood to add his two bits.

"Stoney, nobody could have guessed things would unfold the way they did." Jackson tossed his coffee in the fire and stowed his cup in his saddle bag.

"That's for damn sure. Have you guys…killed people before?" Martin and Henry exchanged glances.

"No. Never." Martin shook his head also. Stoney continued to pack up his effects and load up his horse.

"I've been doing a lot of thinking, and I'm not going North with y'all. Benjamin made me an offer to come be a ranch hand on his property out in California, so I'm going to ride out that way. I have no reason to run, alright? I didn't shoot that rancher or the kid! And I sure as hell did not shoot the sheriff." He lifted his saddle onto his horse's back and cinched it tightly underneath.

"If you leave, there's nothing I can do to help you, you understand? Sanderson too, you tell him that!" Rhodes pointed at him aggressively, a bead of sweat rolling down his temple in the chill morning.

"Good luck, Martin. Rhodes." He tipped his hat and set off on a leisurely trot with the sun to his back. Martin and Rhodes watched

Stoney leave for several seconds before they returned to their campfire and their plans.

"One of them is leaving westward. Can't know for sure, but I think it's the youngest one, John Jackson."

"They're splitting up? What do we–should we follow him?"

"Let's just wait and see what Rhodes and, um…uh the Mexican, Martin, do. Rhodes is our target afterall."

"Can you hit him from here?"

"Not even in my dreams. I can barely see him through the scope, much less, shoot him."

"Could Pa have shot him from here?" Vaclav smiled in the corner of his mouth and glanced at Andras for a moment. Andras was looking through an old brass telescope, his face scrunched in concentration.

"Maybe. If the wind was right. And he didn't eat too much for breakfast." Vaclav suppressed a chuckle and continued to watch through the scope. Andras propped himself up with his elbows and studied Vaclav, trying to discern if he was kidding.

From down below, the remaining two riders set off northward. "That's right, gówniarz, run home to daddy," Vaclav whispered. Beside him, Andras gasped quietly.

"Pa would've given you such a smack if he heard you just now."

"Oh, are you fixin' to tattle on me?"

"I might. Seeing as we're hunting down dangerous outlaws in the wilds of America, we might see him soon." Andras chuckled at his own joke alongside his uncle. Vaclav nodded to the right and nudged Andras.

"You're too young to joke like that. C'mon. Let's talk. Stay low." The pair crawled backwards several yards before standing to walk back to their horse.

"Let's go! We can catch them!" Andras struggled to get his foot in the high stirrup and ultimately failed when his uncle smacked the stirrup away from his boot. "Hey!" He laughed at his uncle's prank, but Vaclav wasn't laughing. He had on his thinking-face, and his forehead was all bunched-up.

"We can't catch up to them before they're home free, or they spot us and start shootin'."

"What are you saying?" Andras's voice got low and cautious. Vaclav held out his hands placatingly.

"I'm saying we aren't going to catch Rhodes by chasing him down on horseback in open country. There's two of us plus both our packs on *one* horse. They'll beat us in a chase." Andras looked at their already heavily-laden horse, and he nodded in consensus. "What I'm saying is we go West and follow Jackson a ways and see if we can figure out another way to lure Rhodes back out of hiding." Vaclav crossed his arms and waited expectantly. "Well? What do you think, partner?" It was both their decision. As much as he desperately wanted to end

Rhodes, Vaclav's tactical expertise was not to be taken lightly. Andras conceded.

"You're right. Let's go west." It wasn't only the sound logic that so easily convinced Andras, but the alluring idea of being able to kill one more of the men who murdered Pa. "Can I take the reins for a while?" Andras delivered his closest approximation of what he would deem a "cheeky smile", but, to Vaclav's eye, it was more a hardly-contained baring of teeth, a feral threat.

"Gah, yes, fine, just don't bite me or drive us over a cliff, you egg," Vaclav surrendered with palms raised. After preemptively begging the horse's pardon, he hoisted Andras into the saddle and climbed on behind him with much difficulty and poor directions. Andras checked that his boots sat correctly in the adjusted stirrups and scooted as far up as he could on the saddle. Vaclav watched with genuine admiration as Zimo's son saddled-up like a real cowpoke.

"Ready?" Andras asked over his shoulder as if he was speaking to a much younger Vaclav.

"I really thought I was. I wasn't, but now I am. Let's take it nice and slow, pard'ner. We don't want to make too big 'a dust trail, so they see us coming." Andras nodded and turned the big roan's head with the skillful hand of one who learned to ride on the back of a very sleepy, stubborn mule. He clicked his tongue at the horse, whose ears perked at the familiar sound, and he nudged the horse gently in the sides. "I'll be damned..." Vaclav muttered under his breath. The two trotted down rocky switchbacks to patchy hills that glimmered with quartz and sturdy flowers that would outlive the coming cold. Vaclav patted his nephew on the shoulder and asked,

"How much did your pa teach you about firearms and shooting?"

"All that he could teach me. I haven't had much practice since…" His mind wandered to smoky jail cells and the smell of burnt brains on the back wall.

"Since they killed your pa, yeah, I figured as much. I have an idea that I think is going to sharpen up those skills and get you ready for some safer action."

"What do you mean?"

"I want to teach you how to use the rifle." Andras's excited vibration caused the horse to also stop and turn to look simultaneously.

"You're not teasing?"

"Absolutely! Teaching you to use the rifle keeps you fed in the winter and safe in the spring. Besides, if one of these cowboys starts flinging lead, I'd rather you be flinging it back from further away than that six-shooter can."

"Alright! So, what do we do?" Andras's hand rested on the exposed butt of the rifle that hung in its sheath on the saddle.

"I'll tell you what we did back in Ukraine during the uprising, eh? Back then, before you were Clara's favorite, your dad and I were doing a run across the border through this old village where the traditionalists lived. He told me that it was customary to kill and prepare a gift of game for them as a sort of peace offering, asking for permission to pass through or some other small favor. You and I will hunt–"

"A traditionalist?"

"–a deer, dress and clean it, and–what? No. We're going to give it to any locals who don't mind us passing through."

"Sorry, I'm just really nervous about the part when you were talking about them flinging lead at me." Vaclav put a heavy hand on Andras's small shoulder to emphasize his words.

"That–" he pointed his thick, crooked forefinger directly between Andras's eyes, "–is your vital instinct. Trust it. Those 'nerves' will keep you alive, if you listen to them, but be careful not to let them take over, else a smarter hunter will use it to spook you into a trap. Hear me?" Andras did not nod immediately. He pondered his Uncle Vaclav's words like he was trying a new food.

When Andras thought about his vital instinct, he remembered it being cold. He felt the dry, splintering wood beneath his hands as a ricochet narrowly missed him. He remembered crawling on his belly in a wagon and then the awful keening of the dying mule. He remembered sitting up, a swollen mouth full of sand, wailing at the sight of his own gunshot wound. Each time, he had chosen to reject his baser urges to hide, faint, or flee, and instead, chose to survive. In the jail cell, in Asher Milan's final, mewling moments of shame, Andras remembered the look in his eyes. The look was that of a trapped animal. This was something Andras determined never to become.

Andras nodded. "Good," said Uncle Vaclav, "eyes on the trail now, before we careen into some ravine." Andras laughed and pulled the right corner of his hat a little lower.

To the north, two riders gallop on old, dusty roads to familiar hills and forgotten ghosts.

To the west, a man feels, for the first time in a long while, a little lighter. He breathes easier knowing that he chose to leave behind a path of destruction for one of honest work and rewarding labor.

Not quite as far west, two riders on one horse veer from the path of destruction on a detour to follow the scent of an unrepentant sinner.

Chapter 18

To think about the years that had passed, about the way he had left, and about his final words to his son, it was like falling in an early Spring river. It had been a long time since he had felt it. Now, here where the sun could see him, he felt the puha around him like long grass made of lightning, but it did not cause pain, only warmth.

He smiled as the wind lifted him for a moment, feeling lighter than he'd felt in years. Even before he left the Basin, he had been afraid to go to the High places or to look up at the mountains too long for fear of finally hearing their call and refusing to listen to its truth. He left his hat on the cart and he unlaced his tattered boots.

When he felt the earth beneath him, he felt the puha stirring just below the surface like a new child nearing its time. Below the initial surge of warmth and familiarity, he could sense a deep longing for an ear to hear its song. Tavibo felt the weight of the song within him, and he cried out as a young warrior shouts after their first battle or they've stolen their first horse. His shout did not waver, but endured as he struck his drum once and listened.

Beneath the earth, the insects, the roots, between the stones where the heart of the earth can be heard; Tavibo beat that heart upon the skin of his drum with a simple mallet of agave root. The drum rang like his voice, and he let the puha flow through him, as his song joined the earth's.

Below him, he saw the ancient, sacred place where the stone trees always sleep, but never fall. At dusk, when the mist slithered about one's ankles, it was said that one could see the spirits of the ancestors-past, and, if you were wise enough, you could follow their footsteps back to your fire. When the sun set, the shadows of the trees could not hide the glory of the heavens. The mists swirled about the massive red, white, and amber marbled trunks, but Tavibo sensed an alien presence. Within this sacred space, an evil lost spirit was slithering amongst the ancient stone titans, its shadowy stain leaving a sickly, bleached wash where it passed.

As the shape poisoned and consumed the puha that lived there, it took shape and dissolved into the shadow of the largest petrified pillar. In the moonlit gaps between trees, the spirit walked noiselessly like a hooded monk in a temple to some forgotten tree god. Each time the moonlight washed over the spirit, its silhouette twisted and morphed so that knees twisted and bent to become antlers, and a human face melted and stretched into a snarling, hairless wolf's.

Tavibo watched it prowl the darkness, bleaching the holy trees and searching for a shape to fill. Like a malignant filth, the pale stain stretched up the stone trunks so that they shifted and threatened to crumble like a canyon wall in monsoon. To his horror, the desecration did not stop at the holy place, but continued to stretch across the rolling black hills until nothing could be seen but the pale sheen of death.

In the fragment of a moment that it took for his mallet to rebound, Tavibo had seen it all. He stopped his beating and listened as the ring of his voice and drum melded into the call of the wind. He had not had a vision in many years, but now, he feared that it was too late.

The sweat that had beaded on his brow rancold and skated across his clammy brown cheek. His hand shook and he clenched his fist tightly to stop its trembling. Laying a hand on his bare chest, his heart pounded in silent fear beneath his heaving ribs. Gathering up his shirt and shoes, he walked hurriedly down the hill.

His breathing still shallow and ragged from his sobering vision, he drove his cart deep into the old woods where the fallen trees could lie in peace, where the twisting slot canyons prevented any mounted rider or wheeled cart from passing.

Even in his alarmed, panicked state, the pahu thrummed and rippled in the earth and stones. So far from the noise of man and civilization was the true sound of life: peace and stillness. Chaos existed in the form of a balanced machine that pushed and pulled on itself like the ebbing of the lake's tide. Tavibo breathed easier upon seeing the stillness of the surrounding woods undisturbed, but paused at the silence of the trees. With the coming cold, the Autumn ravens should be calling, and the small birds would protect their caches noisily.

So full of the ecstasy of his heightened senses, so deep in the medicine of his people, he laid his hand on the ground and allowed the grass to pass between his fingers. On the tip of his tongue, he sensed blood in the air, and inhaled deeply. He smelled no rot or fresh dropping nearby, and heard no scavengers bickering. Somewhere nearby, a predator had made a fresh kill. Crouched low, Tavibo advanced on the hidden entrance of the slot canyon that guarded the way to the stone grove, the place he saw in his vision. He pressed himself against the cold stone wall and shimmied his way through the claustrophobic crush.

Once inside, the passageway widened, creating a funnel of wind that seemed to push him back the way he came. He inhaled the cold, dry air and again smelled the blood and… something else. He navigated the slot canyon as quietly as possible, pausing at each tiny tumbling pebble to listen for signs he'd been detected. Each time he stopped, all he heard was the heaving of his own breath and the blood in his ears. The deeper he ventured into the dim passageway of stone, moss, and hanging vegetation, the colder the air became, until his flesh erupted with a shiver of goosebumps that was partly from the cold, and partly from what he saw. He turned the final corner and beheld the stone grove illuminated by a single beam of sunlight that shone down through a circular opening above.

Dust and mist floated through the golden beam like motes of pure light sinking in water. He ran his hands along the stone wall, transfixed by the sacred sight, momentarily forgetting the scent of blood and dark presence. Within the largest chamber, myriad petrified trees stood in solemn, statuesque silence, memorials to the land that once was. The power in the grove was tangible, like humidity or the moments before lightning. Beneath his foot, something soft squished and slipped. When he lifted his foot, he saw a shiny, wet stain of bloody moss and a trampled bit of offal. The blood he smelled.

"It's not polite to sneak up on people," rasped a vile voice like metal on stone. Spinning around, Tavibo turned to face the massive antlered head of a deer, its mouth and jaw twisted wide and crusted with blood. Its wide eyes gazed blindly in different directions, and its fur was shiny and black with its own gore. A fly landed on the eye and began to slurp.

Blood dripped freely from the severed throat that drained blood onto the stained ground. Behind it, the rest of the deer hung from a stone tree, skinless, its abdomen sliced open, and blood pouring onto the ground from the neck as it rotated slowly. Its legs were spread wide and tied with a sturdy branch that was suspended by a rope. On the ground below the gutted deer was the rest of it, looking as if the deer merely split open and dumped its innards at the base of an ancient petrified tree that still stood to this day.

Stepping out from behind the tree was like an image of death. Long, thin legs, a lithe body like a puma, and a face in such stark contrast with itself, he could hardly look away from his eyes, like open graves. He was dressed simply, black boots and pants and a white collared shirt he had opened at the collar and rolled up the sleeves. His hands and forearms were sticky and red with deer's blood. He held a crude, black stone blade in one hand, and a mass of dense muscle and tissue in the other.

"Leave here now," Tavibo warned sternly. His face did not change although his mind itched and his heart raced. He could think of nothing but the vision and the malignant spirit that haunted the place.

"It's not polite to not introduce yourself when meeting new people either." When he spoke again, it was the sound of a branding iron on cold, wet flesh. The stranger turned to walk to a pile of his nearby effects, a black hat and gun belt on top of a coat. Tavibo spied the ugly disfiguration of scar tissue and malformed flesh pulled tight.

"This is a sacred place for the people of this land. Why are you here, white man?" Tavibo mirrored his path and kept a stone pillar between them

"I was just cleaning this deer for my supper. Had I known I was expecting company…"

"I heard no shot," Tavibo challenged him. Vukašin met his gaze.

"That's right," he nodded once and lifted the mass of meat to his mouth. The wet pop of teeth through tissue and then the dull crunching of heavy muscle. Tavibo glanced back at the deer carcass. The severed neck had several deep, jagged lacerations in the meat that implied the cutting began while the deer was still moving.

The white man took another wet, crunchy bite of heart and placed his flint skinning blade on the ground beside his other belongings. Slowly, lazily, he donned his gun belt while holding the gnawed deer heart in his mouth, like a half-eaten apple. Now armed, Ilíc turned to face Tavibo, his lips and chin smeared with blood. Tavibo was regretting he had not brought his rifle.

"Take your deer and go home. Blood should not be spilt here." The rage in Tavibo threatened to ignite his hair and consume them both, but his face betrayed none of it. The white man did not budge either.

"No, I don't think I will. I like this place. It suits me." Hush looked around the dim cavern with fascinated interest, nodding as he surveyed and ripped another tough chunk of cardiac muscle from its whole.

The moment his back was turned, Tavibo drew the knife from the band of his pants and lunged forward with one step, closing the distance in an instant. As Tavibo's old body pounced like that of a younger man, Hush's gun was already drawn and aimed at Tavibo, so that his forehead rushed forward to meet the barrel of the black and blued pistol. They froze. A drop of blood dribbled from the hexagonal contusion on his forehead, but he did not drop the knife.

Hush pulled back the hammer of the pistol still pressed against his forehead threateningly. Tavibo did not duck away, dodge, or move to attack. Tavibo inhaled through his nose, filled his chest, and let out a loud, threatening war cry and showed him the inside of his mouth in a great show of force. He was not afraid of this white man, and he would not allow him to chase him away. He raised his knife and shouted again, stamping his foot and beating his chest, showing Hush that he was not afraid. The white man smirked at the primitive and squeezed the trigger to a satisfying *snap* of the hammer. One tiny puff of white smoke and a flash was all that came from the gun.

Hush's expression transformed in that moment, from a wry jungle cat to that of something that had never been seen on earth by human eyes. His black eyes widened, and the muscles and tendons in his neck tightened, so they looked like his head was held onto his shoulders with rope. His hands, once relaxed, now curved into animalistic claws for grabbing and tearing. He leaned forward onto the balls of his feet and pounced at Tavibo who was already bringing the knife down on Hush.

When he collided with Tavibo, a low rumble emanated from his chest. With a soft thud, the blade of Tavibo's knife buried itself into Hush's back so that only the handle of the knife was visible. Hush seemed not to notice. He scrambled on top of Tavibo and brutalized him with a single punch across the cheek that made him see stars and lose his bearings.

In a moment, Hush was off of Tavibo, writhing on the ground, hissing and squealing like some angry beast, reaching for the protruding handle in his back. Kicking and thrashing on the ground, he rolled like an alligator and collided into the side of one of the petrified trees. Tavibo righted himself again and felt the gash on his cheek where Hush struck him. He pushed to his feet with a war whoop and met Hush on the ground, his hand immediately finding the knife handle, so that Hush quivered and twisted. As the knife lodged between his ribs wrenched this way and that, Tavibo could see the ribs flexing and spreading. He twisted the blade one more time to pull it free and finish off the intruder, but the handle came free in a sudden snapping.

Hush rolled away and drew his second pistol, firing blindly at the direction he knew he was. The stone tree beside Tavibo exploded a shower of red and white gravel over him. He pressed his back against the tree and listened. The hammer of a pistol locking back, and then it fell quiet. In the silence, he heard a single muted grunt of pain and smelled the tang of fresh blood again. What he heard next made his skin crawl.

In a high metallic pang that ricocheted as it struck stone, the broken blade of Tavibo's knife bounced onto the ground nearby and skated to a stop, leaving a wet streak where it landed and splattered.

Tavibo ran. It was no white man that haunted this sacred place. It was no man at all.

Tavibo didn't care about being silent anymore. He scrambled through the thin slot canyon, shoving, grunting, and climbing as he needed. Behind him, Hush fired over and over, seven shots, from both his guns. Bullets snapped and ricocheted off the dozens of tight corners, but Tavibo finally spilled out of the mouth of the narrow canyon and flew through the old woods that he used to know.

Echoing through the trees, amplified by the sacred cavern, Tavibo heard a ghastly howl that churned his stomach as it lashed his ears. His ox lowed anxiously and tugged the yoke against the cart's handbrake. In a great clumsy dash, the two were headed down the road while Tavibo, breathing heavily, checked himself for wounds. Free of anything beyond superficial scrapes and bumps, he noticed his hand trembling.

"My son was right. The people must dance. I didn't want to believe it. I still don't want to believe it."

Hush cursed under his breath as he emptied the spent shells from his pistol one by one. He chuckled a wet, gurgly laugh at his own theatricality. He swaggered over to the fragmented blade and picked it up, measuring it beside his hand for approximate size. He twisted and looked at the gaping, gushing gash that was leaking dark blood through his once-white shirt.

"То није добро. *That's not good,*" he said calmly to himself. He pressed the heel of his palm against the leaking hole on his back awkwardly and bit down on the soft brass cartridge of a pistol shell. He widened the shirt hole gently and tipped a meager amount of pinkish vodka onto his wound with a sharp inhale. Pinching the bullet out of the cartridge with his teeth, he carefully poured the fine black grains onto the ground in front of him. He did not flinch or cry out as an aching spasm of pain jolted up the right side of his spine, making his right ear ring as if he had been cuffed.

He gathered a small pile of tinder and built it around his black powder. Pulling out his wheel-lock striker, he wound the spring so that the sparks showered across the tinder, but with no ignition. He gritted his teeth in frustration and anticipation of the coming agony. Vukašin knew he could bleed out if he did not address the wound. He wound the spring again and struck more sparks across the tiny kindling altar. A slowly creeping glow turned to slithering white smoke that Hush fanned gently and gathered more light tinder around.

In moments, the tiny fire was lit, and the brass shell in the fire slowly began to glow a dull orange. He inhaled deeply, and then twisted as best he could to see the wound in his back.. He squeezed the ends of the stab together and inserted the glowing, crimped metal into it, using a smoking leather glove. Hush exhaled loudly and quickly through filthy gritted teeth as he burned shut any blood vessels that still leaked.

When the smell of cooking pork began to nauseate him, he tossed the shell into his fire again. He used the moment of pain's reprieve to heat the repurposed fishhook and curse loudly while repeatedly smacking his forehead against the nearest stone pillar. Vukašin threaded the twisted fishhook with the same thread he used to repair his dungarees.

Once the metal was hot enough again, he squeezed the gash shut, plunged the hook into one side of the wound and shoved it into the flesh of the other side so that it punched back through with a painful tugging. He secured the tail of the stitch and pulled tight the first of seven pungent sutures. After one more set of reheating and cursing, He took a long, deep pull from his bottle of beet vodka and then spit a tiny mouthful on to the messy stab wound.

Hush was satisfied with the results of his field-medicine mattress stitch and took another swig of vodka. He licked the blood from his fingers, sucking each one clean before returning to his hanging deer with a faint limp. If those damned natives wanted him gone so badly, nothing short of an act of god would remove him.

Chapter 19

September was threatening to bare Winter's teeth, it seemed, as the first snow surprised them one evening while the pair guarded their small fire from a cold wind. For the past few days, Andras had struggled to orient himself when the clouds blocked all his useful stars. When before, the Mountains always indicated West, now, mountains surrounded them from all sides. Just when he was starting to memorize some of the more prominent features of the area, they were all now white-washed.

It was true, what his uncle had said all those months ago. "In America, you fight America." Even the terrain seemed more aggressive. During long stretches, Uncle Vaclav would choose to walk instead of riding, giving the horse a rest on the harsher roads.

It was late one humid September afternoon when Andras's inner dialogue spilled into his and Vaclav's conversation.

"How long did we rent this horse?"

"Er uh…a while I guess. I hope they don't reckon we stole it."

"I'm only asking because we've been riding this same horse for a good, long while now, and we've only ever just called it, 'horse' on account of we don't know the real name. Do you reckon we should give it a name?" Andras leaned forward and scratched the horse between the ears. Vaclav looked up at him, his face all scrunched up in confusion.

"Doesn't it already have a name?"

"Yeah, but we don't know it! How can we call it a name we don't know?" Andras's pleas were beginning to verge on frantic, so Vaclav diverted his focus.

"What would you call him? It needs to be a good name." Andras stroked his imaginary beard and hummed audibly as he pontificated.

"It needs to be a good name," Andras repeated. "Something strong that sounds like we mean business. What was the name of the first king of America?" Andras asked, struck by sudden brilliance.

"George!" Vaclav answered confidently, snapping his fingers at the quickness of his own wit.

"Hold up there, wasn't that the British king?" Andras struggled to remember the American history he had learned so far, and he found that he confused much of his European history along with it.

"No, no, I'm certain that he was the general who defeated the British king; George… something-the-third," Vaclav corrected. His voice seemed to waver along with his certainty. The two Poles wracked their brains in mutual silence for several moments before Vaclav finally snapped his fingers again.

"Vernon. George Vernon the third," he answered, his confidence having returned.

"That sounds correct, I think," Andras conceded. "For some reason, I kept thinking 'Whithaus.' We should name him George after the American general!"

"I think George will be a fine name until we have to give him back," Vaclav nodded and trudged along, a peaceful smile across his hairier face. He'd not shaved since he arrived in Colorado, and he was forming the shadowy foundation of a proper Polish beard.

Andras rubbed George's thick neck as they trotted down the stony path. After another half mile or so, Andras dismounted, and they led George off the trail into the impenetrable brambles and hills made from boulders. As they neared their destination, Andras felt the warm wetness of nerves on his palms, and he was breathing heavily as though they had been trekking uphill for a mile.

They finally reached a tall lookout spot covered in thick, twisted branches and roots that overlooked the side of the adjacent mountain. The view was a chaotic, geometric kaleidoscope of shadowy cracks and shaded hues. Andras laid on his belly and crawled into the base of the bushes and branches.

Uncle Vaclav handed the rifle from behind once he was well-hidden. Holding his Pa's rifle, the Winter Viper's own venom, it seemed to vibrate and thrum with energy like he imagined a magic sword might feel. Andras took a deep breath, steadied himself, and the vibrating lessened. He pressed the butt of the rifle against his shoulder and leaned his cheek on the stock. He kept both eyes open like his uncle showed him and he counted the seconds of his breaths: eight second inhale, eight second exhale. Slowly, almost imperceptibly, Andras scanned the mountainside.

"Alright, we'll see if you're right, wild man," Vaclav mocked, skeptical condescension gathering in a pool beneath his words.

"You'll see," Andras responded with a smug smirk. He didn't look away from his mountainside. Behind him, Vaclav lay on his stomach with a spyglass extended in the same direction. Silence fell over the mountainside as they waited and watched. Every shift or rustle was amplified in their silent world, until the loudest sound was the wind on round leaves and their hearts beating in their chests.

Vaclav had been relentless in his tutoring of Andras in the art of shootistry. Andras asked if he had meant "marksmanship," but Vaclav insisted that it was, indeed, shootistry. The amount of hours that Andras had spent looking through this scope had begun to give him a headache.

After Andras gave the Ute the gift of his very first hunt, they were so pleased that they showed Vaclav and him a path through the Wasatch mountains. Andras noticed that, beneath their smiles and helpfulness, they were cautious and reserved. He never saw a village, a fire, or any indication that more people lived nearby, but it was clear they were being led away. Vaclav and Andras allowed themselves to be led away, seeing as it would be safest for everyone.

The next day, Andras shot a large, curly-horned ram that posed itself proudly on a boulder, exposing his profile. Before they could reach their quarry, the ram's corpse had disappeared, leaving behind a faint, bloody, drag trail to where the ram had been stashed in some brush fifteen feet above them.

"Catamount" was the new word Andras learned that day as well as the name of his new nemesis.

For days now, they had tracked and stalked the big cat, laying eyes on it once thus far. Finding predator scat and prints was enough to convince Andras of their likely success.

"What better way for me to learn how to hunt a predator?" he argued. Vaclav had rolled his eyes and massaged his temples while he tried to think of a better argument than "it's too dangerous." Afterall, he was the one who agreed to take him on a manhunt for a murderer.

Now, lying on his belly in a bush staring through his ancient, scratched spyglass, he couldn't believe his eyes.

"Son of a…" Vaclav muttered to himself out loud. "High left, just below the big barren tree." He heard Andras's breath catch in his chest as he slowly panned his scope left and searched for the aforementioned tree.

"The big gray tree? With the twisty-branches?" he asked quietly.

"Mhm," Vaclav confirmed. "Look closely. He's the same color as the rocks. Try to spot the movement of his tail or his–he's moving!" Vaclav hissed a whisper.

"I see him," Andras replied with a voice like a winter breeze, soft and cold. Andras did not race to the trigger, but followed the puma's path along the ledge. He knew that the cat would not stay in the open for long, but he had to wait for the right moment. Two thin, black lines intersected directly over the cat's eye, then behind its shoulder. The puma stopped on the ledge and lowered its head down, laying its paws on the stone wall, preparing to descend the steep cliff.

"You're gonna lose 'im."

The puma's tail flicked to balance its jump.

"No, I'm not."

The puma loaded onto its powerful hind legs. Andras's finger slowly found the trigger, and he held his eight-second breath. He squeezed the trigger slowly and steadily, waiting for the kick and smoke. The gun jolted in his hands, but he kept hold of it. The cougar cleared the ledge and dropped out of sight.

On the wall where the puma has crouched, was a dark, red splatter.

"Niezły strzał, Zimo!" Vaclav exclaimed from behind. He sighed and began to rise from his spot, a wide smile splitting his scarred face. Andras was struggling to free himself from his bushy blind, so Vaclav grabbed his ankles and slid him out on his belly. "You nearly lost him, you hesitated so long: why?"

"Because I didn't want to have to climb."

Together, they trudged through the thick stalks of wild bushes and trees desperate for water where the puma lay, blood on its chin and between the shoulder blades. Andras involuntarily skipped and giggled when he saw the great predator lying on its side, but Uncle Vaclav reached out and grabbed Andras by the shoulder with a cautionary hand.

"Many beasts are still dangerous after they're beaten, Andras. Be cautious," Vaclav warned. Andras nodded and glanced at the knife on his uncle's belt before reconsidering, and drew his pistol instead.

He aimed and fired the pistol once at the supine puma, and leapt back when the big cat seemed to flip and scream at him, lashing forth with a deadly swipe of its spread claws. With ears laid flat, long yellow teeth bared in their fullness, and its eyes mere golden rings in blackness, the cat gave its last rebellious groan and laid its head on the ground, finally dead.

When Andras came to his senses, he found himself gripping his uncle's shirt tightly like a frightened child. Both of them had drawn their pistols and were recovering from their near-fatal jump-scare. Andras nodded. He slowly released Uncle Vaclav's shirt and approached the dead puma cautiously.

The cat lay still, its warmth slowly sapping into the cold ground. Carefully, cautiously, Andras reached out and lightly brushed his fingers across the tan fur. Even dead and lifeless on the ground, the beast was impressive. Its teeth and claws were designed to grab and crush bone and sinew alike. Its fur was perfectly-colored to disappear against stone or brush.

"Wow," Andras whispered aloud as he marveled at the massive cat. When Andras turned to call Vaclav, he saw a warm smile and relaxed posture. Vaclav watched with a nostalgic peacefulness that led him to remember earlier memories in the forest with his father.

As Andras began to struggle to wrestle the puma onto its back and begin the long process of skinning and cleaning, he spoke up conversationally.

"Is that how Pa learned Ukrainian?" Vaclav's mind almost fell out of his head from the mental whiplash of the question. He shook his head to clear it, and replied dumbly.

"Huh? What do you…"

"A few days ago, you said that Pa and you used to hunt deer for the traditionalists in Ukraine, while you were there." Andras's question was innocent enough, but Vaclav's stupor caused him to wonder.

"He did learn in Ukraine, yes. When did you hear your dad speak Ukrainian?" Andras cocked his head as he carefully cut the tough hide around the puma's ankles.

"The note Hush sent him was written in Ukrainian. That was the first time I heard him talk it." Andras paused from his messy process to ask his uncle candidly, "do you know Ukrainian?" He shrugged and nodded his head.

"Yes, I know Ukrainian. I *am* Ukrainian."

"You are!?"

"Yep. I was born on a tobacco farm in *Chernigov,* near the Pripyat."

"I always thought you were Polish. That doesn't make us…enemies, does it?" Vaclav laughed loudly and exaggeratedly to emphasize the preposterous nature of the question. He walked to Andras and spoke very seriously and softly.

"Politics be damned. If the Lord God, in all His glory," he began to say, as he crossed himself and knelt in front of Andras, "were to come down from His lofty throne and command me to harm you, then I would commit a Great sin against the Lord that day. Not even the gates of Hell would stop me from getting back to you. Do you believe me?"

"I do believe you, Uncle Vaclav. You're the only family I have left." The moment hung in the chill air as the two felt more like brothers than uncle and nephew. Uncle Vaclav smirked and winked at him and nodded at the dead catamount.

"Are you going to skin it, or are you waiting for it to get stiff?" Andras cracked a churlish grin.

"Are you going to help, or are you just going to sit there like an egg?" Vaclav glared at him with a comical rage as he rolled up his sleeves.

"An egg, huh? Look here, partner: catamount hide ain't the same as deer hide." The sooner they finished up with the puma, the sooner they could deliver their prize to their Indian friend.

With the puma skinned, cleaned, and quartered, they returned to where they last saw their Paiute guide, who offered to lead them to the *Sosone* land, where they would pass peacefully within a few miles of their suspected target. Shortly before sunset, their guide appeared on horseback, with a friendly smile as before.

His dark brown skin seemed to glow like polished copper in the late-day sun. His beautiful, long, black hair was tied back with a tightly bound ribbon, and he wore comfortable clothes that were clean and almost seemed laundered, but the weapons he wore offset any message of formality or peace. A pistol, a rifle, a tomahawk, and a knife that they'd only seen used to eat an apple. Wilson had a charming smile that was as disarming as it was charismatic, and he spoke English better than Uncle Vaclav.

He slid off his horse with a wave and plopped himself down beside them like an old friend. Andras liked Wilson, but he could tell that Vaclav was cautious of him, so he kept his wits about him all the same. He took off his wide, flat-brimmed hat and set it on his knee.

"Back already? I was praying for your fruitful hunt, but that soon would be too miraculous. Tell me the news." Wilson leaned on his elbow and searched the items around the fire. Andras suppressed a smile until Vaclav gave him the nod. Andras brought his hand from behind his back and opened it to reveal four hooked puma claws. Wilson flopped onto his back with a comically surprised face, and Andras laughed at his surprise.

"We came upon him completely by chance. He nabbed a ram that Andras had felled, so we tracked him a few days until we got our chance," Vaclav explained proudly, nodding to Andras who nodded proudly in confirmation.

"I had to shoot him twice. He scared me the second time," Andras giggled nervously, remembering the defeated puma's last lash of defiance. Vaclav produced the cat's hide, rolled and tied-up with twine. He handed it to Wilson over the fire who stroked the fur reverently.

"There are some who believe that Brother mountain lion is a guardian of powerful dreams. Those who wish to gain power this way, it is said that the lion and snakes come to test their bravery. The fearful run away, proving they are not deserving, but the brave…they overcome." As he spoke, Andras felt compelled to listen.

There was no one he had met yet in America who were more confident and at-home on this land than the Indigenous. Their confidence was not a domineering ownership or lording-over, but the peaceful comfort of being surrounded by family.

Wilson looked at Andras and held out his hand for the teeth and claws that he had collected as a favor for him. Andras delivered his prize proudly. Wilson glanced at the many light-colored remains, and he clutched them to his chest.

"This is really going to help me get back on the good side of my *puhagim*. There was this awful mix up with a coyote and–nevermind, you don't want to hear about that," he said. He leaned towards Andras and whispered, "Do not let a coyote get into the old, fermented fruits. If they eat too much, they might just scare a few superstitious aunties into thinking the end of the world is coming." He rolled his eyes, and Andras laughed and fell over, absolutely charmed by Wilson.

"Hey, New York City, I like your boss. He thinks I'm funny," Wilson called to Vaclav from across the fire. Vaclav snorted a chuckle and shook his head at Andras who was sitting exactly like Wilson now.

"Too bad we didn't come all the way out here, in the middle of Paiute territory, at nightfall, just to trade jokes," replied Vaclav, his tone still friendly and casual. Wilson knew when a white man was nervous though, so he nodded and shrugged.

"It is too bad. I know some pretty good jokes," he said and then nodded for them to follow him. Together, they stood and walked to where Wilson's horse nibbled at a thin, spiky plant. Wilson cupped his mouth and made a popping noise with pursed lips, and the horse sauntered over, towing along with it a second horse, attached with a lead line. It was noticeably younger and thinner than Wilson's, and it had a very thin, cushioned saddle cinched around its waist. Its coat was the color of late-Autumn clouds and a fire's first billows of smoke when doused with water. The mane was black and shone like a raven's feather. Andras stared, transfixed by the ghost-like apparition.

"Who's your friend?" Vaclav asked, nodding at the second horse.

"His name is Pukayuc. He is very fast, and I am not so young. When we saw you both riding on poor, old George there, I felt dearly for him, so I want you to take Pukayuc with you." He turned his attention now to Andras and said, "He will not easily allow you to fall. He's not just any horse: he's your Numa partner. Treat him that way, and he will return the favor." Wilson handed Andras the reins of Pukayuc and lifted him under the arms onto the silver horse's back. Still stunned, Andras struggled to catch his balance before finally taking hold of the reins and planting his other foot in its stirrup. Vaclav stared agape at his nephew astride the beautiful silver stallion. He stopped Wilson with a point and took three quick steps toward him.

"Are you really giving him that horse?" he asked. Wilson cringed at his pointed finger. Vaclav withdrew his hand.

"Yeah. Consider it a token of the People's support of your crusade. We don't want murderers living in our backyard either." Wilson smiled at him and elbowed him gently. "Besides, this was really a favor for George. Mount up, cowboy. We're burning daylight."

They rode through the night along mountain ridges shaded by jutting cliffs, game trails disguised by heavy brush, and one very impressive stone tunnel that was so dark; they could only march forward by the sound of hooves and Wilson's soft humming.

When they finally reached the end of the tunnel, the darkness of midnight had never seemed so bright. Andras watched curiously as Wilson extended a familiar hand towards the moon in thanks. He paused, squinted up at the distant celestial body and waved shyly for a moment before he mimicked the popping sound that Wilson had done and spurred onward.

The longer they rode together, the more Andras realized how incredibly intuitive Pukayuc was to his movements, conscious or otherwise. It only made sense that Andras began speaking to Pukayuc quietly as they rode, communicating observations at first, as a spotter, and then, slowly, he began sharing his ideas with Pukayuc. He was never expecting Pukayuc to respond verbally, but Andras knew that he understood. Even after hours of riding, his excitement had not subsided, but Andras mostly remembered to maintain a controlled composure.

Minutes before sunrise, the three riders stopped to have breakfast and rest before parting ways. Andras brooded darkly as he contemplated the spoonful of beans that was going cold. Pukayuc stretched an exploratory nose over his shoulder, focused on the offered beans. Andras started, and the horse bolted away, taking a bouncy lap before returning nearby to nibble some long grass innocently. Andras blinked and noticed Uncle Vaclav and Wilson looking at him.

"Forgot your yeast, Andras?" Vaclav asked. He poured a cup of dark coffee and placed it near Andras.

"I'm trail-ready, boss. I just need a little *Arbuckle'* on my boots," Andras replied with sleepy enthusiasm. He swirled the black liquid in his cup as he waited for it to cool and watched the fire. Wilson produced a cup of his own and sat beside Vaclav.

"So, why the kid?" Wilson asked quietly. His voice was as low as the crackling of the glowing coals. Vaclav filled the cup and offered him a small tin of sugar. Wilson shook his head and smelled the cup.

"What do you mean?" Vaclav replied, equally as quiet. Wilson reconsidered and took a pinch of sugar. By the look on his face it didn't help much.

"I can understand the need for blood and the weight of retribution, but those are poisons for old men, not for children. He wears and carries a gun like a soldier, rides like a cavalryman, and drinks this…like a cowboy. Why bring him along?" Vaclav watched Andras who had fallen asleep immediately after reclining on his saddlebags. He rubbed his cheek and sighed as though pressed by a heavy burden.

"His father and I were like family. We met when we were very young, and we survived…too many battles together back in Europe. Eventually, there was nowhere else to go as a wanted man, so I left. I had a little cash from some jobs we worked together, and we planned it all out. After I got settled, I'd help him and his. I did everything I could to give them the life they deserved, the life *he* deserved. We picked the most beautiful li'l plot, bought a real covered-wagon and arranged a team of mules, paid for the lumber and goods to build them a real home– not the rat-holes they'd been hiding in. I even paid extra for a team of real craftsmen to build it for them." As Vaclav spoke, his words became labored, like something bloated that had sat hidden for too long. He sniffed once, took off his hat, and continued. When he spoke now, it had a renewed vigor of justice.

"Try to explain this to me," Vaclav said. He held up a thumb. "Clara dies of fever on the crossing." He raised his forefinger. "Zimo gets murdered in front of his son by some… *suka khuylo,* Hush." He raised the next finger. "Those same fucking drifters torched the house," he raised the next finger, "and then shot the child they just orphaned." Vaclav held up the last remaining finger. "And nobody did fucking-shit about it," Vaclav hissed, struggling to maintain his grasp on a whisper so to not rouse Andras. He squeezed those five fingers into a trembling, white-knuckled fist.

"So, I did the only thing I could do: I went out to kill the men who took Andras's life away. I have asked God for forgiveness in preparation for the things I'm going to do, but what else could I do with Andras? He has no one else, anywhere. I can't send him away, and I can't leave him alone. The only way I can both protect Andras and do what needs doing is to bring him along. I know it's idiotic, but there's no choice that makes sense." Vaclav sipped his coffee, cringed, and then tossed it away into an unlucky plant. Wilson nodded slowly, processing all that Vaclav had shared.

"I know what it feels like to hate, deep down in your bones. I know the feeling of losing your home to strangers from far away. And I know how it feels to watch the last of a generation fighting and bleeding for any scrap of hope or goodness." As Wilson said it, Vaclav knew that he truly could understand. He could understand why Wilson would be sympathetic to their plight, and why he wanted to protect Andras. Wilson's low voice brought his mind back to the present.

"You don't have to be a prophet to see that this is going to end in death."

"I know it is. I'm counting on it. I'm not returning home with this unsettled. When I bring Andras home with me, there's not going to be some monster waiting out west for him."

"Only ghosts," Wilson added. Vaclav absent-mindedly drew and checked his pistol.

"Yeah, that's right, only ghosts. He's so young, he still has a chance at changing things and making things better for himself."

"He's *so* young. He'll need you, won't he?"

"It ain't about me anymore. This whole god-dammned mess is because we ran away from our past instead'a dealing with it. Doesn't he deserve better than that? If I get shot or…killed, I reckon that'll be the Judge closing my account," Vaclav said matter-of-factly. He poured another cup of coffee and sipped it carefully. "You can really taste the sock this morning," he added after a quiet moment. Wilson silently mouthed the word, *sock*, before offering up his cup again.

"That's what it is, the sock. *That's* what I hate so much," he said after his second sip.

"Maybe that's why they call it 'barefoot,' eh?" Vaclav chuckled to himself. Wilson lowered his cup slowly, his face stern and steely.

"What do you mean, 'barefoot'?" he growled. The air grew tense for a moment before he cracked a churlish grin at him again and smacked his knee playfully. "Nah, I'm just fuckin' with you, New York City. I like you," Wilson said before he exploded into loud, high, infectious laughter that started Andras awake, making Vaclav and Wilson laugh all the more.

Once his heart slowed down, and he poured himself another cup, Andras finished his morning coffee in three gulps and began packing Pukayuc quickly. His sudden realization that he would probably never see Wilson again caused him to pause mid-brush. Pukayuc side-stepped closer to Andras.

"Mr. Wilson?" Andras called. Wilson turned attentively.

"Mr. Andras."

"Can we see you again if we come back this way?" he asked hopefully. Vaclav cleared his throat from where he was packing George and cut in.

"Andi, part of our agreement with Wilson and the Numa was that we would *not* come back this way." Vaclav cringed, preparing for an argument, but Andras merely said,

"Oh, alright. That makes sense. We want to respect our neighbors. Then maybe I'll see you again somewhere else, not this way."

"I look forward to that day. We *are* neighbors, afterall. Travel well." Wilson yanked himself up onto his horse and spoke to it in Numa before trotting off down the opposite trail, headed east. Pukayuc knickered and pawed the ground, stirring up dust and small stones.

"Don't worry. I think we'll see them again," Andras whispered reassuringly. He leaned forward and stroked Pukayuc's neck, giving it a solid pat-pat at the end.

After trotting down the stony hill into the grassy valley, Andras turned back to see if he could spot Wilson, romantically waving atop the highest peak before his noble steed reared regally like he had seen in all those paintings of dukes and barons. But there was no sign of Wilson at all. Not even a dustrail remained to tell of Wilson's path, or if they would ever see him again.

Chapter 20

Tavibo's cart bounced noisily and progressively slower the further he and his ox got from their haunting encounter with Hush. Tavibo knew that he had barely escaped with his life, and that he wouldn't survive a second encounter with Hush one-on-one. By now, he could feel the medicine had mostly burned out of his mind, and he felt more present in this world. His mind sprinted and juggled the many thoughts he was considering.

The terrain had transformed as he drove through the night. Tall, centuries-old trees morphed into scrubby bushes and prickly plants. Strong, surging rivers thinned to shallow unpredictable streams, and sticky mud transformed into bright, shifting gravel and sand. The air was still cool, but much more dry.

Tavibo wasn't looking for just anyone. He was looking for a warrior.

Many of the morning's rock formation silhouettes were visible with the first light splashing bright pinks and purples across the sky. Yet the beauty of the morning could not assuage the deluge of horrific images that melded together to haunt him when he shut his eyes.

He saw the bloody, gore-splashed deer head speak to him with the voice of a demon and transform into a vision of death. It moved faster than any human he'd ever seen, ate the dripping flesh of the dead, and was unperturbed by mortal weapons. He remembered watching how his blood seemed to sap life from the earth and spread like a lightless fire. The creature that now inhabited the Ancient Stone Grove was the result of the world's imbalance. Certainly, more like him would come. The people needed the dance.

Seeing the shattered horizon, jagged with mountains like so much broken glass, Tavibo felt both at peace and tentatively anxious about being home and about seeing his family. The day he left had been filled with shouting, tears, and broken promises. It was not a spontaneous clash of passion, but a conglomeration of many tiny stress-fractures over time. Like an old tree, grown over many years, when many people work together to bring it down from all sides, it falls quickly. The day he left had been the culmination of decades of bitterness, unspoken regret, and quiet resentment. It was all his fault. He walked away. He chose pride and bitterness over forgiveness and family.

For years, he let himself rot alone in that cabin, haunted by the ghosts of his words, knowing each day he did not return home was another wedge of separation. For years, he hoped to die just as his son had said all those years ago, "fat, old, and alone, surrounded by the remains of your *real* family, empty bottles." For years, he tried to oblige his son, but he kept waking up.

The drink silenced the call of the mountains and the cry of his people as they suffered. He did not have to look himself in the eye if he couldn't see straight. Now, like a wound that had been improperly dressed and forgotten, it may be too late. He had punished himself for long enough. Today, he would face his son and the rest of his people.

If they did not accept him back, so be it, but they must know about his vision and the evil in the Ancient Stone Grove.

When a nomadic people are forced to centralize, the middle generation takes it the hardest. Children are adaptable and the elders are happy to be around family and a good chair. The parents of the adaptable children were raised on horseback, following the weather and game, living the way their ancestors lived, learning the way the ancestors learned, and teaching the way their ancestors taught, but now, the parents don't know what to teach, what to learn, or how to live. Resistance is natural. The Europeans want to tell the Indigenous how best to live on their own land and how to be "civilized". Before the Europeans came, they woke up when they wanted, fished when and where they wanted, made love when they wanted, and ate what they wanted. Now, there are water-rights, claimed stakes, punch-cards, subsistence farming, share-cropping, mining, labor strikes, and a federal government who demands payment to live free. They were free before. Now, they were… something else, but not free.

One by one, the tribes were being quarantined to keep from infecting the rest of the country. Those who doubt need only to see the hundreds of miles of Cherokee roses to understand the scope of the decimation that was taking place. The people were growing weaker with each passing generation. On that, his son and he agreed. Who would know their history when their language is forgotten, and their stories are replaced?

Looking down, Tavibo noticed his hand was shaking again, and sweat beaded his temples and ran down the deep wrinkles in his face.

He pulled the reins tight and beheld the village of his people before him. Dozens of wickiups and smaller dwellings dotted the brushy landscape. From here, he could see many of the people without the restraint of European clothes, still living as they had before. To his relief and heartbreak, the people were exactly where they had been when he left. He cupped a hand around his mouth and let out a loud cry to announce himself. The ox rumbled forward again toward the village, where three riders rode out to meet him.

Before they reached him, Tavibo stood and waved, waiting for them. The first two riders, smiles spread wide, leapt from their horses and embraced Tavibo with tight hugs and strong grips.

"*Look who it is! You haven't aged a day!*"

"*You're back! It's so good to see you!*" The warmth of the greeting was welcome, but the hard part was coming. The third rider finally closed the distance, dismounting calmly and walking slowly. He had beautiful, long hair tied back, and that ridiculous flat-brimmed hat. He was dressed like the other young men but also wore a fringed buckskin shirt painted with the traditional depictions of a dark bird. The other two fell silent as the tension impressed upon them as well. Tavibo took a deep breath and a step forward.

"*Son, my only boy, I've–*"

"Father, *I'm* sorry!" he interrupted, flinging his arms around his father and pulling himself onto his father's shoulder. Tavibo was stunned, speechless, clueless about what to do next.

"Quoitze, please, I had something I wanted to say to you– well, I should have said it long ago." Tavibo's words became thick and cluttered in his mouth. His son pulled away and looked at his father with still-wet red, teary eyes.

"Quoitze, when I, um, all those years ago when I, uh… *My son, I'm sorry. I was wrong to speak to you and your mother that way. I lost my chance to apologize to your mother, and I wasted your youth. I have spent so many years deafening myself to the cry of the land and our people. But I am listening once more, and I fear it is too late. I have seen an evil vision, and we must act as quickly as possible.*" The fear crept back into Tavibo's voice like frost on a lake. Quoitze's face grew grave, and he nodded. He placed a hand on his father's shoulder, and his expression transformed to that of a wise leader and grown man.

"*I, too, have seen dark visions lately. I have already begun preparations.*"

"Preparations? The Circle dance?" Tavibo asked, his gaze drifting to the ceremonial shirt he wore. Quoitze smiled again and displayed his shirt proudly.

"*Something new. Something that will bring peace. I've seen it,*" Quoitze said with such faith and confidence, Tavibo began believe him. *"But we can talk more about that later! You must be thirsty. You must let me make you a meal to share, and, once we are fat and happy, we'll talk about dreams and spirits."* Tavibo's mouth felt heavy and strained as his face bent into a smile. He nodded enthusiastically. His face did not feel strained because he was pretending or forcing himself to smile. He had not truly, contentedly smiled in so long; it felt labored and foreign.

"I am already fat, and I am happier than I have felt in a long time, but I would like some water and any bread you have. It's been too long since I had Numa bread..."

Within Quoitze's wickiup, Tavibo reclined on the floor and listened as his son carried-on about all the recent news and gossip he could remember.

"–and when they got back with everyone else, she was already pregnant!" Quoitze guffawed, nearly falling over while trying to keep his voice low. His father chuckled on the floor, shaking his head in disbelief.

"Where did they all go for so long?" he asked curiously. Quoitze's face darkened, and a muscle in his jaw visibly flexed. He sat down beside his father and shook his head.

"I'm sorry you'd not heard earlier, but I'm glad to be with you when you hear it. The federal government reserved a valley for our people in Oregon. It was good enough for some, but others were concerned about the soil, and others just didn't want to leave their homes. It

sounds terrible to say, but I'm glad I was working on that ranch when they all left because I might have gone with them," he said darkly, that charismatic spark missing from his eye. Tavibo reached out and touched his son's shoulder.

"Why? What happened in Oregon?"

"The same thing that always happens. The settlers nearby needed more land. More of our land, to be precise. The American president had to side with his people, and... the water was soured with blood. Let's just leave it at that," he said, looking down, avoiding his father's gaze. Tavibo's wrinkled, old hand took hold of his son's arm with the grip of a warrior, and he shook it.

"You tell me, dammit! Tell me of every son and every daughter whose cries I have ignored for so long. Break my heart as it should have back then, so that I may grieve with you."

"The Pannakwati, whomever survived, are headed north to the Idaho Territory for good. Things went bad for the Shoshone, and Chief Buffalo died. Ehegante followed after him, but he died too."

"Both of them?! How?"

"The Imatalamɫáma from Yampapah betrayed them. The Army was pressing them, and betraying Ehegante was the only way to save themselves," he said sadly. It was a fact he had reminded himself of over and over to keep from poisoning himself with hatred. He did not hate the Imatalamɫáma. Ehegante was born in the same valley near the Yampapah. When he was older, he would fish in that river. He must have been a great chief, for however brief a moment. Quoitze's mind wandered to a possible future before his father's hoarse voice encouraged him, saying,

"*And then what? Do not spare me.*"

"*I do not hesitate for your heart's sake, but for mine. To retell it is to relive it, in some small way.*"

"*Then I shall wait until your heart is steeled.*"

"*No, Father. I must never allow my heart to become hardened to the spilling of People's blood.*" Quoitze took a deep breath and nodded once before continuing. "*As the Pannakwati and Shoshone tried to regroup and organize, nearby settlers ambushed them with hunting rifles and farming tools. Soon, the soldiers caught up. Every single warrior that died did so, bravely. As did those who survived. Many of them have agreed to surrender to the reservations, but others...*"

"Others would rather die," Tavibo said, completing the thought. Quoitze nodded sadly.

"Would *you* go?" Quoitze asked him, now in English. He knew many neighbors nearby did not speak English well enough to eavesdrop. Tavibo sighed deeply now, reviewing all the times he had considered that same question.

"I'm not sure. I think it would depend on what was waiting for me there."

"The survival of your people: that's what's at stake. Sooner or later, for better or worse, our last stand is coming, and for once, I'd like to choose how it happens."

"How can you say that life on the reservation is our people surviving?"

"Because our *children* will be alive there, Father. You know that I value the Old Ways and traditions of the elders," Quoitze said with the firmness of an ordained minister. Next, he spoke in their native Numa, saying, "*If we do not make sacrifices now, we will have no one left to teach.*" His father nodded sadly as a single tear careened down the jagged wrinkles of his cheeks.

"*I know you are correct. You are as wise as I am stubborn. For my own benefit, I must be stubborn. Clinging to the past is how we ensure it's never lost. My fear is that... I do not know who we will become. I am afraid.*" Together, father and son sat and pondered each other's words for a moment before Quoitze turned to face his father.

"Tell me about your vision," he said. Tavibo also turned to face his son with a stony look.

"It was a vision... and an encounter." Quoitze's eyebrow arched inquisitively.

"Your dream was confirmed?" Quoitze suggested. Tavibo withdrew a beautifully adorned knife handle inlaid with exotic woods and a leather sheath splashed with blood. He lifted the handle to reveal the missing blade.

"He cannot be hurt by our weapons," he said gravely. Quoitze took the handle and studied it, smelling the dried blood and inspecting the broken end. Tavibo took back the broken knife and said, "But I may have a solution for that already."

Chapter 21

Nightfall came like a fresh linen sheet pulled under a chin. It laid cooly across the landscape, blanketing the fruited valley in a silvery sheen of moonlight. Acres of beautiful, rolling hills, surrounded by miles of fence, protecting his herd. He couldn't see them right now, and for the first time in his life, that didn't make him nervous. He'd finally knocked back enough of the neighboring farmer's distilled mash-liquor to convince himself to sit down.

Benjamin had a controversial theory. It wasn't controversial in a way that had provoked arguments amongst friends. He'd not voiced this theory out-loud because to do so would bring into question not only his age, but his sanity. While Benjamin's sanity had not recently been called into question, he had begun to ponder it introspectively. Were he to voice this theory, he'd be branded an "old coot" for sure.

He chuckled as he pushed off the floor with the toe of his boot, and the rocking chair groaned into rhythm beneath him.

It wasn't that Benjamin disliked dogs; in fact, he liked dogs very much. He had bought himself a dog almost immediately after he had signed the last of the paperwork for this spread of flawless California landscape.

His theory was this: mankind's best friend is not, in fact, the dog, but the lowly rocking chair. The rocking chair needs neither food nor water and does not tussle with skunks. The rocking chair is supportive and restful after a long day's work.

The dog sits firmly in the second position, but the place of best friend should belong to the rocking chair.

Benjamin smiled at his own silly, secret joke and lit a cigarette. He swirled his cold liquor in its canning-jar tumbler, rocking in his favorite chair as he exhaled the first drag of a perfect, hand-rolled cigarette. This was it: manifest destiny. All his hard work had culminated to this exact moment of peace, and he knew that he was deserving of it. He hummed a familiar tune as he gently blew across the glowing cherry of his cigarette. An ethereal wisp of paper glowing with ember danced away from him and landed on the floor near him. On his next rock, he stepped on the small light, snuffing it for good.

There was a metaphor in there somewhere; he was sure of it.

He was expecting John Jackson any moment now. "Stoney," as everyone had come to call him, was an exhaustive play on the ridiculousness of his name, so Benjamin had resolved to merely call him "Jack" or "Jackson." It was the least he could do to treat Jack as a professional. He'd always been respectful to Ben; whether it was for his age or his merit, he couldn't be sure.

A squeak from the porch grabbed his attention and jolted his fingers to life. He perched the lit cigarette on the lip of his glass and cocked-back both hammers of the shotgun that lie across his lap. He aimed both barrels at the hand-carved door, and said calmly, "It's open." Jack pushed the door open and immediately disappeared behind the wall, loudly exclaiming,

"What's the big fookin' idear, Sanderson?! It's me, Stoney!" His accent relapsed when he was anxious or talking to other Irish. It was his mother's accent.

"It's alright, Jack, come on in. Not to worry, kid, these aren't for you." Jack's empty hands appeared in the doorway before his head did. Sanderson uncocked the shotgun and laid it back across his lap.

"Who'n the fuck are they for?"

"They're for what's comin'. How was your ride? Any trouble with the locals?" Ben took another sip of his drink and shuffled his broad mustache as he sniffed the bite away.

"Shit, no. I wasn't fixing to risk it. I took the northern way over Paiute country. With the Bannock and 'Shone all riled-up the way they are, I figured the less folk I piss off, the better." Jackson hung his hat on the antler of the buck over the mantle. He sat at the table and took a long moment to drink from his can. Ben resumed his rocking.

"Anyone follow you?" he asked. Jack wiped his chin with a wrist and shook his head vaguely.

"I wasn't exactly covering my tracks, but I didn't see anyone tailin' me all the days I was on the trail. Hardly even saw another rider for days. 'Uardo was the first person I talked to when I rode in earlier today. He showed me to the longhouse, and I scrubbed up a bit a'fore I got your note about coming over after dusk." Ben nodded slowly as he exhaled a long, slow breath of smoke. Jackson stood from his seat and peeked out the closed curtain.

"We expecting trouble, Mr. Sanderson?" Jackson shifted nervously from one leg to the other. He wasn't wearing a gun, and he began to regret that decision. Ben shrugged vaguely.

"Expecting, anticipating, deserving; take your pick. Jackson gave him a strange, sidelong look.

"'The hell you talking about, Benjamin? Did something happen? 'You losing the ranch?" Jackson asked, his face betraying vexed confusion. His question seemed to recall Ben back to reality because he finally made eye contact with Jack and smiled like a tired old man.

"In a way, yes. I had a dream the other night, and I haven't been able to get it out of my head."

"A dream?"

"Yes, a dream. I crossed the desert with a sack of silver coins, not knowing the silver was dripping out of a hole in the bag, turning into a trail of blood that followed me everywhere I went. As the dream went on, I couldn't help but feel like I was being hunted. I began to run and run and call for help, until I eventually just give up and let it get me." Jackson listened, wide-eyed, mouth slackly ajar.

"Let what get you?" he asked, almost whispering.

"Not sure. I never turn to look. I always wake up right when it catches up to me." He sipped his drink again, rocking all the while. Jackson shivered with a chill and shook his head.

"'The fuck is wrong with you, Sanderson? Why'd you ask me here?"

"Because I think someone is coming to kill us for what we did to that rancher and his boy."

"You mean like a marshal or a bounty hunter? Like the one that plugged Rowe?" Jackson's voice dropped sadly as he remembered. "Do you reckon he was the same one that shot Asher?" Ben stopped rocking suddenly.

"Who plugged Rowe?" he asked curiously. Jack shrugged. Upon noticing Ben's dog flatulently slumbering on a rug near the fire, he approached and crouched to scratch its belly.

"Some feller from back east, I think. He wore a flat cap, and he was a wicked-fine shot, from what Martin said. He irrigated Rowe right there in the middle of the street. Right after that, Martin, Rhodes, and me, we high-tailed-it north," Jackson explained, trying his best to be distracted by the dog who had awoken and requested more pats. "What's the dog's name?" Jack asked.

"Whipple. He's got a favorite stick over there. Well, it's actually a thick, knobby root, but he don't know any better. So, you didn't get a good look at the killer?" Benjamin asked. Jackson retrieved the gnawed stick and proceeded to scratch the dog's round belly with it. He shook his head and sighed again.

"No look at all, more like. After Asher, then Rowe, I wasn't sticking around to capture a likeness. Just south of Dakota, I split off and went my own way. Say someone was tracking us from Colorado; they're looking for Rhodes, not me. I'm ready to put all that bullcrap behind me and finally make some honest money." Jackson stopped scratching Whipple's belly and sat on the milking stool beside the fireplace. Whipple groaned his disapproval and pawed the air in desperation. Benjamin nodded slowly again, and the tension in his jaw and temple seemed to slacken.

"Maybe you're right after all. I pray you're right. It ain't justice, us getting away from that unharmed like we did, but I'm grateful. I'd like to think I'm wiser for it, and I hope to do right with the chance I've been given. I feel much more at peace about it, having talked about it. Thank you, Jackson." Sanderson commenced his relaxed rocking. His finger remained on the trigger. Jackson let out a relieved chuckle and teased the cattledog from where he sat.

"I'm glad to hear that, Mr. Sanderson. I was glad to walk away. I'll be even more glad if I never see those bastards again. I feel so much better and more rel–"

Both men stood to face the open window behind Benjamin with a silent start at the sound of a rustle. With his shotgun leveled at the window, Benjamin walked as silently as he could on the boarded floor. He cautiously locked back the hammer on each barrel and leaned to peek out. Leading with the gun, Benjamin tilted out and swept a wide arc. He retreated back through the window with a chuckle and shuffle of his mustache.

"It was a damn skunk," he laughed, thumbing towards the window. "I saw him bobbing away around the corner of the house. Damned thing, got us so jumpy." Benjamin shook his head and ran a hand through his silvering hair. He sat back down in his chair and began rocking again. Even Whipple seemed to relax again as they sat and continued talking about the plan for the week. Benjamin poured a drink for the two of them, and Whipple commenced his rude noises by the fire.

Whipple lifted his head, his ears pointed towards the front window, moments before the lower left pane suddenly shattered, splintering glass across the floor. The two cowboys and their dog were on their feet.

Whipple barked at the violent disturbance from the safety of the bed while Jackson barreled his stool over and took cover by the door. Benjamin leaned against the other side of the doorway, his shotgun ready.

Jackson's shouted questions, Whipple's relentless barking, the crunching glass underfoot, the loose trigger guard on the shotgun; Benjamin's head was a blur of noise and panic. Benjamin roared at Whipple to shut the hell up, so he could think for a goddamned second. The dog snarled in concession and disappeared under the bed. A voice from outside called inquisitively,

"Hello? Is everyone alright in there? I'm sorry if we disturbed you, but we didn't know if you were armed, and I didn't want to find out after knocking."

Jackson held up his fingers like a pistol and mouthed the word, *gunbelt*, to Benjamin. He pointed to the chest at the end of the bed and turned his attention to the voice outside.

"We're alright, you son of a bitch, and we're armed to the teeth. The next words out of your mouth better be an apology and an offer to replace that window."

"Am I speaking to Benjamin Sanderson and John Jackson?"

Jackson returned to his place by the door, pistol drawn.

"You know our names, but we don't know yours!" Jack shouted in reply. Ben cringed at Jack's bold confirmation of their identities to a mystery assailant. Jack immediately cringed upon realizing the same.

From outside, a tickled, genuine laugh echoed from behind cover. Benjamin risked a peek for a moment. Crates, a barrel, bales of alfalfa, the open hayloft of the barn, the slanted roof of the bunkhouse; the dim, dusky light washed everything in shadows and shapes, so that even his own home obscured the attacker.

"That's true," he called back, laughter still in his voice. "I'll make you a deal: if you guess my name, I'll confirm it like an idiot, too." Jack and Ben exchanged looks. Ben shrugged and shook his head. Jackson thought hard, and then he shouted.

"You're that gunman what shot Asher and Barnabus back in Foothill. Fixin' to plug us too, and drag our stiffs back to town for a bag of coins, right? You best watch your ass out there, cowpoke, 'cause the rest of the ranch hands certainly heard that." Jackson smiled at his own wit and checked the cartridge in the pistol. After a long, quiet moment, the voice responded.

"...No, that's not my name. Besides, I only shot Barnabus. Nobody is paying a bounty for your sorry hides. And you needn't worry about your army of ranch hands: Eduardo and his son are tied up in the barn, healthy as oxen." Ben gave Jack an exasperated look and held up a hand.

"Sarna: is that your name?" Ben guessed. Air seemed to grow thick with tension. The pause felt far more loaded with potential. His voice sounded less musing when he responded.

"I was hoping you'd remember me, Sanderson. I should have followed you when you left that Russian silver on the bar, you coward."

"How's this going to end?" Ben called out, taking the lead in the conversation. "You're going to kill us both, an old man, and a young kid who never done nothin' wrong, and for what? How do you win?" Jackson slowly pressed the latch of the door and opened it barely an inch. He peeked quickly before letting it swing open as he pressed against the wall again. No shot came as Jack had expected, but he was grateful all the same. He nodded at Ben, pointed to his eyes, and then nodded outside. Ben nodded vaguely in reply. When Vaclav responded, his voice seemed to be coming from a new hiding place.

"Label me conservative, if you will, but I don't think folks who play accessory to murder should just walk away, unbothered. You shot a boy, Benjamin. He was seven. You held him while they murdered his father, and neither of you said a damn thing to stop it."

"The boy was alive when I left him," Benjamin shouted loudly, partially confessing his lie to Jackson. "When they told me to go'n finish him off, I couldn't do it, so I told him to lay still and play dead, and I shot the dirt by him. He was bleeding but breathing when I left him. I spared his life, Sarna!" Benjamin did not look Jackson in the eye, not from shame of his lie, but from the shame of defending his shooting and leaving a child to die alone on a burning ranch. Jackson wasn't looking at him either.

"I didn't lay a hand on neither of them," Jack negotiated. He holstered the pistol and held two empty hands out the door for Vaclav to see. Jack hissed a whisper to Ben as he half-stepped into view, saying, "I'm going to try to get him to reveal himself. If you get a clean shot…" Ben nodded gravely. Jack called out to Vaclav loudly again.

"If I come out, you're not gonna shoot, are you?" He waited, his hands still exposed in the doorway. When Vaclav responded, it was quieter, more unsure.

"Alright, I won't shoot."

"How do I know you mean it? You could just be waiting for me to step out a'fore you plug me." Jack nodded to Ben again. They both watched through their tiny slivers of view as a hand raised a pistol to the air from behind the hill of alfalfa bales.

"Got my gun in the sky. I swear on my dog that I will not shoot you." Ben spotted an arm, a shoulder, and a head. With any luck, the buckshot in his scattergun would hit all three. He crouched and leveled both barrels at Vaclav while Jack concealed his movement.

Behind Vaclav, a flash and loud crack of gunfire from the dark hayloft revealed a small boy lying prone, staring down the barrel of a large rifle. Locking eyes with the markman through the fist-sized hole in Jackson's middle, Benjamin dropped to the floor. Clutching his shotgun to his heaving, pounding chest, he pressed his back to the wall, keeping his head out of view. Benjamin raised his shotgun over his head and fired blindly out the broken window in the theoretical direction of the hidden marksman.

"Oh, shit," Vaclav cursed quietly to himself as both barrels appeared from the window and exploded in an echoed blast, like a massive drum. He dove to the ground quickly, burying his face in a loose pile. He didn't trust these bales to stop bullets. Spitting dry alfalfa from his beard, Vaclav stayed low, waiting for Andras's plan to unfold. Everything was set and prepared almost completely without a hitch.

There was a moment earlier when Vaclav feared that he would sabotage the entire operation and maybe get himself killed. He had crawled on his belly fifty yards, agonizingly slow, to the corner of the ranch house, where he could plant the payload of dynamite and nitro in the space beneath the floorboards.

With a mouth full of creosote, a head dripping with sweat, and boots full of sand and gravel, he began to shimmy silently beneath the house. From ahead of him, a terribly familiar scent caused him to look up into the pig-nosed, beady-eyed face of a black-and-white striped skunk. Equally as surprised, Vaclav shielded his face and pressed himself against the nearest wall he could find as quietly as he could.

The skunk, also anxious and alarmed at this awkward invasion of space, pressed itself as far away from him as it could: nearly twelve inches. Waddling as quickly as skunkly possible, it turned right and snorted as it crawled over the top of Vaclav's shin.

Instinctively, Vaclav withdrew his legs in a sharp jerk, and the skunk scurried away. Above him, the conversation had fallen silent, and one of them was directly above him. He held his breath and froze every muscle he knew how to control in his body.

After a long moment that felt like hours, the conversation started back up, so Vaclav took a breath and removed the bundle of dynamite. Exactly where Andras and he had decided, he slid the apple crate so that Andras could see the bundle of brown paper-wrapped sticks tied around the small glass jar seated within.

The moment he released the box of explosives, he immediately felt as if he had aged a decade. He shimmied slowly backwards, checked for any returning residents, and slowly crawled away to his position. Besides that, the plan was working perfectly.

Andras inhaled a deep breath and released it slowly, trying to catch his breath again as he rested Pa's rifle along a saddle resting on a crate. It wasn't the most-hidden spot, but, from here, he could see the glint of the glass jar nestled in a wreath of brown paper packages, tied up with string. He called out loudly to Benjamin, signaling Uncle Vaclav he was in position.

"Sanderson!" Andras called, trying his best to shout and not sound almost-eight. Staying low, Vaclav scurried from his bales to his next position.

Benjamin held his breath and listened again. He cracked open the breech of his shotgun and slid in two new shells..

"Sanderson!" The call came again. It wasn't only his imagination.

"Who's that?" Ben called. He closed the shotgun and cocked-back the hammers.

"You killed my pa," Andras yelled back. He was fixed on his target. Vaclav should be on the other side, covering the other exit. "And then you shot me, and you left me all alone to die out there on the prairie."

"Son of a bitch…" Ben swore to himself in disbelief. That little bastard survived. There was a spark of satisfied joy, contentment, upon learning that the little boy he had spared had made it after all. That bright, beautiful, joyous spark was immediately snuffed by the wake of realization that he was being murdered by a child. "Andi, right?" Ben shouted. His finger danced alongside the trigger, his conscience locked in a contested grapple with mortality. Somewhere, Sarna was out there too, but maybe he could convince them both...

"That's right," Andras replied. "How did you remember?" he asked, genuinely surprised.

"You're joking, right?" Ben replied back, a smile spreading beneath his quivering mustache. "Ain't a day goes by when I don't wake up, remembering you on the ground, crying and shot. When I was walking away that day, I was praying to whatever god would listen to an old bastard like me, that you would survive and find peace someday."

It was all horribly and terribly true. Sanderson was haunted. In many ways, the upsot-wagon-moment of his life was the day he watched his fellows murder a rancher and burn his home. Staring down the barrel of his pistol at the blubbering, begging boy before him, it broke him. He swore to pursue a peaceful existence from that day on.

Today was Tuesday, and he already unloaded and reloaded his shotgun with the intent of killing the same boy. Deep, deep down inside, Ben knew, were he to survive this ordeal, he would remember this being ironic.

Andras squeezed his eyes shut and remembered the sweet-smelling sweat and rough, calloused hands that held a gun to his head as they killed Pa. He remembered how he shot him, shoved him to the ground with a rough boot, and pointed the gun at his face. Andras thought that he died that day.

"I do remember. You told me that you hoped I would find peace when my dad, my horse, my house, all of it was gone. Where was I going to find peace? You took everything away, and left me there, all by myself, when I was shot in my leg by your gun!" Andras felt the anger rising in his chest like hot bile. It spilled onto his words as he spat them at Ben. Despite the boiling hatred in his throat, his hands were steady as a statue's. The crosshair of his scope never wavered from the glint of glass beneath the floor.

"Andi, I swear to god, I never wanted any of that to happen to you. I'm begging you to have mercy on a penitent old cowboy who turned away from all that." Ben's hands trembled as he scooted slowly toward the wall where he heard Andras's voice.

"I don't give a fuck what you wanted to happen. Just because you're sorry, doesn't mean what you did is gone. What you did followed you to your home this time, and now I'm going to show you mercy like you showed me: with a bullet, *mudak*."

Andras hardly felt the heavy push of the rifle as he leaned against it. In the dusky dim of sunset, the heavy white cloud of his gunsmoke was parted by a ground-shaking detonation that momentarily blinded him a second before it deafened him. He felt the ground jolt once beneath him as the echoes of the detonation returned from distant hills. Scraps of wood, bricks, and the tattered remains of home furnishings began to rain down in smoldering chunks. Andras dipped beneath his saddle rifle-rest and watched the shards of Sanderson's and Jackson's new lives pepper the ground like falling stars.

Vaclav cried out and stumbled from his cover toward Andras.

"Are you alright?!" Andras cried, standing from his hiding place and jogging to his uncle. Vaclav nodded and guided him back to safety. The shrapnel had nearly finished raining down, but there was no rush. The two ranch hands would slip their ropes eventually and are free to do as they like. Andras hoped they would stay and rebuild a home for themselves.

"What's wrong?" Andras asked Vaclav. His face was pale, and he was holding his stomach gingerly.

"Yes, I think I'm…" Vaclav, doubled over again, clutching his mouth. "Sanderson's body landed real close to me, almost touched me, and I got sick to my stomach, and we need to get the hell out of here." Andras nodded, his mouth hanging open in amazement and his eyes lost.

As the pillar of smoke rose into the darkening sky, the two riders rode east beneath a dark red shadow.

Chapter 22

November arrived in a cold wind that didn't let-up until the frost began to settle. The Dakota Territory was never described as "peaceful" or "gentle", but the people who chose to live there called it "theirs." In the last decade, towns and camps had seemingly appeared overnight. Families from every corner of the world were flocking to the Sioux lands in hopes of winning some of that Indian gold. Most of the Sioux had been moved East after the war ended, and gold was discovered on their land.

Hank didn't understand why some of the Sioux chose to stay. If he were them, he would leave to find freedom elsewhere, but he didn't know where that was for people like them.

Coming home had felt easier and smoother than he anticipated. As his hand hovered over the doorknob to his father's chamber, his heart churned in his chest, and his mouth felt dry and sticky.

The broad mountain of muscle and authority who had purchased him all those years ago was no longer. Syphilis had eaten away at his sharp business acumen and steely gaze. In its place was a frail, old coot in too-big clothes, stringy, untidy white hair, and lips that always glistened with moisture.

Rhodes had come to see his father twice since he had arrived; once when he first rode in, and again last week to transfer power of attorney over to the oldest living heir, Henry Earnest Rhodes III. The entire estate and surrounding town seemed to sigh in relief when Hank and

Martin rode in. Big Hank's impending death shaded everything with an unsure air of instability, like a glass teetering on the ledge of a table. Riding into town felt surreal as he inspired hope and peace in the townsfolk with only his presence. He would lead his father's town when he passed, and every ounce of his gold would buy everything his father ever denied him. He had only to wait for the frail, old toad to croak.

Most of New Rhodes was the Rhodes's estate, a gaudy Georgian plantation house lined with pillars and patios. The surrounding land was beautiful, green, tended lawns and gardens, fountains, and courtyards where the finest horses in Dakota lived. Many of the animals on Rhodes Estate lived and ate better than the rest of the people in town.

The remainder of New Rhodes was a muddy town that continually expanded without improving. Like a growth, the unplanned and uncontrolled expansion sickened everything around it, until the filth of unchecked mankind scratched at the gilded walls of Rhodes Estate.

Hank's arrival marked the advent of a new era of the Rhodes dynasty, with Hank III bringing along his strong worker's ethic, well-traveled experience, and charismatic charm of youth. He'd yet to claim a wife for himself also, and the eligible ladies of New Rhodes prepared themselves to battle with perfume and rouge for a place by the side of the next generation of Rhodes leadership.

The saloon in town was perhaps the next largest building after the plantation. Like the town, it had grown, expanded, and transformed into a town center where the men of New Rhodes could stand on a jury of their peers, and then buy a whiskey on their way out. Simply referred to as "The Beaver Dam," when any of the Henry Rhodeses came in, they drank for free. It wasn't long before Martin Xochitl-Tlajuillakan was recognized as the "number-two" of the new regime, and people began respecting him for it.

For a young Mexican boy raised in Texas, he could hardly believe whenever someone stepped to the side for him or tipped their hat with a friendly smile. The entire town viewed him as New Rhodes's newest badge and the newest lieutenant to join Big Hank's ranks. Wherever Henry went, Martin was nearby, watching the door and holding down the darkest corner of the room. He hadn't needed to draw his gun once since they had arrived. Even with the roving band of dopers, everyone recognized Martin as the next Big Hank's muscle.

Being respected was new for Martin. He'd been feared, avoided, hated, liked, and even loved once, but never respected. Martin was a simple man who took nothing for granted, and appreciated each opportunity for what it was. It had been a long time since he had felt content enough to call somewhere home, but New Rhodes was beginning to look like everything he ever wanted.

Hank and Martin sat at the bar of the Beaver Dam, truly relaxed and wearing genuine smiles. Around them, the atmosphere was warm and at-ease. Townies laughed and drank as though a great celebration was near, and the anticipation was already leaking through. Each day felt closer and closer to the fulfillment of a dream with Hank's father slipping further and further into unhealth with each passing day.

Leaning on Martin's shoulder was a beautiful Sioux woman whose raven-black hair cascaded down past her waist where Martin's arm was wrapped. She sipped on his whiskey as they flirted. Henry was talking loudly about the instance a buffalo gored his horse, and he had to kill it and walk back to camp over the course of three days. It was a tale he borrowed from a Cheyenne he met years ago, but it was always received well. He had perfected the story by now, so that he knew when the bartender would bring his next drink, and when the ladies listening would gasp.

From the poorly-hung, swinging saloon doors, polished shoes coated in dust carried a tall, thin-framed man with a short beard and wire-rimmed bifocals into the saloon. He wore fine clothing and a buttoned coat, and he held a derby hat in one hand, the same one he had removed when he entered the building. In the other hand, he held a document bag that was also polished but now dulled by a coat of fine dust. The stark contrast between this polished member and the rest of New Rhodes's population was glaring.

He allowed his eyes to adjust for a moment, adjusted his glasses on his nose, and then crossed the room to where Hank and Martin sat drinking. Troy Bundin Esquire was no stranger in New Rhodes. Although never armed, he was never harassed. Upon the rapid decline of Big Hank's health, a lawyer was sent-for to finalize the papers and prepare the transfer of Rhodes Estate over to its new sole beneficiary.

For the past week, the lawyer had documented and taken inventory of all of Big Hank's assets to ensure the security of the Will. When Big Hank quietly passed away in his sleep in the coming weeks, the new day would be marked with a new Big Hank.

Henry waved the lawyer over and dismissed an adjacent patron to clear a seat for him. Henry hiccuped and suppressed a burp as he watched Mr. Bundin open and unpack today's documents.

"How much is it today, school-marm?" he slurred jokingly. The lawyer chuckled nervously as he aligned the corners of the forms on the damp, sticky bar. Bundin filled his fountain pen carefully with the well of black ink, and he scraped the excess from the nib. He handed the pen to Henry and indicated where to sign, explaining quietly with each page turned, knowing Rhodes was not listening. Bundin would have liked to be finished and never have to return to this town ever again. Henry signed blindly.

"This one is the power-of-attorney's authorization form to addendum. This is the final Will and Testament abstract to be duplicated and notarized in triplicate. Sign this one to agree to the division of asset distribution as outlined in the abstract…" Henry signed lazily over and over until the stack of papers dwindled to several sheets. Near the bottom, an instance of his printed name caught his eye, and he paused to inspect it.

"Is there a problem, Mr. Rhodes?" the lawyer asked nervously. Henry pointed to the name with a poorly aimed finger and articulated wetly.

"That's not my name. I'm the third; Henry Earnest Rhodes, the third. This says 'Henry *James* Rhodes', the fourth?" he asked, confusion smeared across his face like drunkenness.

"Yes, sir, that's correct. Yesterday, you authorized the amendment to your father's will through your power of attorney over your father's estate to your half brother, Henry James Rhodes, the fourth." The lawyer froze and waited for Henry's next reaction. Henry shook his head to clear it in case he misheard.

"Adneddum? Addedum. Ande–what the fuck are you talking about, Bundin?" Martin gently shoved the girl from his lap and sat straighter on his chair. She disappeared up the stairs. Martin's subtle shift changed the tone of the table. The lawyer adjusted his glasses with a shaky hand and drew out yesterday's forms.

"Here, sir. You signed these yesterday authorizing your step-mother with shared power-of-attorney. You approved the changed document to include your half-brother under the monopoly statutes, sir, do you remember?" Bundin produced the forms and indicated to the sloppy signatures, unmistakably belonging to Henry Earnest Rhodes, the third. Henry stood from his seat and swaggered in a half circle before he swept the pages off the table and raised his voice in an inebriated stupor.

"I know my own signature, gawddammit, fuckin' lawyer. I don't know who the fuck…" He squinted and read the name on the addendum approval form, "… Henry James Rhodes, the fourth, even is!" he said, flinging the paper so that it spun and flicked to the floor like an autumn leaf.

"Grab him," Henry barked, and then snapped his fingers. Martin lunged forward and grabbed the collar of Troy Bundin's shirt in a grip only a bronco-buster could have. "Let's go figure this out right now, c'mon," Henry said, waving lazily, and he walked out the crooked doors. Behind him, Martin roughly escorted the nervous lawyer who was clutching papers to his chest and struggling to close his bag.

Hank shoved open the tall, black wrought-iron gate leading to the pleasantly curvaceous walkway to the main house. Trees with the last of Summer's leaves clung desperately to their last signs of life before they feigned death for the long winter. The estate's gardeners and hands bustled quietly about their work, avoiding the drunken war path being forged up the road.

At the bottom of the stairs, the house's footman gave a friendly smile and nod and offered a tray with a coffee pot and cups. Hank waved him away like an annoying insect, and pulled the door before pushing it open. At the top of the stairs, his father's butler, Julius, began to descend, speaking in a strong, authoritative voice.

"Mr. Rhodes, the third; what an unexpected visit. Can I help you?" Julius crooned. The creases of his pants hardly bent as he walked.

"I need to talk to my father, right now, Jules."

"Your father is not able to entertain visitors at the moment, but perhaps, for supper–"

"This ain't waiting. I'm heading up. Get out of the way, or get put on the floor, Julius." The butler conceded the stairway, but proceeded to calmly call up the stairs, "Ma'am: people are here to see Mr. Rhodes. Would you be so kind as to assist them with their search?"

"Of course, Julius, you are so kind and accommodating. We are ever so lucky to have you." Appearing at the top of the stairs like a vision of frontier beauty was a damn-fine, handsome woman in a beautiful modern dress with her hair tied-up in a ribbon. Her light brown hair played like the final rays of the setting sun. Her cheeks were the color of fresh embarrassment, and her lips promised a song yet unheard. Reflexively, Henry straightened and removed his hat, brushing his disheveled hair from his forehead. She glided as she walked, like a real lady, but the expression on her face was not as soft as its features.

"As Julius so eloquently informed you, Big Hank is not available for visitors. He is resting for now. Another time would be more appropriate, perhaps," she spit her words at him like ice. Her diction laid bare her education and upbringing. Henry furrowed his brow as he studied her, part furious, part aroused. "Please leave," she said at last. It was not a request. Henry eyed her unstably and climbed three more steps toward her. He noticed the faintest of hesitations as she stopped herself from taking a step back.

"Who might you be to be nagging *me* in this house, ma'am?" Henry arced an eyebrow at her and leaned forward onto the next stair.

"I'm the Lady of this house, sir."

"Lady of this house?' Like a–"

"Mr. Rhodes's wife."

Henry paused as his brain reviewed what she had just said. She crossed her arms and looked down her nose at him.

"His wife?" he asked. "Well, I'm–"

"I know who the fuck you are, Henry Earnest Rhodes, and I would have you unhand the estate's lawyer, Mr. Bundin." She waited. Henry nodded to Martin, and Martin released the frightened lawyer. Mr. Bundin smoothed his waistcoat and composed himself before climbing the rest of the stairs unaccompanied.

"You swindling little slut! You're trying to steal my money!" He barked, stabbing a filthy finger up at her. Mr. Bundin rounded the corner to the bedroom and closed the door behind him. She coughed out a single disgusted laugh down at him.

"*Your* money? It's your father's money, and soon it will be his family's money. I'll make sure you never see more than a bit." Henry mounted three more stairs, until he was eye-level with his step-mother, a beautiful young woman who could be no older than he. As he climbed the last three steps, she was suddenly so small, and she looked so much weaker when he was looking down at her.

"I don't know you, and I don't care if your boy is the son of the Virgin Mary. I'll kill you and your little bastard. Run off back to the whore house, and find another old-fuck to rob. This one's taken." The blush in her cheeks turned pale, like a wet bible, and her bottom lip trembled. She took a half step away from him before following Mr. Bundin into Big Hank's bed chamber.

Within the largest room of the house was a beautiful four-poster bed made from African woods. The curtains were hand-woven linen from Cuba. Lying before a fireplace large enough to stand in was the hide of a bison with its head stuffed to its original size. Big Hank often placed sweating, cold glasses atop the bison's broad forehead as he sat by the fire. The curtains that blocked the fifteen-foot high windows were Chinese silk, and they allowed no sunlight to enter the stale room. Taxidermized animals from all corners of the States guarded battlefield trinkets and artifacts from dead peoples. Neglected paintings of ships, animals, and military officers hung crookedly on sagging hooks. The decor brought to mind something similar to a museum or a dragon's hoard.

The only light in the room came from two oil lamps beside the wide bed. Lying in the top left corner of the enormous bed, it looked like some underdeveloped creature dying from exposure to the sun. The stringy wisps of hair reminded Henry of old spiders' webs. He slept hideously, his leaking mouth, agape to reveal the last surviving teeth in his pale-gummed mouth, like an eye socket. His skin seemed to hang from the sharpest peaks of his protruding skeleton, appearing as if he were melting away, like some wax sculpture set too closely to a lamp. His breathing sounded like a saw being pulled through a pulpy tree.

Henry froze at the initial glimpse of his father before Martin nudged him and indicated he'd be looking around at all the dusty artifacts. Henry nodded and approached slowly.

Hank's newest woman sat on the edge of the bed, speaking softly with Mr. Bundin. Rhodes inhaled a deep breath, burped out a bit of his drunkenness, and assumed a loud, confident walk to announce his aggressive arrival. Again, she stood to confront him, but Henry raised his hands placatingly and gave her his most charming smile.

"Now that we've had a moment to calm down, let's start again. Who the fuck are you?" His tone did not change, but instead, he allowed his words to convey how dangerous he was.

"Helen Rhodes. I *was* Helen Cleary, but I came to love Henry just as he loved me. He was so proud that I gave him a son, 'a proper heir,' he said, when they first met." Henry bit back the malignant bitterness in him.

"What's your angle in all this? You want dope? Gold?" He studied her.

"I want my husband to be well and strong, and for my son to have the good life he deserves." As she spoke, she glanced over her shoulder at the frail, leathery mass in the bed. Henry took another step closer to her, so now she could smell him.

"I can give you both of those."

She looked back at him with disbelieving shock. "Go to hell, Earnest," Helen whispered, and she turned back toward the bed. Henry's hand lurched out, and he grabbed her thin wrist and yanked her closer to him. Mr. Bundin put down his bag and took two hurried steps toward Henry and Helen.

"Mr. Rhodes! Please, refrain from any rash or illegal behavior," Troy said with an edge he'd not heard before. Henry nodded to the lawyer.

"Of course, Mr. Bundin. We're just talking, is all," he explained, conveying the slightest tinge of threat. He squeezed her wrist harder and brought her close to him. She whimpered under his crushing grip.

"Change it back, or you'll be needing a Will next," he hissed to her.

He was so fucking close to being rid of that old bastard and having the money and life that he had waited so patiently to take for himself. She winced in pain, and he released her with a jerk.

"Mr. Rhodes," the lawyer growled, "*must I remind you*, any illegal activity done with intent to change or alter the contents of this Will disqualifies you from it entirely." Henry's fiery glare transitioned to the lawyer, who looked to be ready to throw a punch.

From the bed, a fragile, knobbly arm rose as if suspended by a string, signaling the stirrings of his father.

"Laudanum…" the spindly shape mumbled. His kindly wife glided to his side and unstoppered a bottle. She carefully extracted a dose of dark liquid with a dropper and squeezed the contents of the dropper into his open, waiting mouth, like a baby bird, hatched from syphilis and opium. He smacked his wet lips contentedly and sighed hoarsely. "Who's there? Hm? Don't be a coward. Announce yourself!" Each syllable was a wet cough that made Henry want to drink water. Helen leaned down to the ear of her husband and kissed his forehead before speaking gently.

"Beloved, it's your loving wife, your lawyer, and your son, Henry." She smoothed his wispy hairs. He blindly reached for her, and asked louder now,

"Henry! Bring me my son, Henry" he called, reaching for his son now. Henry took a quick step forward to his father's side as he continued to rave. "Bring my new son to me. Show me my Little Hank…" Henry stopped.

"No, Hank, it's your older son, Henry Earnest."

"Earnest? Hmm…Earnest. Let me give him my blessing. Come forth, boy." Henry moved forward again and bent over his father. Big Hank weakly grabbed his son's shirt in flesh-draped, skeletal digits and held it, rubbing it between his thumb and forefinger unconsciously.

"Father, there's something wrong with the Will, and I need you to change it back to how it was," Henry said softly to his father. From behind him, he heard Helen mutter, "oh my god, he's a tick."

Big Hank's milky eyes rolled around in their oversized sockets before they locked onto his son's.

"You don't look anything like me. You look like your mother. Mother, mother, motherrrrfucker. Makes more legacy. Never forget a face, you fifty-dollar whore-bill."

Mr. Bundin laid a calm hand on Henry's shoulder and said, "He's delirious and in pain, Mr. Rhodes. Even if he wanted to, your father is in no state to conduct business. He must be of sound mind to make any amendments to the Will."

Henry laid a hand on his father's shoulder and shook it gently. "Father, wake up, you dumb bastard," he cursed quietly, shaking him more roughly. Behind him, Helen floated in to intervene, but was deterred with a swift backhand that caught her across the ear and jaw that sent her spinning to the floor. Mr. Bundin rushed to her side to check she was alright. He rose to confront Henry, but was halted by the barrel of a pistol pointed between his eyes.

"I'm going to talk to my father. Get this all figured." Henry put the gun back in its holster, and Martin faded back into the shadows of the gallery.

He tossed back his father's covers and sat him up higher so they could speak. He gently placed pillows behind his back and head.

"You are a Henry," his father began. "But are you one of mine?" he asked, his pale eyes rolling to the right. "Or are you one of hers?"

"Father, someone outside the family has tampered with the Will, and you need to fix it."

"The Will? Impossible. The power of will is within. And a safe." A fleck of warm spittle landed on Henry's hand, and he reflexively wiped it with the covers. He shook his father roughly, and his head lolled and bobbled like a wilting rose. A disgusting, gurgling laugh bubbled from his gullet, and his eyes became wide.

"Stoppit! You'll kill him!" Helen cried from the floor, her jaw already swelling. Mr. Bundin was standing now, shielding her from another attack from Henry.

In a single moment of coherent clarity, Big Hank's eyes locked with Henry's gaze. He grabbed Henry's shirt and pulled him close. Big Hank smelled like cellars, crawlspaces, attics, and outhouses. His first word was pronounced with a bubble that flicked wet onto Henry's cheek when it popped.

"I am so, so disappointed… in you. You could have been someone, but instead, I'm out fifty dollars. What a fucking waste. What…a…waste…" he rasped, and then coughed wetly onto Henry's cheek. Henry stood from his seat on the edge of the bed and drew his pistol. "A true waste indeed," were his final words to his oldest surviving son.

Henry fired six times into the twiggy body that had been eaten away by disease and opium. The warm white linens drank up the bright red blood so that, before too long, he was enwreathed by a halo of red. Hank couldn't believe he ever feared him.

Mr. Bundin removed his bifocals gently and put them in his bag. He closed it with a metallic snap. Helen stood from the floor, her face frozen in a moment of shock and horror.

"You killed him," said Bundin, more a fact than an accusation.

"You're damn right I did, and if either of y–" A loud crack of gunfire and a bright flash from below sent Henry toppling over, onto his side. His head bounced on the floor as he landed. Clutching his calf, Henry moaned in pain as he inspected the hole through both sides of his boot.

To his mind-fragmenting horror, his boot twisted and fell to the floor with the severed-foot still inside. His fleshy, bleeding ankle began to send jolts of agony up his body, so that he couldn't bring himself to rise. On the floor, clutching his leg, he turned to glimpse the shape of a young boy beneath the bed, holding a smoking pistol that was now pointed at his head. Henry's moan turned to a chuckle, and then to a warm belly laugh as he began to understand his situation.

Out in the hallway, the sound of smashing ceramic could barely be heard.

In a strained, pained voice, Henry pointed at Helen, saying, "I see what's going on here. The two of you are in-on-this together, and this little guy here is Henry James Rhodes, am I right? You are so fucking stupid, all of you." The boy rose from under the bed and holstered his own pistol.

Now he could see that he did recognize the small boy, but not from a family resemblance. From a pretty plot of land in Colorado.

Somewhere in the house, an angry shout was heard.

"My name isn't Henry. It's Andras. Andras Walenty. And their names aren't Helen and Troy. That's Mary, and that's my Uncle Vaclav," Andras said to him in a calm voice. Mary still held her face gently, and Vaclav, now no longer acting as Troy Bundin, seethed with vengeful justice at the man who laid hands on his wife.

"You're right: they were in on it together," Andras explained. "Unfortunately, you're wrong about the rest of it. Uncle Vaclav isn't a lawyer. He's never practiced law or seen a Will. Mary didn't marry Big Hank. I'm not the heir to the estate." For days, Andras had lived a silent, reclusive existence with only the plan to ponder. Pretending to be the newest bastard in the house had been as easy as minding his own business.

From downstairs, an exchange of gunfire made Mary start.

"Alright, Andi, let's go. It's getting bad out there," Uncle Vaclav warned grimly. He crossed the room, opened one of the Chinese silk curtains, and opened the tall balcony door, letting the yelling uproar outside spill into the dark bedroom. Andras nodded to his uncle, and caught a glimpse of Martin, crouched in the shadows behind a suit of gothic armor. He did not draw his gun or say anything.

"I was going to shoot you in the head, but this seemed more fair, an eye-for-an-eye. The Will never changed. Your father never married. Your future is gone now too. You killed your father, booting you from the Will. We told all the house staff too, so they're stealing everything they can. You have no more family, no more money, and no future. Now, we're even." Andras did not spare him a second glance as he climbed over the balcony, and onto his uncle's back to descend the rope.

"Martin!" Rhodes called from the floor. His hands were sticky and trembling, and he couldn't stop the bleeding. From the ring of shadow around the bed, Martin stepped out, holding a fancy Meerschaum pipe made to look like a steamship. From his pockets, glints of gold and gems teased his loot. "Help me get up, Martin, we need to kill those fuckers before they get away," Hank pleaded, reaching up with a sticky, red hand. Martin did not reach for the hand. "Martin!" Hank yelled, swiping a hand at him. Just out of reach, Martin studied him curiously like a carrion bird circling suffering.

From outside the door, banging and gunfire could be heard, and the smell of smoke had begun to grow stronger.

Martin clenched his new Meerschaum pipe in his teeth and drew his pistol from its holster.

"What the fuck is wrong with you, Martin? Help me! …Martin?"

Chapter 23

Being in a regular town felt strange after so long on the road, tracking Rhodes. His feet still couldn't touch the ground when he sat in the chair, so he left his feet to swing and kick freely as needed. Andras noticed how brown and dotted his skin had become since beginning this manhunt. Looking at Uncle Vaclav, he wondered what Pa would have looked like with a big beard and "freckles," as Mary had clarified.

Only one remained, and they had no idea where to begin looking, or if he was still in the country. He pushed a slice of tomato around his plate with his fork.

"Andras, are you alright? Is your stomach feeling fine?" Mary asked, leaning to see his face better. Andras nodded.

"Yes, I feel okay. I'm…" Andras shrugged. Uncle Vaclav nodded his head.

"I understand what you mean, Andi," Vaclav said. He nudged him with a playful elbow and gave him a wink. Andras tried to return the wink, but only reciprocated a very difficult-looking blink. Mary grasped Vaclav's hand on the table and squeezed it.

They were far from the Rhodes estate now in a small town a few miles West called Julesburg. It was a tiny railroad town with smatterings of residents, miners, farmers, and ranchers. The townsfolk were more concerned with animal attacks than politics. The smoke from the Rhodes estate was visible from the cafe they sat in now.

Vaclav poured Andras another cup of coffee, and Andras guzzled it down as quickly as the heat would allow him. Vaclav set the pot down and wiped his mouth. "It's hard to feel normal and safe when you're not some regular schlemiel, and we're not exactly doing regular business. Hush deserves to be taken down more than any of the others. A creature like him is likely to leave a trail of bodies behind him or something. We should check in with the fort or the train station. What do you think?"

Mary shook her head, her mouth full of food. The cafe wasn't crowded, but the server was busy with other patrons.

"This coffee tastes…weird," Andras said, looking at his cup. Vaclav laughed and poured himself another cup.

"That's because it tastes like coffee, and not that brown sock-water you love so much," he teased. Andras shrugged. He was probably right. Uncle Vaclav was right about a lot of things most of the time, but when he wasn't right, Mary was.

Andras had been so happy to see Mary after so long. He was not, however, as happy as Vaclav had been when she arrived. Her Polish had gotten so sharp and eloquent, that Andras forgot that she was born and raised in New York.

The night she had arrived, the first thing Mary and Andras did was converse in Polish together. She told him to tell her everything that had happened since last they saw each other. Andras started from the beginning. Mary cried when Andras told her about Ma passing on the Atlantic crossing. She cried when Andras told her about Buck, Piotyr's cloven compatriot. When Andras finally told her about the day Gourd and Pa died, she opened her arms and pulled him into her lap, where she held him tightly as she cried. Andras cried too, and held onto her tightly. It had been so long since Andras had felt motherly affection, and it melted parts of him that had been frozen for too long.

Later that night, Vaclav and Mary had approached Andras with a proposal. Together, they asked if he would accompany them both down the aisle when they were wed. Andras asked if he had to cut his hair, and accepted after they assured him no.

The next day, the three of them went to the church up the way and asked if they could be married. A friendly, old preacher was more than pleased to unite a couple in love. The preacher's own wife sat as a witness for the ceremony while she dabbed the corners of her eyes with her handkerchief all the while. The ceremony was respectful and beautiful, and Vaclav gazed into Mary's eyes the entire time. They exchanged smiles and giggles, and then they finally exchanged rings. The preacher prayed a blessing over them of protection, peace, and fruitfulness. When, at last, Vaclav and Mary kissed, Andras had clapped and imagined his ma and pa's wedding, and how happy they were, together.

Andras wondered what kind of blessing the preacher would give if he knew what they were up to. Would he pray for quickness and sharpness of aim? Is it Christianly to pray for success in killing? He reckoned it wasn't, and thought it best not to ask. The next day, they had completed their journey to New Rhodes.

Today marked one month since Vaclav and Mary's perfect wedding ceremony.

"Hell of a honeymoon," Mary said flatly, bacon in one side of her mouth. Vaclav gave a sidelong glance at the bruise on her jaw and on her wrist where Rhodes had roughed-her-up.

"*Hell* of a honeymoon," Vaclav agreed. Andras suddenly became very excited and withdrew a small paper-wrapped package he had been holding in his vest pocket. It was heavy and could fit in one hand.

"I got you a wedding gift! I almost forgot I had it, but you reminded me. Open it!" Mary did not try to hide her excitement at opening a wedding gift, and froze when she saw inside the package. Her hand reflexively covered her heart with surprise. "Do you like it?" he asked.

"Andras, where did you get this?" she asked quietly, trying to appear as calm as possible.

"They were in a box under Big Hank's bed. I was under there for a long ti–a *long* time, Aunt Mary, and I thought about taking more, but then I felt bad. After a while, I took two, one for each of you, because you guys have given me so much, and I wanted to give you guys something really good." Andras finally shoveled the last tomato into his mouth. Mary handed the paper package to Vaclav, and his eyes went wide with shock.

"Is that go–... What does 'CSA' mean?" Vaclav asked. He covertly pocketed the package with a poorly-veiled grin.

"It means old war and bad blood," she whispered, looking around the room cautiously.

"Good find, *moj bratanek*," he whispered excitedly.

"Gratulacje!" Andras exclaimed as he raised his mostly-empty mug of coffee and drained it. Slowly, the color returned to Mary's face, and she finally laughed, imagining what the gift could mean for their future together as husband and wife.

Behind them, the cafe owner raised his voice aggressively, almost shouting, "no, sir, out with you! We want none of your violence in this place!" Both Vaclav's and Andras's hands disappeared under the table for their guns at the commotion. They turned to see a handsome, bronze-skinned Wilson, dressed in Euro-American clothing and wearing that same wide-brimmed hat as before. His hair was braided behind his head, and it swung over his shoulder like a cat's tail when he scanned the room quickly. He made a hurt face when he heard the rude bartender, and took his hat off so the bartender could recognize him.

"It's the Wilsons' boy, shit-for-brains," exclaimed another patron sitting at the bar. The Indian pointed at the loud patron and waved with a friendly, "Que onda, pard'ner?" The bartender shook his head, half from shame.

The rays that beamed from Andras's smile drew Wilson's attention, and he immediately slackened with relief. Dodging a few tables and chairs, Wilson dropped into an empty chair beside Mary who reflexively leaned away from the stranger, alarmed.

"I saw Pukayuc outside, and I knew I would find you here!" Noticing Mary, Wilson turned to study her as well, but with far less alarm. He leaned to Vaclav and loudly whispered, "which one is this?" Vaclav snickered and made to pour his coffee in Wilson's lap who retreated with a charming laugh. "I'm merely teasing. After all the stories he told of the beauty of his great love in the East, I assumed you to be the sunrise. But of course, you are Mary. You've got yourself a fine man there, Mary," Wilson spoke sincerely, took her hand warmly, and shook it once. She shut her mouth and looked to Vaclav, half stunned, half confused. Laughing, Vaclav wiped his mouth and made the introductions.

"Mary, my love, this is Wilson, a Paiute friend we met in Nevada a while or so back," Vaclav explained. Wilson paused his burglary of Andras's biscuit from his plate with a dramatically wounded expression. Andras snatched back the biscuit and licked it territorially.

"You haven't told her about *me*?" Wilson asked Vaclav. Wilson snatched the biscuit back and ripped off the licked portion before stuffing the rest in his mouth. Andras giggled uncontrollably.

"Unintentionally. It must have slipped my mind while we were hunting dangerous fugitives," Vaclav responded, smirking.

"*Fugitiffs you neffer woul'f foun' wiffout me,*" Wilson mumbled as crumbs tumbled from his mouth. He was still harassing Andras, now attempting to steal his coffee, and Andras was batting his hands away like a cat. Mary was smiling and covered a giggle with her hand as she watched the boys tussling.

"Please excuse my initial rudeness, Mr. Wilson. As you say, I am Mary Sarna, wife to Vaclav. It's just that…" she paused, planning her next words.

"That you've never been this close to an Indian before," he said with an understanding smile. She blushed and nodded, embarrassed. He chuckled, waving away her nerves, saying "I'm glad that your first experience was over breakfast and not in more…unsavory circumstances." Her smile faded quickly.

By now, Andras had surrendered the remainder of his breakfast to their visitor, and was contentedly sipping another refill.

"Did you come all the way to find us just to steal my breakfast?" Andras asked over his mug, dramatized anger furrowing his brow.

"Just the biscuit actually. The bacon was a welcome bonus. No, you're right, I did come looking for you to ask you a favor. It's deeply personal and important to me." The tone around the table shifted as Mary, Andras, and Vaclav leaned in to listen to Wilson as his voice lowered to a serious timbre.

"As with all things, there is good news with the bad news. The good news is that my father has returned home after many years, and his wisdom is helping our people find hope. The bad news, unfortunately, is what brought him back home. My father and I experienced the same…prophetic dream. It told of an evil that spreads like pox and steals life everywhere it goes, and it's living in one of our sacred places." Andras's eyes went wide.

"What do you mean?" Vaclav asked, "Like a specter or a…demon?" His hesitation echoed with anxiety. Wilson thought on his question, staring up at the ceiling. He took a drink of Andras's coffee.

"I'm not sure. My father had a dream, he went to investigate that dream, and he found someone there. He buried a knife in his back, and the guy fought him off and threw the blade back. My father and I agree, he needs to go, but we also agree that it shouldn't be one of the Numa." Vaclav leaned back in his chair, nodding.

"Why not?"

"My father is convinced that our weapons won't work. I'm inclined to believe him. My father is getting upward in years, but he's a warrior to his bones. If my father says he buried his knife in him, and it didn't work, I believe him." Andras was almost on top of the table, listening anxiously.

"Did your pa say what he looked like?" Andras asked, so quiet, it was nearly a whisper. When Wilson met his gaze, Andras knew.

"Father said he wore black and had black eyes. He moved faster than any man he'd ever seen. He mentioned that he was very scarred and malformed," Wilson remembered.

"Were the scars on his neck and face? With a coat made of wolf's fur?" Andras asked again.

"I came to the right cowboys after all. Some of the locals told me about a notable amount of folk going missing in these parts, so I had to come investigate."

"He goes by *Hush*. He's a Serbian marksman who worked for the Russian army during the uprising nearly a decade ago. We don't know his real name, or where he is, but we've been looking for any trail leading to him. He, um, killed Andras's pa and razed his home," Vaclav explained darkly. It was Wilson's turn to nod. He pointed at the pair of them.

"It *must* be you. You're the ones who have to get rid of him. There's no other way to explain it."

"We'd be glad to!" Andras blurted out, "Where is he?" Vaclav had to restrain Andras back into his chair. Vaclav leaned in close to Andras so that only they could hear.

"Are you goofy? I'm not taking you with me."

"You're not leaving me behind! Besides, I've seen him shoot before! And you'll need me for back up. I'm a good shot now, even you said! Please, Uncle Vaclav. He's the last one before this is over."

"And then what? What comes after? After you've killed them all, what then?" Vaclav asked him with a sharp snap. Andras lowered his eyes and shrugged.

"I'm not so sure. Do I go to school?"

To be honest, Vaclav hadn't thought about it either. He'd been so preoccupied with their hunt that he hadn't given much thought to the future. He'd barely been married a month, and he was already having to make arrangements for a little boy to become part of their life. At least he would avoid the toilet-training stage.

"Yes, you'll go to school. And you'll learn a craft. We're going to do everything we can to give you a normal child's life," Mary declared confidently. The moment she had said it, she wished she hadn't.

"What does a normal child's life look like?" Andras asked.

"Whatever we make it look like," Vaclav said. He rested his hand on Mary's knee, and she nodded. Wilson slapped his thigh, inserting himself back into the conversation.

"So it's settled then," he said, smiling. Vaclav studied Andras for a moment. He nodded to Wilson. Mary did her best to veil her fear, but a cold shiver ran through her.

"I'll take a stage back to Foothill and arrange for our travel back home," Mary said with a brave voice. She stood and held her husband's face between her two hands. "Wróć do mnie do domu, Vaclav. *Come back home to me, Vaclav.*" The kiss they shared was fearful, hopeful, prolonged, and savored. Vaclav held her hands after they broke apart. If it would be their last…

"How long of a ride is it from here?" Uncle Vaclav asked Wilson, beginning to gather the dishes.

"Not a full day's ride, I reckon," Wilson calculated in his head. "If we leave soon, we'll arrive before dusk."

Three riders rode South toward familiar mountains and prairies haunted with the ghosts of possible futures. Andras found that the countryside was far more beautiful and peaceful when accompanied by a native of America. In Wilson's presence, shady, craggy passes were a welcome sight, and the dust of a passing band of Bannock hold-outs was more beautiful than terrifying.

By late afternoon, the Rocky Mountains loomed skyward, and the alien rock formations gradually transformed to rolling hills and ancient forests. Vaclav noticed a vaguely concerned expression on Wilson's face as he watched four coyotes trailing them from a nearby hill.

"What's wrong? Worried they'll catch up?" Vaclav asked, squinting to see the coyotes. Wilson scrunched up his face and shook his head.

"No, it's not that. It's probably nothing. Coyotes are bad news sometimes. Let's keep going."

As the last of the sun's rays settled behind the highest peaks of the mountain range, the three riders trotted quietly through the ancient forest. Crickets chirped, and evening birds called from far off, but all the trees around them were silent.

"I've not been here since I was very young. My father brought me here to see the old stone grove once. Now, I fear we may be the last generation to keep it. I'll go no further while the taint remains in the grove. I'll set up camp here and wait for you to return. Andras, are you sure you don't want to stay here with Pukayuk and me?" Dismounting, Andras patted his horse's neck and pulled his hat down tighter.

"I'm sure. If I don't defend my family, then I won't have anything," he said boldly. The words did not sound like a child's coming from his mouth, and he was surprised. Vaclav's face was pale and rigid like stone. He reminded Andras of the heroic statues that dotted the courtyards of the town where he was born.

Uncle Vaclav loaded his pistol and put all eight rounds into the repeater he reclaimed from Rhodes. Andras loaded his own pistol silently, watching his uncle. He left his coat and satchel on George, and Andras stuffed his hat into Pukayuc's bag. Together, Andras and Vaclav walked into the darkness of the forest. Andras looked over his shoulder one last time to see Wilson lighting sage by the fire, his song to the horses barely audible.

The forest air was cold and reached through their clothes to sprout goosebumps each time the wind passed them. Just like Wilson had described, they found the entrance to the slot canyon, a narrow split in an overgrown cliff-face. Vaclav looked at Andras silently, and Andras nodded.

Vaclav tugged the right side of his cap down and unslung the rifle. He had to squeeze and twist to contort his body into the narrow passage, but he noticed the ease with which Andras traversed, walking almost completely unimpeded. The wind sighed as it slowly coaxed them back to the entrance, and a foul, rotted smell caused both of them to pause and wrinkle their noses. The nauseating odor of old death and recent decay made their skin feel slimy and filthy. Vaclav turned back to Andras and held up a finger to his lips. Andras mimicked locking his mouth with a key.

The first indication of evil was a smeared bloody handprint on the wall, not at chest height like one would expect, but above Vaclav's head. Beneath Andras's feet, the fine, silty sand began to crunch and jab the bottoms of his boots. Looking down, he spotted many bones of small animals, rodents, birds, and some larger bones that could be deer or sheep.

Vaclav crouched and inspected the splintered end of a larger leg bone. It had been broken open, and much of the marrow had been scraped and sucked out. Evidence of gnawing and teeth was present. Vaclav thought it best if he didn't point that out to Andras. Looking back to check on him, Andras's attention was focused above them.

Hung like paper lanterns during a street festival were many scalps, blonde, brunette, black, short, long, curly, coarse, smooth, and straight. While some had shriveled and dangled from dried hair, others gleamed silver in the moonlight with fresher blood.

Vaclav swallowed down his nausea and tugged the front of Andras's shirt to regain his focus. Andras blinked, freed from his mesmerized horror, and nodded. His eyes were wide with fear, and his bottom lip trembled.

The end of the narrow passage was before them, and the rising moon's light had just now begun to carve a beam through the darkness. Silhouettes of ancient marble and stone pillars grown gnarled and feral emerged from shadows like so many bars in a massive cage. Vaclav crouched down to speak to Andras one last time before entering the main chamber. He placed a wide, heavy hand on Andras's shoulder and locked-eyes with him. He spoke low so only Andras could hear.

"Remember: both eyes and both ears open. Trust your instincts, but don't let them contr–" a quick rustling like a rattlesnake caused both of them to look down before a fragmented deer's antler sprang upward by a concealed wire. The booby-trapped bone spike lanced through the fabric of his trousers, hooked deep into the flesh of

Vaclav's thigh, and yanked his leg from under him, bouncing his head off the ground once before dragging him away from Andras into the inky blackness of the grove, as if snatched away by some unknowable monster's massive claw.

It was so quiet. Andras froze and covered his mouth, not daring to breathe.

Andras knew that Uncle Vaclav was dead. He'd never seen a grown-up snatched away like a baby bird before.

It felt like minutes before he breathed again. From the darkness, he could hear the quiet scuffling of someone moving carefully and he knew it wasn't Uncle Vaclav. Andras drew his pistol and muffled the mechanical cylinder with one hand, as he cocked back the hammer with the other.

The quiet shuffling in the black stopped. Andras ducked low, moved into the chamber and planted his back against the closest fossilized trunk. The moonlight in the sacred chamber cast long shadows as it floated higher until Andras could make out the shapes moving in the darkness. Peeking around the tree, he took in his surroundings.

A deep groove in the ground where Uncle Vaclav was dragged away led to the back of the chamber. He wasn't sure where Hush was, but finding Vaclav's body was a good start. Staying low and hugging the wall, Andras moved through the darkest patches, obscuring his shape from view.

Like jagged claws over stone, a voice slithered across the cavern walls to find Andras. "Is someone there?" "A new one with an old face," the voice whispered to itself absently. "Is it true, or is it a memory? It feels real. A Ukrainian returns for vengeance, or to die with his pet snake?" "Or is he the pet?"

Andras held his pistol out in front of him, ready to fire. He hugged the wall and moved quietly. Slowly, he saw the limp form of Uncle Vaclav, suspended upside down by the antler-hook in the flesh of his thigh. Blood ran from the side of his head where it hit the ground, and his trousers were growing more red by the second.

Crouched in front of Vaclav, craning his neck to study the unconscious face, was the gaunt and filthy Hush. He was naked from the waist up and had adorned himself with shapes and symbols. The scar across his shoulder, neck, and face was splashed with brownish-red that had begun to flake off. The way he crouched before Vaclav reminded him of an owl or the gargoyles that used to scare Andras on his baba's church.

Hush grabbed a handful of Vaclav's hair and brandished a shiny black flint-knife. Vaclav's face contorted with pain as he groaned under Hush's harsh yank. Hearing the angst in Uncle Vaclav's groan filled Andras with a desperate, spurting, burning hatred for Hush.

His iron sights aligned over the shirtless, painted body of Hush, and he squeezed the trigger. A sharp explosion obliterated the silence of the ancient stone grove. When the smoke of his pistol cleared, Hush was gone. Slowly stirring to his senses, Vaclav was groaning and cursing in Polish, Ukrainian, and English, trying to unhook the antler-spur from the flesh that was suspending him from the snare. He blinked away blood and sand and agonized with every twinge of movement that further tore his leg.

Andras made to rush to his uncle's side and help, but Vaclav thrust out a hand and shouted, "No! Don't!" Andras immediately realized his mistake and ducked back into the shadow of a petrified tree. A vile, moist chuckle echoed from somewhere close. Vaclav wrested a knife from the back of his pants and slashed the cord that held him aloft. Crashing to the ground in a dusty, disoriented pile, he stumbled to his feet and drew his pistol from its holster in an uncertain hand.

Behind cover, Vaclav took hold of the carved antler hook and breathed in and out quickly. He pictured Andras, crouched in the darkness as Hush snuck up behind him. The surge of emotion strengthened his hand to yank out the hook with a wet sucking noise. He cursed loudly in a fourth language, and immediately inspected the tip to ensure it all came out. Satisfied, he limped away from his hiding place, trailing black pools of blood behind him.

Andras surged from cover to his uncle's side, breathing heavily. "Uncle Vaclav, I'm really scared," Andras whispered, his teeth chattering, but his hand steady like steel.

"I know, Andi, me too. Trust that feeling. It's trying to keep you safe." With Andras's help, he cinched his belt tightly onto his leg above the deep, stretched wound. Hopefully, it would be enough. Vaclav clawed the sand, digging for something to hold onto, as the too-tightly-cinched belt began to do its job.

Below him, Hush saw a familiar firearm. It was not that he was familiar with the model or make of the gun, but the actual individual firearm that lay below him was familiar to him. Like remembering a face in a dream, this rifle played a role earlier in his recent life.

He finished packing ash into his gunshot and climbed silently down the stone trunk like a puma. Crouched low, he scooped the rifle into his hands and skittered back up the trunk where his perch was obscured from view.

He rubbed the smooth wood against his cheek intimately, as he pulled it into his shoulder tightly. The familiar gun belonged to the familiar face, and then, like some neglected memory dusted free of cobwebs, Hush remembered.

"Poor Rhodes…"

"Would've liked to see him die."

"Who killed him?"

"Didn't you see his face? None other than the peasant-Viper's New-Yorkrainian."

"Rhodes stole from the snake, and the snake bit back."

"Fucking dumbass," he said.

"Fucking dumbass," they agreed.

"Shut the fuck up," Hush rasped in a gravely, wet timbre. He pushed forward the lever and cycled the first round into the chamber with a satisfying sound. He bit his lip.

"It's nice."

"Like it was made for me."

"But it belonged to the Winter Viper."

"Previously. No longer."

"It will remain the Viper's fang until you use it for something greater."

"They're going to hear you," Hush warned in a sharp hissing whisper. Hush held the rifle in one hand as he climbed to the adjacent column. He'd learned which roots could hold his weight, and he tied simple rope loops between others to help him traverse above the heads of anyone who would stumble into his lair. There are two of them. He nearly had the flesh of one before the other shot him from behind.

"Stupid."

"Sloppy."

"We'll see if he hit anything important by the morning, s'pose." Turning inward, Hush felt the sharp ache of the bullet still inside him. The bullet had entered his side and remained somewhere within his abdomen still.

"Who's the other?"

"Someone quiet. Someone small. A woman? His woman?"

"Harmless."

"Weak." Hush nodded in agreement. The Ukrainian was the heroic type, and he didn't see him endangering a woman he cared for lightly. He needed a closer look.

Andras pushed the hair on his forehead to the side and slowly peeked around the edge of the stone column he had grown so comfortable leaning against. He didn't see anything. It was like Hush disappeared into thin air. Uncle Vaclav slumped over in a limp flop. Andras pulled him back up and watched his uncle struggle to focus his eyes.

"I-I-Iiii think that chewed-bastard poisoned me when he stuck me. In my leg." Vaclav's face went colorless as his eyes rolled back, and he seemed to fall into a cold sleep. Andras struggled to hold him up, his hands full of Uncle Vaclav's sleeve as he clung to him. "I'll stay here. Go-go-go get him…" Vaclav slurred from the ground. Andras nodded. He took hold of his uncle's belt and pulled him onto his side.

"I'll be back," Andras promised. "I'm going to get you to a doctor." He leaned over and kissed his Uncle Vaclav's forehead and darted away into the black.

Where is that sneaky bastard? Dashing from shadow to shadow, he struggled to keep his unconscious partner in view in case he should circle back to him. His gun felt odd and heavy in his hands, and the sandy floor made his feet feel heavy even though his footsteps were all but silenced. As God intended, it was one predator against another, the older and wiser against the younger and sharper.

Hush quickly grew tired of the invisible hide-and-seek game they were playing and decided to change the rules. He dropped to the ground noiselessly and swallowed a chestful of air. The bullet ached terribly inside him: he swallowed the pain, too. Expelling all his air and pain, he released a horrifying, yowling shriek that gave him goosebumps.

"Who *are* you anymore?"

"Wrong question, loves."

"Ah, yes, please rephrase."

"Who are you becoming?"

"Much better," Hush whispered, wiping blood from the corner of his mouth. It probably wasn't good that he was coughing up blood, but he would have to address one problem at a time.

Andras shivered and felt like he needed to throw up. Hush was trying to scare him, and, holy shit, it was working. Andras was pretty sure he had hit him before, but now he was howling like a beast from one of Baba's stories. Andras gathered all the sour taste in his mouth and spit it in the sand in front of him, expelling the fear that fastened him to the ground as well. He rounded the pillar, pistol first and fired blindly, his left hand already pulling the hammer back for an aimed shot.

Hush dropped prone to the ground and aimed down the sights at his opponent. He fired, and the shot strayed high, over the head of the tiny gunman. Andras's bullet disappeared into a puff of coarse sand behind Hush.

"A child?"

"Don't be ridiculous."

"Ridiculous? We've killed children before."

"Yes, but none of them were shooting at us."

Andras moved to the next tree, dropping his two spent shells and replacing them with two fresh cartridges. On all the cartridges he'd brought with him, he'd carved the letter "H," for Hush, onto the flat tips of them with his pocketknife. Uncle Vaclav said this was to help the bullets find their way. He'd hardly missed a moment ago. Hush was quick, but Andras was pretty sure he could be quicker. He locked back the hammer and listened, waiting to peek out.

Hush rolled and got to his knees before moving to the next angle. He'd circle right, forcing his opponent to aim left. Child or not, he'd add his scalp to his collection.

"If you want to survive the winter, you'll hit the target."

"Who is more dangerous? The wolf?" Or you? Hush pressed hard on his ash-covered wound before violently striking it twice with a scabbed fist.

Andras looked up. The walls were scrawled with letters and symbols he didn't recognize. More importantly, he noticed the handholds and ropes suspended between the stone trees. Andras glanced down at the shadow-splashed ground and then up at the moon, whose light cast everything in a ghostly sheen.

"Are you still alive, little one?" called a mocking voice, sounding like a hand on a stove. Andras exhaled steadily.

"Yeah," Andras called back, trying not to sound frightened. The quivering in his jaw was audible enough. "Are you shot?" Andras called out to Hush, expecting him to lie.

"I am. If I don't find a doctor soon, it may kill me. I hope you don't mind if I take your horse after I kill you."

"I do mind. Pukayuk is special to me, and I don't think he'll like you–" The wall behind his right ear exploded into shards of coarse gravel that peppered his face. Andras ducked to the floor and rolled to his left, landing on his stomach with his pistol extended in front of him. Andras fired a shot and watched Hush disappear behind another pillar. Andras scurried to the next tree as Hush emerged from the other side and fired the rifle three times with amazing speed.

Andras quickly looked himself over to find himself unharmed, but his shirt had four new holes where two bullets had narrowly missed him, and pierced his shirt instead. He exhaled the quivering nerves in his chest and sprinted to the next pillar, trying to close the distance between Hush and him. Andras fired three more times into the petrified tree that he saw Hush behind and began reloading the moment his back hit another wall.

"That rifle doesn't belong to you," Andras called out, masking the sound of his reloading.

"Which of its owners' deaths haunt you most?" His question was a slimy sound, like pulling a body from a lake.

"Mój ojciec. *My father's.*"

"Ah. Walenty. Myślałem, że nie żyjesz. Trudniej cię zabić niż twojego ojca. *I thought you were dead. You're harder to kill than your father.*"

Andras emerged from his cover and fired three more times at the tree Hush was behind. He rounded the edge with pistol locked and loaded, but he found no one but his Pa's repeater leaning where he expected Hush to be. He glanced upward first, holstered his pistol, and then scooped up the rifle. He swung forward the lever and checked the chamber. As expected, Hush had shoved a cartridge in backwards to intentionally jam it. He slung the rifle over his back and drew his pistol again.

Hush noiselessly rounded the column that Andras had left Vaclav lying limply. From his spider's-point-of-view, Vaclav looked like a trapped, helpless insect, unable even to beg. He crawled down the pillar like a spider, head first, finding handholds he'd hook his fingers into.

He was titillated at the thought of ending Vaclav with Vaclav's own gun, and then collecting him with the skinning blade he'd made. He'd leave something for the young boy to find. When he was barely a meter away, he turned himself and dropped onto the ground in front of Vaclav. As expected, Vaclav was still weak and helpless. His eyes struggled to focus on Hush, and his hand flopped for his holster like a fish trying to fling itself back to water. Hush put a finger to his lips and pulled Vaclav's useless wrist away. He peeked around the column cautiously, keeping track of his wayward opponent.

When he grabbed for Vaclav's gun, the holster was empty. He felt around behind Vaclav and finally pulled him over to check for the gun beneath him. When he righted the drugged cowboy, a crooked smirk and silly chuckle from Vaclav made him pause.

"You think that's funny? I don't need a gun to kill you, Ukrainian. Maybe I'll take your eye all the way out first, finish the job I started all those years ago. Is that funny?" Hush threatened, holding the flint blade centimeters from his scarred eye. Vaclav continued to chuckle and then floppily nodded. From above them both, a sharp, distinct, "*mudak*," caused Hush to reflexively leap backward like a retreating bobcat.

Andras had followed Hush's route from above and gotten the drop on him. Andras fired, not where Hush was perched atop Vaclav's limp form, but eight feet away, where he expected him to roll or dive away defensively.

Hush flung his flint knife at Andras, where it sliced through the air, ricocheted off the cylinder of his pistol, and sliced a long, jagged cut across Andras's cheek. Andras fired again and again, six times, each time, aiming and squeezing the trigger slowly and accurately. When his pistol was empty, Andras dropped down from above Vaclav and holstered it.

He wiped the blood from his cheek with his sleeve, checked his sleeve, and then wiped again, surprised at the amount of blood.

Hush lay on his back, chest heaving with each labored breath. Counting the first shot, he'd been hit seven times; in the left kidney, in the left leg above the knee, in the left elbow, his right clavicle, his right wrist, in the right hand, severing his thumb, and in the right hip. Plus, some Indian stabbed him. He was properly irrigated and dying fast. He watched Andras with wide, feral black eyes.

Andras drew Vaclav's pistol from the back of his belt and handed it to his uncle. Weakly, he grasped it. "I got him for you, Uncle Vaclav. I got him," Andras whispered. Vaclav smiled crookedly and tried his best to nod. Andras helped his uncle to a wobbly knee. Hush coughed a bubble of blood onto his chin and spoke up, his voice like piss on embers. Andras refastened his aunt's locket around his uncle's neck.

"You really are Kyrylo's son. A killer through and through," he goaded. His voice wavered with agony, like a burning log being smothered with water. Andras paused and locked unblinking, boring brown eyes with Hush's empty. "That was your father's real name–

well, his *first* real name. Before he abandoned his home and his people and became a gun-for-hire. A filthy gun-runner. He was a weapons smuggler, a coward, a murderer, and a thief. The Russians sent me to stomp out a criminal, not a hero."

Andras only bled. He wiped the blood from his cheek again. "What's your point?" Andras asked flatly when it seemed like Hush had said enough. Hush's expression melted into confusion. It was not the reaction he expected. "You already killed him. I'm nobody's son now," Andras explained to Hush. "And you're gonna die knowing you got beat by a seven-year-old, and *another* soldier you failed to kill all those years ago." Andras helped his uncle aim the pistol, allowing Vaclav to brace his elbow on his shoulder. Vaclav chuckled again. "Actually, I'll be eight next month," Andras clarified, and he helped his uncle pull the trigger.

The final bullet punched into Hush's chest, leaving a crater littered with rib fragments. He lay still, his eyes, like two empty graves.

In a mix of the poison's effect and the finality of the act, Vaclav collapsed to the ground. A single tear skated from his eye as he struggled to sit up. Andras wrapped his uncle's arm across his shoulders and squeezed his hand, saying, "It's over. We actually did it. How do you feel? My cheek is bleeding."

Vaclav did his best to nod and walk, and Andras spun an endless string of questions and observations faster than Vaclav could listen. Vaclav recognized the fire of war in him, burning hot, and it was all too much for him as he began calming down. After Vaclav's first battle, he remembered feeling like he was vibrating, and the whole world was a little too quiet and far too slow.

"Can you tell me more about what Hush said about Pa?" Andras asked, and then he waited. Vaclav was stunned at the sudden silence and discovered he could speak.

"Uh, um– Sure, Andi. Remember when I told you that I was born in Ukraine?"

"Yeah. On a tobacco farm by the river."

"That's right, good memory! Your Pa was born in Ukraine, too." Andras flinched in surprise.

"In the same village as you?"

"No, a very different village." Vaclav was nervous about how to broach the subject, not knowing how Andras would react. They had plenty of time to talk as Andras helped his still-clumsy, recovering uncle navigate the narrow slot canyon. Vaclav smacked his forehead against the wall of the canyon more times than he can remember. "Ow. Dammit, I hit my head again. Your pa grew up with his own people far away from other towns. Do you know the word 'cossack?' They were secluded– Do you know what I mean when I say that word, secluded?" Andras shrugged and tugged his uncle's knee around a tricky corner. "They were very different because they didn't see a lot of other people. They were very religious, and they were fierce warriors."

"Is that where Pa learned to fight?"

"That's where he began learning, yes. He left his village and ran away from home when he was young, about fourteen or fifteen years, I think."

"Is that when you met him?"

"Shortly after that, yes. I heard your father speaking Ukrainian in Poland and saw his peculiar clothes, so I befriended him. After that, we joined the army." Andras nodded as he listened. His face was screwed up in thought as he pondered hard.

"Pa's real name was Kyrylo?"

"Kyrylo Strilyaibaba, yes."

Andras mouthed the name to feel it on his tongue.

"Is what he said about Pa true, too? About the smuggling and guns?" Andras asked, not looking at his uncle. Vaclav reached out and stopped Andras in the narrow corridor.

"Yes. All that was true. After the uprising, your pa and I began to buy and smuggle guns over the border from Hungary for our soldiers. After a few months, we were getting guns from many places, and then it wasn't only guns, and then we weren't buying them anymore." Andras thought hard as he listened.

"Did you hurt people?" he asked softly. Vaclav nodded. They both knew the next question to follow, and as much as Andras didn't want to ask, Vaclav didn't want to tell him.

"And Pa?"

"Yeah, he did. That's why he got the name, 'Winter Viper.' All through January and into the Spring, your dad and me would lay in wait to strike at the perfect moment. He was so deadly, the Russians told ghost stories about him. Some even thought he could transform into a white snake to escape." Vaclav smiled as he remembered, his eyes still sad. "But then he met Clara, your ma, and he wanted to leave that life behind. He worked a few more big jobs, saved up money, and started planning his new life. He changed everything for you."

When they finally emerged, Andras collapsed onto a fallen tree to rest, and Vaclav collapsed onto the ground due to his body's slow recovery from whatever was on that gnarled bone hook.

"Pa, Kyrylo Stril-something, was a Ukrainian warrior who abandoned his post, smuggled guns, and killed a lot of people during the uprising," Andras told himself, mulling it over. Andras nodded. "Okay," he said after a long moment.

"Okay?" Vaclav asked, craning his neck to look at Andi.

"Yeah, okay. All the things I know about him, it doesn't change the good dad he was to me. Plus, he's dead now. It's not like he can pay for what he did any more."

"Truly? You're not angry or confused?" Vaclav strained to sit up, but managed it with several embarrassing moans and grunts.

"I'm not angry. I'm… surprised, I suppose. But I don't see how it changes anything. At least, I don't think it changes me. Pa and you and Hush and Big Hank; whatever y'all did in your life doesn't have to be the same as what I choose." Vaclav was impressed all over again.

"Damned if that wasn't the most profound thing I've ever heard." Vaclav shook his head and collapsed back to the ground. "Now, run and get Wilson. Tell him to bring George." Andras jumped up and ran toward the distant glow, and Vaclav laid back down and listened to an owl hooting nearby.

Chapter 24

Andras closed the pocket knife and returned it to the hole in the heel of his boot. He thought it was a clever place to hide a knife, and the hole had been a happy accident. He brushed the last remaining splinters away with his thumb and blew lightly to clean it. Inspecting his handiwork, Andras nodded and couldn't help but smile. Carved into the finely polished stock, as nicely as Andras could manage, was the name, "HUSH," commemorating, not only the monster he slew to claim it, but also give the name a new purpose.

It was a quality firearm and easy to handle, but, most importantly, it was meaningful to Andras. The legacy of the rifle was legendary already; he'd taken it from Hush, who'd taken it from Uncle Vaclav, who'd taken it from Rhodes, who'd taken it from Pa, who'd received it as a gift from Uncle Vaclav.

"Ready?" Vaclav asked, appearing in the doorway of his room. Andras inhaled a deep breath and exhaled it slowly. He returned the rifle to its place on the wall and turned to his uncle.

"Ready," he said.

Andras had made his uncle promise that he'd walk him all-the-way for his first day of school. All the other children knew the teacher already, and already had made friends with each other. He was sure many of the other children would know English better and be able to read and write better than he. In Europe, he didn't go to school because the Russians had burned it down. Now, the schoolhouse was visible from their front yard, so he was without excuse.

Vaclav kissed his wife goodbye, and Andras hugged his aunt. Vaclav had been preparing for the barrage of excuses and questions Andras had prepared for this walk. Vaclav handed Andras a tin cup of hot black coffee. He sipped it long and deep before he pulled away and swallowed.

"Ow. I burned my tongue."

"You still have to go to school."

"I know. What kind of stuff do you think we'll be learning?"

"Let's see; you're eight years old now, so I reckon you'll be learning arithmetic and literature." Andras stared at the ground as they walked the wet, dirt path. He kicked a small rock. It bounced off the road into the grass.

"I've heard those words before, but I don't know what they are."

"Books and numbers, Andras. You're good at reading, and you know your numbers alright."

"Kind of alright," Andras said under his breath. Vaclav slyly bumped the heel of his boot, so he tripped over his own feet and stumbled. "Hey! Watch it, partner," he warned like a tough guy, laughing between words.

"Listen, Andras. Today, just focus on observing. Watch the kids, watch the teacher, learn how the day works, and maybe see if you can make some friends. You're going to do great," Vaclav encouraged warmly. Andras nodded and looked at the ground again. When they started walking again, Andras occasionally tried to trip his uncle in the same manner.

"How do I make friends?" he asked. Vaclav paused. That was a very good question, and he wasn't sure he knew how to answer it well.

"Well…er, when you become friends with someone, it's usually because of something you have in common. Like your Pa and I: we both rebelled against our officers and fought back against our Russian captors. And your aunt Mary and I were drawn together by our love of horses."

"I thought you said it was her hair and her eyes."

"It can be more than one thing, Andras."

"Okay, so what-in-the-hell am I going to talk to the other eight-year-olds about? Dead parents? Killing outlaws? Guns?"

"You have a point," Vaclav conceded. He stroked his beard as he pondered. "I wouldn't recommend any of those on your first day. What about horses? Pukayuk and you have a special bond."

"I guess…" Andras agreed. Vaclav stopped them on the road again. A group of boys of Andras's age jogged by, rolling a barrel-hoop alongside them with sticks. Andras watched them with annoyance and jealousy as they laughed and enjoyed their game together.

"Your whole life, one of the hardest things you will do is learn to exist around other people. You don't master it in school, and you get it wrong a whole lot. Aunt Mary and I will always be okay with you getting it wrong, alright? You don't have to be just like the rest of the kids, because you're not just like the rest of the kids." Andras nodded. That did make him feel incrementally better.

"Observing and watching today: got it." They were quiet the rest of the walk, enjoying the cool morning air and watching the gathering throngs of school children. Andras tipped back the rest of his coffee and passed his empty cup to Vaclav. He hugged his uncle tightly and asked him so only they could hear,

"You promise you'll be here as soon as school is done?"

"I promise. How is it you can face down killers and outlaws with gun in-hand, but you're petrified at the thought of numbers and letters?"

"Because the worst thing that can happen in a gunfight is I die. I have to go to school *everyday*." Vaclav laughed at Andras's reasoning and nodded in agreement.

"I suppose you're right. Okay, I'll make you a deal. Go to school for this whole week, and if, at the end, you hate it, you can go back to working at Pete's cafe, deal?" Andras considered the deal and stroked his chin like Uncle Vaclav did.

"It's a deal," he concluded. They hugged once more before Andras turned and walked inside.

Within, rows of students sat at desks, some conversing while others polished and cleaned their slates. Andras chose a desk on the far side of the room, but quickly gave it up to another student who claimed their stake to it.

He finally found an empty desk and sat silently, watching the kids around him. They were so small and their voices were high and noisy. They played singing games and smiled at each other while some threw small items at each other playfully. He wasn't dressed like them. Many of them wore short-pants, laced-shoes, and caps. Andras wore his canvas riding pants, a belt, a linen shirt and his wide-brimmed hat.

Looking closely, he noticed the girl beside him had a scar on her cheek similar to his. A boy in the front row had a badly crippled hand. Another boy sitting near the door was missing an ear. Each child had a small keepsake of their life's suffering thus far that they carried with them forever. He imagined who the boy with a cripple hand would become, and what would become of the girl with the scarred face.

The teacher rapped her measuring stick against the lectern and greeted the class. The class collectively greeted her in turn, and Andras blushed under his ignorance. Immediately, her hawk-like gaze and long nose focused on Andras.

"Children, today we have a new student with us. Come here, son, where we can all say, hello." His heart caught in his chest, and his mouth felt dry, like he'd never had water. All the students stared at him, as he stepped out from his desk and made his way forward. Some of the children turned to whisper to each other, and Andras hated them for it. He came to the front of the room and thought about how he'd rather be riding Pukayuk with a pistol on his hip. Andras glanced at the teacher, unsure of what to do.

"Tell us your name," she said slowly, enunciating in case his English was weak.

"Andras Walenty."

"Where do you come from, Andres?"

"Pols– Poland," he corrected himself, trying his best to display his English skills, but he couldn't remember any words. The teacher nodded and smiled.

"When did you come to the States?" Andras remembered the motion of the ship on the waves and how it would make Mama quite sick to her stomach. He remembered the smell of New York and the first time he met Uncle Vaclav.

"Only a little while ago."

"And how long have you called Foothill home, Andres?" Andras thought about the time he rode into Foothill, bloodied, filthy, and freshly-orphaned. He remembered killing Asher in the jail cell and the smell of his own vomit and gunsmoke. He remembered the color of blood on the dusty Colorado prairie and how he felt when Paul Becker hugged him. He remembered the smell of his house burning and the pillar of smoke that stretched to the stars.

He remembered his father's words about a home, how a man who did not defend his home belonged nowhere. For months, Andras had lived on beans and coffee with a gun on his hip. He shared most of his food with his horse, and he slept under stars. When he thought about home and what he defended, he finally understood what his father meant so long ago.

"I live here, but Foothill isn't my home. My home is coming to pick me up after school."

www.ingramcontent.com/pod-product-compliance
Lightning Source LLC
Chambersburg PA
CBHW050059170426
43198CB00014B/2396